Women of the
Mediterranean

Women of the Mediterranean

edited by
Monique Gadant

translated from the French by
A.M. Berrett

Zed Books Ltd.
London and New Jersey

Women of the Mediterranean was first published in French as an issue of *Peuples Mediterraneens* in 1984. This English edition was first published by Zed Books Ltd., 57 Caledonian Road, London N1 9BU, UK, and 171 First Avenue, Atlantic Highlands, New Jersey 07716, USA, in 1986.

Cover designed by Lee Robinson
Printed and bound in the UK
at The Bath Press, Avon.

British Library Cataloguing in Publication Data

Women of the Mediterranean.
  1. Women—Mediterranean Region—Social conditions
  I. Gadant, Monique
305.4′2′094   HQ1233

ISBN 0-86232-527-7
ISBN 0-86232-528-5 Pbk

Contents

List of Contributors

Dr Monique Gadant, the editor, is a lecturer at the University of Paris. As a researcher at the National Centre for Scientific Research, she is in charge of the CNRS-CRESM programme on Women, Time and Money. She has published many articles on the political and cultural life of Algeria in *Les Temps Modernes* and *Peuples Mediterraneens*.

Dr Sossie Andezian and **Dr Jocelyne Streiff-Fenart** are both researchers at the National Centre for Scientific Research where they specialize in the study of North African women immigrants.

Dr Maria Minicuci is professor of Anthropology at Messina, Italy.

Yamina Fekkar is an Algerian midwife who practised in Algerian hospitals and villages for over ten years. She now lives in France where she has taken a degree in Psychology.

Dr Didar Fawzy has been a member of the editorial committee of *Peuples Mediterraneens* and of the secretariat of the Henri Curiel Association.

Gaye Petek Salom and **Pinar Hukum** are Turkish social workers with extensive experience of the problems of immigrant communities.

Pepita Carpena was a militant during the Spanish Civil War and remains a member of the CNT.

Dr Malika Zamiti-Horchani is a psychologist and editor of the journals *Architecture et Urbanisme* and *Medecine, Anthropologie, Sciences Humaines* in Tunis.

Marie-Christine Aulas is a journalist who has contributed to *Le Monde Diplomatique* and *Merip Reports*. She lived in Cairo for many years.

Rossana Rossanda was a PCI member of the Italian Chamber of Deputies from 1963 to 1968 and is now a columnist for the daily newspaper *Il Manifesto*.

Dr Mirjana Morokvasic used to lecture in social psychology at the University of Lille. She now works at the Centre for National Scientific Research, specializing in international migration and women's studies.

Evelyne Porret is a potter who has lived for many years in the Fayoum.

Mai Sayeh is an official of the Union of Palestinian Women.

Khaoula Mokhtar lives in Paris where she is working on her thesis.

Anne-Marie Quastana and **Sylvia Casanova** are Corsican feminists.

Abdolrahmane Mahdjoube, the only male contributor, is an Iranian sociologist.

Introduction

Monique Gadant

The family structures of the peoples that live in the Mediterranean basin are characterized by the power of the extended family over individuals, with its greatest weight falling on women for whom motherhood is defined as the sole means of fulfilment; by the power of the mother who obtains social recognition for her function as reproducer (not only of the lineage but also of the patriarchal ideology); by the power of men over women who are excluded from the political arena and confined to domestic matters; by the strict control of feminine sexuality in which men place their honour; by the position of women as stakes of power for men, eternally objects and means, never (or rarely) subjects except to be subjected, deprived of speech save to gossip, backbite, spread the secrets of the tribe . . .; women of whom men are suspicious and whom they dare not love too much; women who are trying to find themselves and want to define their own identity, to be something other than 'Mummy-Whore' . . . rejecting saintliness and abasement, 'to be simply women', as Italian women say.

We shall not discuss in this book the similarities between the various family structures of these peoples, nor shall we try to explain their source. Most contributors mention these similarities and it can be said that they make a mockery of the barriers constructed by religion and state.

Yet, if we had simply wanted to stress these common features, however important they may be, we would probably not have thought about putting this book together. Across the Mediterranean, wherever petroleum circulates and men have gone off to sell their labour power in the countries of the North, relations between the dominant and the dominated also circulate. *Mare nostrum* . . . our sea [the Mediterranean] is no longer a place of adventure, of dream, of voyages, it is no more a place for poets, Ulysses sails it no more. 'The old sea; the sea of many years ago, whose servants were devoted slaves and went from youth to age or to a sudden grave without needing to open the book of life . . . That was the sea before the time when the French mind set the Egyptian muscle in motion and produced a dismal but profitable ditch.'[1]

It seemed to us that in fact there was a great difference between the various countries of the Mediterranean — the difference that separates the developed capitalist countries along the northern edge from the others (whether Christian or Muslim), those which have been left behind in

1

industrial growth or were former colonies. (Italy is split internally by this division.) Feminist ideologies have developed in the former. They followed the advances of individualism from which capitalism benefited and in turn accelerated.

Capitalism has emancipated men and women from the authority of the family and the elders and liberated them from the control imposed by the village community or tribe. It is true this emancipation was paid for with loneliness and the absence of solidarity; class solidarities are abstract when compared with the powerful bonds of the extended family. The immigrant who haunts the suburbs of the great industrial cities knows this price; sometimes too he learns in his position as a worker the burden of a family that has remained in the home-country, and is tempted by the idea of breaking away.

The women are the ones who stay behind and who provide reassurance, because the men want them to do so and have loaded them with their fantasies. Incarnations of the Earth, of the Fatherland, women 'the keepers of the traditions', they say . . . Nationalism asked of women a participation that they were quick to give, they fought and were caught in the trap. For nationalism is frequently conservative, even though it appears to be an inevitable moment of political liberation and economic progress which women need to advance along the path to their own liberation. The contributions of Malika Zamih-Horchani (Tunisia) and of Lebanese and Palestinian women on this issue link with the concerns of Corsican women and raise common questions. Under what conditions does their liberation require activism? What does it mean for women to be active in political organizations? The example of Algerian women is there to remind all women that participation does not necessarily win them rights. From the point of view of those women contributors who have grown up after a war of liberation, everything is still to be done. Yugoslav socialism, for example, while opening up to women access to work and establishing egalitarian laws, has left the patriarchal mentality intact.

Pepita Carpena's experience of an anarchist and proletarian movement (Free Women) during the Spanish Civil War seems to have been very far ahead of its time . . . if such an expression has any meaning. The existence of an independent women's organization, and the nature of the relations between the parties and organizations claiming to be part of the revolution presupposes a calling into question of the family, and a consideration of the ideologies of the left (which is already leading women to challenge male predominance in the political and scientific fields). The situation of women in underdeveloped countries is quite dissimilar. There, despite its oppressive nature, the family is still a refuge against the destructive effects of industrialization; the working classes scarcely exist as a political force and in most cases the existence of single-party states militates against any forms of organization other than bureaucratic ones that tend to censure and repress any initiative that they do not control. The enormous will for change among women is a potential political force that all parties seek to use and which can be harnessed to conservative ends. Women may wonder whether this conservatism defends their interests: this is what Ouardia (Algeria) asks herself when she thinks of the women who join organizations like the Muslim Brothers. But we must be wary of simplistic responses and look at the social class of those who support Islamic fundamentalism and the reasons for their support. Sakiné (Iran) uses Islam to criticize her father who prevents her from being the activist she wants to be and makes a case for the forms of religion practised in the villages, as opposed to that of the 'Westernized' towns. For her, the veil is not a restriction, but a liberation.

An authoritarian modernization, of whatever political hue, has not only positive effects for women. Iran demonstrates this most strongly; but so also does Egypt (Veiled Activism). Culture and religion incarnate national identity. A voluntaristic intervention may have negative or no effects. Did the secularization of social life and the reforms imposed by Ataturk change the life of Turkish women? Is Islam cause or effect? Is it not the state of particular societies which brings about a conservative Islam, used, when it suits them, by existing regimes? Whatever the case, today Islam is hostile to Western societies, to the rulers of yesteryear (or of today) whose domination is not only political and economic but also cultural. Women in the South, however, look to the North for models of behaviour; and the models they find there are not necessarily wholly pure. Hence the ambiguous attitude sometimes made up of envy and aggressiveness, of women in the South to those of the North. It should not be a matter of surprise to see in the writing of an Algerian or Lebanese woman examples of these totemic couplings: Aragon–Triolet, Sartre–Beauvoir. 'What other models could I have had?' asks Malika (Algeria). Corsican women dream of leaving Corsica; but they do not want to become Frenchwomen.

We therefore thought it useful and necessary to put together a few guide-lines for studying the ways in which feminist ideologies are articulated with the various social realities with which women are confronted. In the non-industrialized countries there are home-grown feminist demands that are sometimes out of phase with the ideas and struggles in the developed countries. These demands rarely find authentic expression, since the cultural domination of the North over the South imposes on them a framework and terms of reference alien to the societies in which they originate.

As far as possible, we have sought to let women speak for themselves. One of the effects of the disappearance of oral cultures brought about by the birth, and subsequent cultural unification, of modern states has been the repressing of women's creativity. Culture has become more male. By becoming the focus of political action by a centralizing state, it has escaped from women. How can they regain it? Are female culture and male culture forever polarized, or is an androgynous culture possible? Rossana Rossanda's chapter offers some reflections on these issues.

We hope that the discussion offered here between women from the various shores of the Mediterranean will lead to a communication that will make it possible for women to go beyond the superficial image that they have of each other and promote (why not?) a real solidarity.

Paris, April 1983

Notes

1. Joseph Conrad, *An Outcast of the Islands* (1919, London, J.M. Dent, 1949 edition, p. 12).

Becoming Liberated in Beirut

Khaoula Mokhtar, assisted by Marie-Christine Aulas and Monique Gadant

In the 1940s my father had a piece of land and a house in the Bekaa, in the north-east of Lebanon. It is there that I was born. I went to school at Mount Lebanon with the Sisters. When I passed my *brevet* [tr. approximate equivalent of 'O' level], I was sixteen. My father did not want me to continue my education. I had ten brothers who were going to school with the Marist Brothers (Roman Catholic educators) (it is quite usual for Muslim families in Lebanon to send their children to Christian schools). It was a heavy burden for my parents and my father thought that I should stay in the house to help my mother. I said to myself then that if I stayed in the house my education would be finished forever. So I thought of working. I had to discuss it with my father. So I tried to explain to him that I wanted to continue studying and at the same time look for a job. A girl cousin of mine wanted to do the same thing. My father said, 'No! You will both stay in the house!'

I was very unhappy and didn't try to hide it. I said to myself, 'What is going to become of me? With the *brevet* what on earth can I do?' I went to the Teachers College and I was rejected because you had to be eighteen. My cousin had the idea that we should both look for a teaching post somewhere where we had relatives. It was possible to find a teaching position with the *brevet* alone, without going through the Teachers College, if you went outside Beirut. My cousin's parents agreed. Her mother was a Christian, and was more open-minded. She said to her, 'You want to work? Why not?' My father spoke to them and in the end was won over.

We were posted to the Syrian border, in the north-east of Lebanon, in a state school. In the day time I did my job as a teacher, and in the evening I studied for my baccalaureat. I sat it as a private candidate and I passed the first part in 1958.

In the village where we had been posted we lodged with relatives. If we had not had relatives it would have been impossible. It was already difficult enough in these conditions since women almost never went out or, if they did, they went veiled. People were very closed and conservative. We were young. I can still see myself with my plaits! Yet the villagers accepted us and in the end they came to understand us, because we knew how to behave. We had to have a sense of responsibility and not commit any moral transgressions that would discredit us in the eyes of the villagers.

My cousin and I worked hard for we were in charge of two hundred pupils. Two classes on one side, two on the other. You just had to manage. Give one class written work, and do oral work with the other. But we were happy. The girls, some of whom were older than us, were anxious to study since the school had been closed for two or three years before we arrived. As soon as the school was reopened, they came back at once, and began to talk to us about their problems: that in this world girls counted for nothing, that they could not choose their husbands, that they didn't even have the right to see their own male cousins.

People thought we were very emancipated and it is true that we were. Since our pupils trusted us, we tried to form committees with them. After a few weeks they were full of enthusiasm, they went on strike, they took part in demonstrations. At that time there were problems in Lebanon, and the Arab world was stirred up by Nasserism.[1] The school pupils joined with us for unity. And do you know? Their parents didn't rebuke them. They would say, 'They're doing it for patriotic ends! They have the right to do so!'

Later I went to Beirut, but I had a lot of problems with the Ministry of National Education because they didn't want teachers getting mixed up in politics and trying to influence the children. But my cousin and I were full of enthusiasm and we thought that it was our duty to be political. We talked to our pupils about the freedom and independence of women and we explained to them that our homeland had to be defended because Lebanon was becoming an American colony. (In 1958 the Americans had come to Lebanon with their fleet to help Chamoun.[2])

In Beirut I passed my baccalaureat in philosophy and I entered the Lebanese university where I read law and political economy. I had Kamal Jumblatt[3] as teacher for philosophy of history and we became good friends.

My father had allowed me to go to the university, it was almost automatic. I should also say that as soon as I started working I sent almost all I earned to my father so that he could continue to send my brothers to school or university. Those who were ten years or so older than me were still students and earning nothing whereas I was working and helping him. He was very proud and would say to people, 'See how good she is. She is studying and working at the same time and she's also helping me!' My father thought that I knew how to behave myself. As I've said, he had a piece of land in the Bekaa and when he settled in Beirut he had rented a shop, but he was not a wealthy man. He had agreed that I should go to university but didn't want me going out in the town. He didn't want me hanging around after classes, he was afraid for me at night. When I began to be active in student circles, it was worse. It must be said that at that time people who got involved in politics were running risks. Many young people were imprisoned. Once, a student was killed in a demonstration, so my father was afraid even though he trusted me. While the other women were saying, 'Why is she getting mixed up in such matters? Why is she behaving like the boys?', he would reply, 'She knows how to behave herself!' Yet he would say to me, 'Be careful! Don't demonstrate too much.'

At the university I met my husband who was, like me, a member of the Ba'ath party. At that time, throughout the Arab world, the Ba'ath was the party that had most support. Its aims were the unity of the Arab Nation, freedom, democracy and socialism. We were all working hard for those objectives, but it was a difficult time. The Palestinians had been driven out of their homeland and had come to Lebanon. In the party we wanted to liberate Palestine, it was obvious to us that the future of all Arabs depended on the future of this people. We believed that the Israelis were threatening the whole region and defending American interests. We were pro-Soviet but we knew that the Soviets would not liberate us just like that and that we had to rely on ourselves. Women who wanted more freedom were active in the political parties. In this way they could assert their personality and say to their parents, 'We are fighting for our homeland!' Otherwise it was forbidden for girls to go out.

There were not really any feminist struggles separate from this political struggle. In Lebanon, in Syria, in Jordan, girls thought that politics was the way to free themselves and win dignity. You can't imagine how parents treat girls who have no personality or political ideas. They can't express the least opinion!

At that time, young people who were for the new ideas challenged everybody and everything from parents to the state. There were no doubt some brave women who were for the rights of women; but how were we to fight for these rights? How to represent women? There were a few feminist associations.[4] It was then far too idealistic to say that women should be recognized socially and represented in Parliament. The ones who really wanted to fight understood that everything had to be changed and dignity achieved for everyone for the status of women to change. Some women fought for civil marriage. This was very brave because priests and sheikhs play a very important role in Lebanon. Hackles rose. 'They're attacking religion!' But the women didn't really know how to go about things.

In the 1960s, everyone at the university was reading Sartre and Simone de Beauvoir and wanted to know about existentialism, to know what it meant 'to be responsible for one's existence'. At the same time we were fighting for our society and we wanted to be up with everything that was happening in the world of culture. We were afraid to say what we were thinking but we still discussed among ourselves, to decide what we approved of — at least in what we read.

Now there is Nawal Es Saadawi.[5] She is very important to Egyptian and Arab women, even for those who are not fighting politically. What she writes influences most ordinary women; but most Arab men criticize her and argue that now is not the time for the battle between the sexes nor the time to give priority to the problems of women; priority should go to the national struggle, the struggle for national dignity and change in the backward areas that oppress both men and women. Yet today we can feel very clearly the problems between the sexes. They are now more important than before. People are also beginning to look more favourably on women's demands for greater freedom and more rights. Except of course for conservative people with closed minds who never agree to anything.

Many things have changed politically since the 1960s. The Arab world is no longer what it was then and it is open to question whether women have retained what they won in those years. Today Palestinian women and Lebanese women who are combatants have had a first-hand experience of the struggle. In a way, the Palestinian Revolution has compensated for the decline ...

During this war, women have changed. They have become accustomed to struggle and dialogue. Before, they had no ideas of their own. Many of them were influenced by religion. Like everybody else they thought they were defending their religion but like everybody else, too, they ended up questioning religion, the role of the Americans and their relationship with Israel and the future of Lebanon. This war is like yeast ... it raises ideas!

When the civil war began my three children, three boys, were about seven or eight years old. My husband had to go abroad for his work and I stayed with them in Beirut. There was no longer any decent public transport and I had to run about all the time to take the children to school and then go to work. I was working in a ministry. If there were bombardments, I had to run and find the children. My house was in the Arab university quarter and it was precisely there that almost all the Palestinian leaders lived. So there were often bombs there. At the beginning the children nearly died of fear. When they heard the missiles and bombs coming down they would cuddle up tightly against one another in the corridor. Sometimes I slept the night with them in the corridor and I covered them with my body to protect them. Our house was hit, like everybody else's ... and the children eventually got used to it. Then, instead of hiding themselves, they began to watch.

One day, at a nearby crossroads, a street vendor, with his little car, was working as usual. Around him children were buying eggs ... and then a bomb fell on him. The car flew into the air ... the man was hit in the back and the children ... a whole family was reduced to little bits and pieces of meat scattered against the surrounding buildings. My children saw it all. They were sobbing breathlessly. It was the first time they had seen anything like it. And I was saying to myself, 'My God! Suppose it was them who had gone to buy eggs downstairs!' And yet people would go out despite the bombs, they ended up getting used to living with danger.

Another day a little girl was walking along holding her brothers by the hand, as all little girls do in our country. By the time they are eight they are already behaving like women. The little girl cried, 'Where are my brothers?' One of them had disappeared and she was running around like someone mad with blood gushing out of her like a fountain. She took a few more steps and collapsed.

The children saw many scenes like that. After the Tell El Zataar massacre we saw terrible things from our third-floor flat. Lorries went past with women, children and old men who were groaning and screaming and then again lorries with bodies with or without heads, bodies piled up by the hundred pell-mell. You could see one's hand sticking out, another's foot ... and the faces you could see ... the faces of people ... Oh, my God! Once a lorry was coming back from Sabra where it had been to deposit bodies and had forgotten a foot which was still there, at the bottom of the truck. One of my sons cried out, 'Mummy! Look at the leg they've forgotten!' Do you realize? How can these poor little children be normal? Sometimes, at night, they would call out to me, 'Mummy! There's a bomb in my bed!' I had to sleep with them to reassure them.

My mother came to help me and I was then able myself to help the Palestinian women whose Federation was near where we lived. I was a member of the Relief Committee of the Executive Council of the Lebanese National Movement. We combined our efforts. We took in refugees from south Lebanon who were flooding into Beirut by the thousand. There were also people affected by the bombardments who had to be helped. Everything was well organized in Beirut by the Palestinian Revolution (PLO), and Palestinian women, together with Lebanese women, played a full part.

I devoted all the time I could to relief work. I drove round with my car. I went into the areas along the sea front where people from the south were rehoused and in the evening my children would say to me, 'So, Mummy, did you work well?' Later, they wanted to help, especially the oldest one. At eight or nine years old he would say to me, 'I'm coming with you, you can tell me what to do.' So I took him along and he was happy.

My God! What terrible times we went through. And yet ... I am telling you about the civil war. It was terrible, but not so terrible as when the Israelis came. In that summer of 1982 we lived through times we never thought we'd see. We'd seen it in films about the Second World War, but this ... in Beirut ... During the siege, it was hell. We were being fired on from all directions, from the sea, from the mountains, from the sky. This noise ... a terrible noise, a continuous thunder as if the earth was going to fall in.

My eldest son was fifteen when the Israelis entered Lebanon. He said to me, 'This time, Mummy, they are there, in the South. Before when I said that I wanted to join the fighters you told me, "You must stay here to defend our houses." And now they are there ... they've come as far as here. It's like a test for you, Mummy, to see if you are really sincere, if you are a patriot. I want to go and fight. I'm grown up.' 'But do you realize that you've only done a week's training? It is not enough. You don't know all the modern arms that are used in the front line.' He said to me: 'OK, OK!' And he went off to school — he never came back. I contacted one of his friends who told me that I might find him in one of the volunteer Lebanese student centres for the South. But the students in these centres had had a good training. It was the day the Israelis surrounded Sidon.

My brother came with me, we ran all over the place and we found him. The volunteers were ready to set off. I explained to the officials that this lad was not prepared, that he would die pointlessly. My son didn't want to come back with me. He said that the time had come for him to act according to his own convictions. 'You don't want me to because I'm your son. All mothers are the same, each will come to find her son. Mummy, our whole family is from the South, we must go and defend the South. It's not just a Palestinian business.'

So I went back home alone, and I asked my brother to go back alone to speak to my son. He said to him, 'If you go, I go with you even though I have three children. Your father is not here, so I am responsible for you. If you will just think about it, it would be better if you stayed here where you can do something useful.' My son gave the impression that he had thought about it and he came home. Then he began to cry out. 'Why do you want me to stay here? It's my country. You'll see, we are going to be like the Palestinians. We'll be driven out like they were if we don't defend ourselves.' I said to him, 'But you can fight here!' The following day he wanted to go to his uncle's. But he had arranged with some friends in the district to follow the fighters. That day was one of the worst days Beirut has ever seen, the day when there were the most horrors and the most victims. Bombs and shells were coming from the sea. It was hell!

At midday, he had still not reached his uncle's. I began to get terribly worried. I thought that he must be crushed under a building. I went out with my brother to look for him and we learned that he had gone off with the fighters ... impossible to find out in which organization. We asked the Palestinians, and the Lebanese to at least find out whether he was still alive. For five days, no news. I was crazy. Finally, I learned that he was near the airport, of which a quarter had been pounded by bombs. He went through a terrible experience, but it seems that he very soon learned how to protect himself from the bombs and also how to attack tanks. He told me that he was afraid but at the same time he felt very proud.

He had given a false name, which was why we had been unable to find him. Friends had looked for him in vain, neighbours even went to hospitals to look at corpses ... I was like a woman who'd gone out of her mind. His two brothers said to me, 'Mummy, you're going too far! Look, see the fighters down below. I'm going to help them. I'm going to fill sandbags', and the smallest one added. 'I'm going to make coffee for them'.

My children were only doing what everyone else was doing. Everyone found something to do. The people of Beirut were marvellous, especially the young people. The adults were afraid for the young people, but they were all ready to sacrifice themselves to fight the Israelis. All this energy was not exploited as it should have been. Other Arab countries didn't help the Lebanese and the Palestinians. If only there had at least been an Arab policy, a minimum of mutual assistance! Why didn't they think of using the oil? They could at least have said something, faced with the destruction of Beirut! The Arabs were all around us and the Syrians were even inside our country! Hundreds of fighters without clear instructions were killed in the very first days because they did not know what to do. And yet how they fought, the poor things! And they were massacred. As the Palestinian radio repeated all day long, 'Where are the Arabs? Why do we not hear the Arabs? They hide their money in foreign banks. Are they afraid that the revolutionary climate here might spread to their countries?' All that was clear to us in Beirut that summer. We blamed Arab governments and not the peoples they were gagging.

As for my son, he eventually telephoned me after six days:'I'm fine. Don't be afraid. Do your duty!' And he hung up. But where was he? Eventually the fighters brought him back and I was able to leave Beirut with my children before the Sabra and Chatila massacres.

When I think of the children during this war! During the siege, the Palestinian committee had established a small makeshift hospital near where we lived. Despite the danger the children of the district came to play in the small garden as soon as the bombardments subsided. One day when they were there the bombs arrived. A boy disappeared. His sister shouted, 'Daddy, Mummy! Come here! My brother . . .' The parents came down and looked for their son under the ruins. The second bomb arrived and the father was there with his legs blown off and the mother had disappeared. The little girl was petrified, holding her mother's glasses in her hand and calling out, 'Mummy, Mummy!'

Paris, January 1983

Notes

1. In January 1958, Egypt and Syria decided to unite into a single United Arab Republic, led by Gamal Abdel Nasser. This precipitated an internal crisis in Lebanon, where supporters and opponents of Arabism and the West clashed. The Lebanese president, Camille Chamoun, appealed to the USA which sent in its marines on 15 July 1958.

2. Camille Chamoun, born in Lebanon in 1900, President of the Lebanese Republic from 1952–8 and leader of one of the right-wing Maronite factions.

3. Kamal Jumblatt, a Druze, was the leader of the Lebanese Progressive National Party. He was assassinated on 16 March 1977 in an ambush set by Syrian agents.

4. However, some women were fighting for their rights (between 1952 and 1968): the right to participate in political life (to be elected to parliament), and social and professional life (to be civil servants, judges), the right to travel, to trade without their husband's permission. They had succeeded in forming a few feminist associations. Among them were Laure Thabet, of aristocratic origin, and Emilie Fares Ibrahim, of working class origin.

5. Egyptian, doctor of medicine. Published several novels in the 1950s and 1960s on the female condition; they were a great success in the Middle East. Since 1972 her work has taken a more theoretical turn; some of her works, translated from Arabic, have been published in the West.

Decisions of the First Congress for the Lebanese Women's Rights Charter

Beirut, 5 February 1983

The plenary sessions of the First Congress for the Charter of Women's Rights.

- After having examined the numerous reports and studies presented to the Congress concerning the situation of women in Lebanon and the discrimination of which they are continually the victim, in law as in practice, and after having listened to the discussions which took place during the Congress confirming this discrimination;

- the plenary sessions having received proof that Lebanese women are always treated in accordance with the dominant mentality which imposes on them a status of inferiority, so depriving them of part of their rights as women and citizens, restricting their field of activity and their creative possibilities, and so doing them great wrong, both juridically and socially;

- the inequalities existing between men and women constituting moreover an infringement of the rights and freedoms set out in the Universal Declaration of Human Rights, valid for all without distinction on the grounds of sex, race, colour or religion, just as they are inconsistent with the Lebanese Constitution, which is based on the principle of the equality of all Lebanese without distinction, and with the demands of democracy that Lebanon has chosen as a regime and way of life;

- the cause of women having so monopolized the attention of world organizations and international society that in 1975 the United Nations inaugurated the United Nations Decade for Women which will continue until 1985, with the slogan 'Equality, Development, Peace';

- Lebanese women being called upon today to play their role, which is fundamental, in the construction of a society and a homeland, so that it is essential to free them from any inferiority complex and grant them freedom and equality of rights and opportunity so that they can work and offer their contribution alongside men;

- since it is essential to communicate the positions that this Congress has adopted on the subject of the rights of women in the form of a Charter which will act as a Constitution for the women of Lebanon, a constitution from which they will draw inspiration for their actions and on the principles of which they would draw for the spirit intended to inspire legislation and regulations relating to women in Lebanon;

● taking as a driving force the aspirations of the Congress for a better society, ruled by total equality, in which the dignity of all would be preserved and which would allow each and everyone to develop fully, as a human being and as a citizen;

The Congress proclaims the following principles and demands:

I. Guiding principles of the Charter

1. Lebanese women must enjoy all the rights enjoyed by men worldwide and all those conferred locally on every citizen. They must consequently enjoy all the rights listed in the Universal Declaration of Human Rights and all the rights granted to Lebanese citizens on the basis of the principle of equality enshrined in Article 7 of the Lebanese Constitution.

2. They must enjoy every possible guarantee placing them in a position to exercise their rights to the full and in absolute freedom, eliminating every form of constraint, violence or victimization. To this end, every means and every facility required legally and practically shall be made available to them.

3. Lebanese women shall be protected as far as possible and particularly against all forms of domination and unequal treatment whether by men or society.

a) This protection must be granted to young Lebanese women from their childhood so that they may enjoy a proper education in a relaxed atmosphere, free from any reflex of fear of possible bad treatment, and be treated on an equal basis with their brothers such that they may be able freely to develop physically, intellectually and spiritually and pursue the acquisition of knowledge at all levels.

b) Women must be protected throughout their lives and especially during their youth against any attitude based on violence towards them, and any form of enslavement or exploitation (commercial or private) of female qualities, whether material or moral, and the necessary measures should be adopted for this.

4. Lebanese women must be assured of the inviolability of their rights which shall be protected from any infringement in conformity with the provisions of the Universal Charters that prohibit any state, groups of individuals or individual from any act aiming, in any way whatsoever, at eliminating or reducing these rights.

II. Demands of the Charter

In application of the principles mentioned above, and in order to mark the attachment of the Congress to the Declaration on the Elimination of All Forms of Discrimination Against Women adopted by the United Nations General Assembly in 1967, the plenary sessions of the Congress proclaim the following demands:

1. *Legally*

a) to expunge from all laws and regulations in force all discriminatory texts establishing one law for men and one law for women in the area of rights, duties and responsibilities, and all texts inspired by a desire for domination or by the sterile idea of women's inherent incapacity;

b) to carry out the necessary studies on the possibility of drafting a progressive Civil Code on the status of persons in Lebanon;

c) to promulgate as many new laws as necessary with a view to strengthening equality between citizens without distinction and protecting mother and child;

2. *Socially*

a) to introduce free and compulsory education for boys and girls;

b) to fight illiteracy in general and among women in particular;

c) to offer possibilities of teaching in general and technical and vocational education in particular such that all, boys and girls, may have access to it;

d) to encourage the participation of women in social activities and public production by ensuring their vocational training whenever necessary;

e) to fight all that harms the image of women, their role, and the significance of their liberation and to work to proscribe books, curricula and information media which do so;

f) to instil into people's minds the principle of the equality of the sexes by all means available and principally through school curricula and consciousness-raising campaigns designed to form public opinion, inspire it to reject customary practices and rid itself of any discriminatory tendency;

g) to create a state agency for women's affairs in general and to represent Lebanon on concerned international bodies as is the case in other countries.

Various women's associations participated in this Congress; all were part of the Lebanese National Movement in its various tendencies: Women's Rights Commission, Union of Arab Women, Union of Lebanese Women, Association of Democratic Women, Association for the Defence of Mother and Child. The Union of Palestinian Women had participated before the beginning of the war with Israel (June 1982) in the preparatory meetings. This organization was absent from the Beirut Congress (having been obliged to leave the city) in 1983.

Fatima, Ouardia and Malika: Contemporary Algerian Women

Interviews conducted and presented by Monique Gadant

'Left to myself, if I'd been allowed to, I'd have liked to stay on at school, but I was not as aware as I am now. Today, if my grandfather told me to leave school, I wouldn't leave!' This is Fatima's regret. She was born 23 years ago at N., a small village in the highlands of southern Oran; 80% of the inhabitants are small, sedentary herdsmen. The men do a little extra gardening for subsistence.

Fatima's family is not rich; but more than the lack of money, it was the prevailing attitude 'before', as she says, that made her leave school. In this rural area unaffected by the beginnings of industrialization, where the nearest urban area, Saida, is 200 km away, people see only one future for a girl: an early marriage and the learning of domestic tasks. 'Knowledge' is not for girls; instead they learn to weave when they are very young.

Weaving is an activity of sedentary people; water is needed for the wool, and the loom has to be in a fixed place for several months. The big herdsmen (nomads or others) normally use female labour (adults or children). Traditionally, an exchange was made between the wool producer and the families whose women devoted themselves to handicrafts, with no money changing hands but with payment in kind and unspoken contracts of mutual aid and service (*touiza*). Over the last several years, middlemen have appeared who purchase the wool and monopolize the labour, thus breaking the traditional exchange and establishing a market. The price of the products (burnous, hangings, woven strips of wool from which tents are made) is fixed and imposed by the middlemen on the makers (men or women). They offer the product to the purchasers and the female labour force is paid only when the sale has been agreed. They thus sell without buying. It needs no stressing that these dealings go on over the heads of the women, since, as Fatima tells me, 'Where we live, as you know, women do not go out.' It is the men of the family who deal with the middlemen. It is no doubt the reason why, when we met, and I was talking to her about this women's work, she laughed, saying, 'Ah! Men! Women work and the men pocket the money!' She is obviously very conscious of how this work is kept in the dark and it is probably that same ignorance that made an Algerian whom I was asking for information about craftwork in this region say, 'All the women in that area are mistaken! They all have the idea that the main source of income is weaving, whereas in fact it is herding.'

It is difficult to estimate this income from weaving because no survey has ever been carried out. Yet Fatima is extremely sensitive to its importance since she knows very well that it is thanks to it that her mother, a widow — her father was killed during the war of liberation — was able to raise her three daughters. Refusing to put up with her mother-in-law, she came back to her own family and her brother (Fatima's uncle), who dealt with the middlemen and gave her the full proceeds of the sale. But it is inconceivable that the product of this sale in the village could be treated as an individual's 'wage'. The extended family is all-powerful and determined to resist erosion.

Reading the interview with Fatima, we get lost in a genealogical tree. Yet she moves about in it spontaneously and easily. Everyone is linked by a complexity of family relationships in which men dominate women and elders the young. These links above all enable the group and its interests to prevail over individuals of either sex. So fathers oppose their daughters going to school, but so too do grandmothers or aunts on both the father's and the mother's side. In the face of these alliances the will of a ten- or fifteen-year-old girl counts for very little.

Fatima, a girl from the rural areas, an orphan (for that is what a girl whose father is dead is called), felt every possible constraint weighing on her. School, for her, remained a hope whereas she is in fact the very sort of person the school excludes. It is true, as Tayeb Kennouche says, that the rural people have a sort of 'disarmed relationship'[1] with the school; it represents a sort of enclave of the town in the countryside which is incapable of using or absorbing it. How could it be otherwise when virtually no educational work is undertaken for the benefit of the rural community as a whole? The result is seen in a conflict between 'modernity' and 'tradition' and by a very high school drop-out rate, while many young people (boys but even more girls) do not even go to school at all.

Whereas the school enrolment ratio rises to 90% and above in the large towns, in the rural areas it may be as low as 51.3% and the illiteracy rate 71.3%. In the *wilaya* that Fatima comes from, one of the most disadvantaged, 49.5% of the girls as against 27.7% of the boys are not attending school. 81% of the girls and 74% of the boys do not complete primary school. 50% of children in the rural areas (according to Tayeb Kennouche's survey) do not progress beyond the primary level (the figure is 60% of children whose father is dead).

If sending a boy to school is an investment that pays (or so people might hope), it is not the same for a girl. School, for her, does not lead to a job (or only rarely — 35% of men and 2.5% of women work), given the lack of vocational schools and the economic and ideological obstacles. It is not at all clear what she would bring in to the family if she were educated. In the rural areas, educating a girl does not increase her value whereas if she is married young, knowing how to run a home and weave, she at least maintains what is already there and what people have always known. 'Exaltation of tradition for the sake of tradition',[2] the assurance provided by conservatism. Fatima reports that fathers say of little girls, 'Let them play a little, that's fine! But let them learn how to run a home.' The withdrawal of girls from school is part of a strategy dictated by economic and social constraints. It is not enough, so Fatima thinks, to build secondary schools where people live so that girls will go to them, when having to be away from home is, as ever, the insurmountable obstacle to their continuing their studies. Yet most of them have already been excluded from school and so the question of moving away never even arises.

But attitudes in the rural areas are not unchanging; the village is not self-contained. 'Now girls know their rights', Fatima said to me, and many of them are attempting to have their own way when it comes to marriage. They are determined to know their future husband, not necessarily to form an affectionate intimacy but rather to be able to assess him, his character and to know the sort of person they are dealing with before embarking on marriage. 'The girls want a boy they know, who has a good attitude.' The demand to live as a couple and to be independent in the management of the home is opposed by the family group which sees this desire as a criticism (even though one of Fatima's sisters apparently accepts that her husband gives a portion of his wages to his father, she keeps for herself enough to buy dresses for herself and 'make gold'). Fatima accepts the husband's authority but sees it as opposed to that of parents. Faced with this awakening of individualistic behaviour, the mother-in-law appears just as great an obstacle as domination by men: 'It's you I married and you are alright for me but your mother isn't!'

Emigration from this region has increased since independence. When she was nineteen Fatima married a man of her choice, a worker who had left her village and been working in France for ten years. One of her sisters did the same, but remained in the country, but Fatima joined her husband a year after they were married. In a way she is glad to have moved away, but would be quite happy to go back home if social pressures did not prevent her from achieving her goal of living quietly with her husband and studying and working. She wants to, just as she wants to give her two children, two boys aged three and six, as good an upbringing as possible. She wants only two children so as to be able to 'look after them'. Contrary to Fatima's beliefs, very few women at present, even of her age, have any such plan, which shows a major mental transformation (the birth rate is 3.2%).[3] It involves a new relationship with the child who is wanted for itself and for the couple, and a different relationship with the extended family which thus loses control over the reproduction of the lineage.

Ouardia and Malika have had what Fatima was unable to have: higher education. Both belong to well-off urban families for whom sending a girl to school is not even seen as an issue. 'It was quite normal!' says Ouardia. 'You will go to the polytechnic', Malika's father told her. Their mothers, who are in their fifties, are both educated. One went as far as the primary school-leaving certificate, the other up to the *brevet* [tr: the equivalent of 'O' level]; in their age group, the 1977 census showed 98% illiteracy. Ouardia is 35,

Malika 34. Ouardia got married ten years ago to a man she had chosen, but there were problems. Her husband died soon afterwards, leaving her alone with a small boy. She lives at her parents' house. She has an executive job in the nationalized sector but she has not been able to have her right to service accommodation recognized. Malika is unmarried and lives and works in Paris. Both analyse their lot and that of women in their society intellectually. They have the education necessary to be able to manage social relations, and yet they are not at ease: their consciousness and their aspirations have difficulty in finding an outlet. To varying degrees they also clash both with women and men of their generation whom they criticize for accepting traditional roles.

They studied at the university of Algiers between 1965 and 1970, at a time when the universities were very lively and activist; and yet neither of them had a committed youth. In those years, girls were a minority, and they have remained so. Their numbers have grown and this can be misleading, since they are visible in the streets in the university areas. There were 2,200 female university students in Algeria in 1968, and 10,000 in 1976 (and no doubt 15,000 in 1980) but in 1976 as in 1968 there were still 23 girls for every 77 boys at the university.

Ouardia and Malika were fully occupied with studying and for Malika it was in the university atmosphere that the break occurred because co-education is an impossible ideal in a society in which men and women are separated by modesty, reserve, shame and honour — an endless list of barriers far stronger than the veil and seclusion; a sudden meeting at the university is not sufficient to break them down. 'In reality, there is a separation. There is no communication,' says Malika. Boys and girls play the sad comedy of seduction and the most progressive ones have no complexes about demonstrating the most reactionary attitudes towards women. Writings about the participation of women in the liberation war propagate a myth, the myth of their liberation. This myth has several functions. On the one hand it has served since independence to stifle all demands by women, and on the other it rebuts the West's implicit accusation that Muslims maltreat their women. But Algerian nationalism has never included in its aims the liberation of women and the very circumstances of the struggle drove it into a very conservative cultural position. Women suffered the consequences of this and their massive participation in the struggle did not lead to a serious feminist movement. Since 1962 politics has remained essentially a man's world. Among these men there have been a few, those most sympathetic to a change in the status of women, who thought that everything would turn out right when socialism arrived.[4] Even though feminist ideas were much discussed between 1962 and 1970 (particularly in the books by Fadela M'Rabet), individual options for emancipation remained few and far between. These ideas have to some extent lost ground today, and while a minority of women have risen up against the proposed Family Code to demand basic rights, the majority are willing to accept the status quo. Ouardia's disillusioned comments on the lack of participation by women (students and intellectuals) in the demonstrations against the Code in 1981 are well-founded. Several of those who took an active part in these demonstrations told me not long ago, 'If a referendum were held among women, the Code would win.' Yet it enshrines in law the inequality of women *vis-à-vis* men.

Women have been overtaken by the general depoliticization which became more marked in the late 1970s. Those from better off families have suffered from their families' pursuit of wealth and social success which recognizes only one place for a young woman, as a pawn on the chess board of matrimonial strategies.

There are few women at work. They are to be seen in the large towns, since it is there that working women are concentrated (in Algiers in particular). Among the working population (those 'employed' in the 1977 census) 94% are men and 6% women, four-fifths of the latter being in urban areas. They are to be found predominantly in the education and health sectors. Their timidity is not surprising and it cannot be held against them if they prefer to recreate a miniature feminine world in the work-place rather than to fight with or against men on their own ground. And yet 'as for power, it's the men who have it, of course! You can't do anything. What you can do is fight on their ground,' says Ouardia, who is impatient with the passivity of her colleagues.

Although at present the participation of women in the return to Islamic fundamentalism is not (yet) on a massive scale, it is still true that, among the middle strata in the cities, many of them do adhere to it. Ouardia is shocked at their presence in a movement that aims to remove them from social life altogether, 'Yes, I ask myself what these women can expect from it . . .'

The National Union of Algerian Women (UNFA), the sole organization (under the aegis of the FLN) authorized to represent women, is severely criticized by Ouardia, as it is by every woman concerned with changing her lot and that of her sisters. Needless to say, it was not the UNFA that organized the protests against the Family Code.

'Yet,' says Ouardia, 'things are changing despite everything. The difference from what happened before is that now women complain. They feel the desire for a different sort of life. But to have this other life, women must put some effort into it themselves and stop complaining. Men are not going to change anything. It's not in their interests.'

Fatima

When she talks about her village, Fatima immediately stresses the importance of women's work.

Monique Gardant: And what do the men do?
Fatima: Ah, the men! Some of them work on a little parcel of land. Some go and work in the towns or in France. Before, it was the women who did most of the

19

work. My mother used to weave. She was alone. My father died in the war. He was a watch repairer, and looked after clocks.

One day during the war the soldiers had given him a watch to repair and he had told them to come and collect it at five o'clock. But a man who knew the maquisards got to know that the soldiers were coming back at five. He notified the ALN and they laid an ambush. The French had one dead and two wounded. If they had all died, there would have been no one to talk about it, but there were survivors and when they were asked where they had been attacked, they said, 'At the clock repairer's'.

The French thought it was my father who had alerted the ALN but my father was not working either with the ALN or with France. But the French came to find him. So he fled to the maquis and died there.

When he died there were three of us left. My mother's first child had been a boy who had died, then there were my two sisters and myself. I was two months old when my father left us. My grandparents, my father's family, took us in at first. And then, the last two, Selima and I, went with my mother to her parents. My sister stayed with my father's parents when my mother wanted to leave her mother-in-law. Then her father said to her, 'Move in with us.' Selima and I were very young. Selima was two and I was a year old. The oldest one didn't want to come. That's not surprising. Her grandparents had brought her up.

So it was mother who worked for us until independence. Afterwards, she had a small pension. What she wove she gave to my uncle (*khali*)[5] who looked after selling it, for as you know in our area, women don't go out. He sold what she produced and gave her all the money. He asked nothing for himself. Today many women still weave but it's not like before. Before, girls of my age used to start weaving very young. There were even little girls of nine who were weaving.

In our area not many girls go to school yet. I went, but not for long, only between six and ten; but I learned how to crochet and sew. I know a little Arabic, but not French. I've forgotten . . . I've forgotten Arabic a bit . . . but if I went back to school I could remember and learn French . . . yes, I could.

I went to the Training Centre organized by the municipality, where we were taught in Arabic. It was to teach us sewing.

M G: Why did you leave school at ten?

F: Because at that time people didn't like you going.

M G: Which 'people'?

F: My (maternal) grandfather. At X., even now, there's still this same attitude. It's like that . . . It's because some people are completely thick. Attitudes to school and learning have not changed.

For them, it's as simple as this: girls don't study! And so today they still don't go to school. My cousin, the daughter of my maternal uncle (*khali*) passed an examination to do a teaching course. Her father agreed. Her grandfather too, there was no problem, but *khalt khalti*, my maternal great-aunt, was against it and her grandfather too.

So my mother said to her brother, 'Let your daughter study.' But there was nothing to be done, *khalt khalti* and the grandfather had said: 'No'. So long as my cousin was studying in X., things were fine. But for her to go to town: 'No'. For them, girls must not move away to study. It's 'No'!

Some girls have done well in school. But they can't go on. I've another cousin and she too wanted to be a teacher. Her father had emigrated to France. Her paternal uncles didn't want her to continue. They sent a letter to her father to tell him: 'Your daughter must not go to school!' Now she's at home. She is married

and weaves. She fought, fought and fought, but in the end she got nothing.
M G: And your sisters?
F: They are in the village, they didn't go to school, except Selima, the youngest, who can read a little, but it's not been any use to her. She studied in French because she was at school in the time of the French. She can't read Arabic. She is married and stays in the house.

My older sister is also married, her husband is in France, she doesn't want to come here. I wanted to come, but she didn't. She stuck by her old ways. But I don't want to stay as before. I go where my husband goes.

Many women in the village don't want to move. Young and old alike, they don't even want to go to Algiers. But going to school, yes, they'd like to go. Many women would like to study and who will allow them to do so? You know very well, as I told you, that girls go to school when they are six and leave when they are ten or eleven.

I have a cousin who's thirteen, who did well and wanted to go to the secondary school (*lycée*). But it was impossible. The last time I was at home, I said to her father, 'Let her go.' But there is no secondary school in X. The father was willing, but there was no school. They've built one but it hasn't opened yet.

There are secondary schools at Y. and Z., but they're far away and there is no boarding-school for girls. People don't know anyone to look after their daughters in town. So they take them out of school. If they open the secondary school and girls don't have to go far away, outside, then perhaps they'll be able to study. For the time being they only study between the ages of six and eleven. It's rare to meet anyone who's completed her studies beyond that age.

The boys go to the secondary school. They have the right (*kein el droit*) to sleep there. They go there and come back to the village for the holidays. But girls haven't been given this right. Many people say that if they open a secondary school in X., they'll send their daughters there. Perhaps they will, but for the time being, not many of them are studying, whereas almost all the boys go to secondary school. They have to have their school outfit, but otherwise everything is free.
M G: How old were you when you learned to weave, to make carpets?
F: I was thirteen when I began. I used to go and play in the street, I wasn't really working. When I saw my mother weaving, I used to watch and learn.

When I was about fifteen, I began to work, but not all the time. Most girls start working at eleven or twelve. It's because of that they stop going to school. People think they shouldn't go out. As I told you, my cousins, the daughters of my uncle (the son of my mother's uncle), their father didn't send them to school at all. When they were six he kept them in the house while he sent his sons to school. One is an engineer, the other is studying medicine. These girls asked to go to school, they tried. Their father said 'No!' He said 'The boys go to school, but not the girls!' When they were small he would say, 'Let them play a little, that's fine. But let them learn how to run a home.'

You know, I can't remember much of what I learned. This is partly because we weren't taught well. The teachers passed the time, that's all. They didn't look after the children properly. Now they've changed the head, and there's no harshness. Things are better. In any case, most girls don't benefit. They stay in the house and their parents marry them off.

Before, no girl met her future husband before marriage. Now they do. Well, not many, but some. Boys aren't forced to marry like before, either. But for most girls, things haven't changed. Look, all the girls of my generation are married and stay in the house, they don't work outside.

21

This Centre I went to was to learn sewing and embroidery. We went there from eight in the morning to five in the evening, there was a canteen. We should have come out at four o'clock but between four and five we were given an hour of teaching. People were against that. They said, 'We want our daughters to learn to do something useful. If they marry, it's good that they learn so that they can work in the house. If you give them schooling in the Centre, we'll take our daughters away'.

That's how it is. When the parents take them away from school, they buy them a sewing-machine so that they can work in the house. It's the parent who sabotaged the Centre. They would say, 'If it's to teach them to work, yes. If it's to give them schooling, no!'

There were two hundred girls in the Centre, aged between ten and seventeen. It was useful to us. In the end, only eight of us were left. Most people took their daughters away because there was an hour of schooling. People are like that. They think that a girl might run away if she learns anything. They don't want their daughters to study. Education wakes the girls up and that's not good!

M G: Do the mothers think differently?

F: Some mothers do, others don't. But most of the time, the problems come from the fathers. Of course, there are mothers who marry off their daughters. Yes, that's true. But many say, 'We lived like that, but you, the young ones, we want you to wake up.' Most mothers would be happy to leave their daughters alone, but most fathers want to marry off their daughters like before.

I stayed at the Centre from thirteen to eighteen and at the same time I was working in the house. I helped my mother, I did sewing and crocheting in the evenings. But I had my freedom, my mother didn't bother us. I could go out alone. I never put on the veil until just before I got married. My uncle (*khali*) asked me to stay in the house. I said, 'No! It is not right. If you were my father, yes. But you're not my father, it's none of your business.' I went out like a boy. I did the shopping. Yes, there are girls who do all that. I had a neighbour, a girl of my age. We used to go out together.

M G: And the neighbours? People in the village?

F: Ah, people! They said that parents didn't know how to look after their daughters, that they didn't respect the traditions. Others used to say nothing even if they didn't like it. Freedom depends on the parents. My mother wanted us to be free. She didn't restrict us. My mother didn't go out, but we did.

Half the girls go out. There are girls who have fathers and don't go out but there are some who have fathers and are not restricted, and are free, because there are people who don't bother with customs and let their daughters go out. People in the village say, 'People who do that aren't normal!' Most have never been to school and they believe that everything should stay as it was before.

Even now there are very few girls in the Centre. Yet it was built so that girls could learn a trade, learn sewing. But almost all the girls left the school very young. At fourteen there are none left because people say that at that age a girl must leave school.

M G: Do any girls go to secondary school?

F: Yes, some do, not many. Their parents? . . . Some of them are working, like most people in the country, but say, 'I've worked like that, but I want my daughters to be different.'

I know a girl who is an engineer. She studied at Oran. She's never come back to the village. Her father had a shop. He moved to Z. and sent his daughters to

Oran. I know two sisters. Their father died and the mother made her daughters study. One is a teacher and wants to be a doctor. Their mother lived with her children at her father's house and he didn't like her sending her two daughters to school and he got angry. When her husband died she was only thirty. She left her father's and began to work on her own. She lived well. Rent is not high in the village and she made a good living since she was known as a good needlewoman. She also did knitting. She worked with wool and with that she paid for her daughters to study. Now one is a doctor and the other wants to be one too. The older one is in X. She's married. The younger one is a teacher in the village but she studies all the time.

You see, that woman left when she was told 'no' for her daughters. The state helped her. It didn't give her money, but it gave reductions for the canteen, and boarding fees. Sometimes the state even pays for the boarding fees, you only have to provide the outfit.

M G: And your women friends and cousins, would they want to let their daughters go to school?

F: Yes! They say: 'Our parents restricted us but we won't do the same thing.' Most women would like their daughters to be free.

M G: How did they get married?

F: Some chose, others didn't . . . Half and half. There are girls who know their future husband well but it is mostly the boys who choose now. There are young people who meet each other outside the home, there are girls who are working, there are some who go out, there are boys and girls who meet as neighbours. Young people see each other and when they agree, the parents of the boy go and see the family of the girl . . . Yes, they meet each other, in the street, or in the neighbourhood.

M G: Openly? In the village?

F: Yes, for example they meet at festivals. Married women don't see men but unmarried girls can see young men. If a girl knows a boy, she can make an appointment with him, and arrange to see him, and go out with him, but there are some who still keep to the old customs.

The custom remains that the elders always ask for the marriage but the time is coming when that will no longer happen.

There are also girls who write letters. They don't put them in the post, they send them by someone they know well . . . and the parents don't know about it. Anyway, parents are not supposed to open their daughter's letters. Of course, some do. Especially fathers . . . But you can't want to marry someone unless you know him well.

Sometimes, young people meet each other for three, four years or more. Marriages made in this way have been successful. Where we live, in the countryside, everyone knows everyone else. You meet a girl who is with someone; it may be her neighbour but you don't really know why she is with him. Young people like that, who know each other, can live together.

I have a cousin (*bent amti*, the daughter of my paternal aunt) who was forced to marry. She was seeing a boy cousin. When we were going to the Centre she would see him with me . . . but she couldn't marry him. This cousin worked in the mayor's office and she used to see him at the Centre. In the summer he used to come and buy us lemonade. He could come because we were cousins, and we'd talk, all three of us together.

She also used to see him at my house, they got to know each other well and

23

wanted to get married. The boy's mother went to ask for her hand in marriage but the girl's father was unwilling because his (the father's) aunt had already asked for the hand of this daughter for her son. My girl cousin wanted to marry the other cousin but the aunt was unwilling: she wanted her for her son.

The girl's mother said to her husband, 'I'm not giving my daughter to your aunt because I know your aunt. They won't get on. And perhaps our daughter won't get on with her son. It is the other one she wants. Let her get on with it. If it doesn't work, it'll be her responsibility.'

The father said: 'No! I'm giving her to my aunt.' And he did so. That was two years ago and she's had a child.

If she didn't want this man, it was not because she did or didn't like him. It was because of his mother. Zoubeida, my cousin, told him: 'I took you and married you without knowing you. It's not the other one, it's you I married and you are all right for me but your mother isn't.'

The son was unwilling to leave his mother and they got divorced because Zoubeida didn't get on with her mother-in-law. As she knew that her mother-in-law was very fond of her grandson, she left the child with her because she knew that she would treat him well. Many people still do this; their son gets married and lives with them.

And so there you are ... today girls want to marry a man they know and can get on with. That's why they prefer a man they know to one who comes from elsewhere. Some men come from Saida or El Asnam because they know that there is a girl to be married ... and she doesn't know *them*. Girls want a boy they know, with the right attitude.

There are girls who married and are working. When a girl gets married it is the husband, not the parents, who control her. If she's found a husband who is educated and sympathetic her parents no longer control her; what she wants to do is decided between her and her husband. In the village there are women working in offices, or at school and also housewives. Mostly, these are women who were taken out of school by their parents. Girls who have never been to school, who have always remained with their parents, stay in the house once they are married. But many women want their freedom and want to work ... even in another town. If their husbands would let them, they would even leave the village and go and work ... And in any case, there are always the mothers-in-law!

Most mothers-in-law want to keep their son while most young women want to live alone with their husband. However, if the woman is free within her husband's family, if she can buy things for herself and no one says anything to her, she tends to stay there even if she has some education. My younger sister lives with her in-laws in the same house and likes them. She lived with her brother-in-law's wife but she's gone away now. There are always the *adjouza* and the *sheikh*.[6] They have a divorced daughter with them, a girl of nineteen, two others about thirteen, one boy of twenty-three and another boy of nine.

They don't bother my sister; she's free, she has her own money. But they eat together. Her husband works, and so does her husband's brother. They give money to their father and he is responsible for everything. My sister weaves in the house but not to sell. The men work, they are nice and my sister says, 'So long as they don't bother me, I'm not leaving them.' Her in-laws are not blood relatives, they are people in the village. She met this boy and they got married. She's not bothered, she has her freedom, she's fine.

She has a boy who's just a few months old and another who's five. When I go home she comes to our house, and I go to theirs. Her five-year-old doesn't want to stay with us, he's happier with his paternal grandparents. He wants to stay there because they brought him up and look after him a lot. When my sister is sick, they look after her well. When she goes on 'holidays' (sic) they keep her room clean. They wash her dirty linen. Sometimes she buys clothes or 'makes gold'.[7] They don't say anything to her.

M G: Would she have liked to work?

F: No! She doesn't need anything. She says: 'I'm all right, I'm fine.'

M G: And could you live like that?

F: Ah! To each his own! Perhaps if I had met a really nice family I would have stayed with them. If I liked my husband's mother, perhaps I would have stayed with her. She is an old woman, I would have done the cooking, and looked after her.

I and my older sister tease her. 'And you? Won't you ever leave this prison?' She doesn't like us speaking like that because they do everything for her. She can go out, she goes to weddings, she can walk about.

M G: But most women?

F: It's often the husband's family that is the trouble. Sometimes the daughter-in-law is spiteful and the husband's family won't accept her and they say, 'Go, and take your wife with you!'

M G: And if you go back to the village, do you stay in the house?

F: Yes, why not? But Mohammed, my husband, doesn't want to go back. Me, I'd be happy to go back, after all it is my village (*bledna*). It's better to be at home with your own people. I could stay in the village if I liked the life, if I had my freedom and no one interfered and I could do what I liked with my husband. If your husband doesn't restrict you, if you get on well with him, that's fine ... Whether I stay here or go back to X. I would like to work. I don't like people saying to me, 'You don't work'. If my husband agrees, I'll work.

M G: And when you go back home, what do your women friends say about you?

F: They say that I've changed. But things must change. You build your own house, you do something for yourself, get something of your own, and you want it to be nice. But there are old people who think that things should stay as they were. Those people say, 'We were born like that, and we'll stay like that.'

And there are poor women who live unhappily like that. They spend the whole day weaving, the husband sells their work and brings them food. And that's all. And they are happy with the clothes he buys them. Yes, there are still women like that today. But there are others whose parents don't succeed in imposing marriage on them, and who end up today having the last word because things are changing.

M G: Because they have been to school?

F: Some who are educated are obedient, but others aren't. Even the girls who are not educated think for themselves. They know their rights; they think of their future.

M G: Do those who have chosen their own husband get divorced?

F: No, for many of them, it works. But for those who have had a husband forced on them, no. They stay three months and then go back to their parents. In a traditional marriage, the parents know each other but the most important thing is that the young people should know each other. They wanted to marry me, they tried for two years without persuading me. But I knew the young man only by sight, so I didn't really know him. It was not my mother who wanted to force me. If I had wanted to she would have accepted it. But it was my uncle (*khali*) who wanted to force me. My mother knew the young man's mother but I didn't know him.

M G: Have you heard of the Family Code?

F: You know, everyone wants their freedom and many women don't want to stay under the authority of a father or husband ... If they find a job, or if they want to work ... And a girl who has no parents, who has a brother and who wants to marry someone, she doesn't have to ask him.

When I went to Poissy, I talked about the Code with Zohra, a cousin who has been in France for 21 years. She came when she was very young, nine years old. Her father had emigrated, and she got married here, to an emigrant. We were talking about the Family Code and Zohra said to me, 'I wouldn't accept it. Here now I am free but if I go back there my daughters won't accept it.'

Zohra's mother had stayed in the country with her two children. Her husband had emigrated to France. One day she decided to ask her husband if she could either live with him in France or separate. Her brother got all the papers for her and she came. Someone went to tell her husband on the work-site, 'Your wife and kids are here, in the room.' He couldn't believe it but it was true. He said, 'What have you come to do here?' She replied, 'Even if we had no children you should not have run away and left me alone. But you have two children, you must look after them or else you must come back.' He said, 'I'm not coming back but if you like, you can stay.'

Since then she's stayed and Zohra has grown up and married her cousin here. She has heard about this Family Code and is against it. Everyone must have their freedom, women as well as men. If this Code becomes law, it will cause a lot of problems for women.

M G: Would you like a daughter now that you have two sons?

F: No.

M G: Why?

F: If Halim, my youngest, were a girl, so much the better. But I want only two children so that I can look after them. Some women have lots of children but can't look after them. They get no education. My sister in the village has two children but she doesn't want any more.

M G: How will she manage that?

F: Do you think people there are ignorant? There's the hospital. She goes to the surgery. If not she goes to the pharmacist. It's free. There are plenty of people who are not completely narrow-minded. Even women who live in the house have heard about that. In the old days, when their children were ill, people left them. Today they want to care for them, educate them, teach them. There are women who are very poor, and very isolated and they hear that you need now have only two or three children.

M G: In your opinion, why do most women have many children?

F: There are some, yes. But they are women who don't think. They produce children and God knows how they are educated. It is mostly those over forty who have lots of children. But women younger than that don't have so many.[8]

Ouardia

O: For me there was never any problem about going to school. I started going to school when I was six as a matter of course. I didn't see it as anything unusual. It was quite natural. This was perhaps because my mother had already had a little schooling. She had passed the CEP [primary school leaving certificate]. That was quite unusual at the time because my mother comes from a small village in Kabylia where girls didn't used to go to school. She was the only girl in her family to have gone, perhaps she did because she was the youngest. My grandfather must have changed his way of seeing things, but a little late.

She would have liked to go on but, funnily enough, it was her brothers who wanted her to stop at the CEP. In any event, in her village, she was the only Algerian girl in school at the time. We have a photo of her class; the two other girls were French and the rest were boys.

I think that even today my mother regrets not having been able to continue her education. She still talks about it. And she once explained to me that it was her brothers [they studied, one is a doctor and one a teacher] who said that she couldn't. That's why I say 'funnily enough' because they went on with their education. In any case she would have had to go to the town . . .

My grandfather was no doubt influenced by his sons. It is often the case that what the sons say, especially the eldest son, carries more weight than what the father says especially for daughters.

So for me then, school was taken for granted. Even when I failed, there was no question of withdrawing me. Because it is not enough to start, you have to carry on! Often, the first failure is an excuse for withdrawing a girl. I lost a lot of girl friends along the way because in the fifth form, at the *brevet*, they had failed and the fathers decided that they should stop there. When I failed the baccalaureat I repeated the year, my sister did too. This was normal. And my parents made no distinctions between girls and boys.

M G: Even in the house?

O: Yes, even in everyday life . . . But no, all the same, there were things that I only realized later. About ten years ago I realized that we didn't all have the same status in the house. A girl is asked to help more and above all she is asked to wait on her brothers. My brothers never used to make their beds. It was my sister and me who used to make them. Yes, I always made my brother's bed. If a brother wants something done — say a shirt washed, he asks his sister. It's quite normal to wait on your brother! Never, I never made a fuss. Now things have changed in our house. If one of my brothers tells me to hurry up and clear the table, I say, 'Do it yourself!'

M G: When did you change?

O: I don't know; but there are just things I no longer accept. I don't know when I stopped feeling that some things necessarily had to be done by girls. But I've taught my son how to make his bed. Now he makes it all by himself. When he finishes his coffee, he gets up and washes the cup. I want this to be something natural for him, so that he does not have to rely on someone else to do it. My brothers have changed too. But perhaps they're different from others. I remember that while we were students, I used to tell them that my friends' brothers were nicer than they were, that they took them to the cinema, and they said to me, 'But it's not our job to take you out, to be your guardian angel. If you want to go out, then go out!'

But it's now that I'm talking about it that I realize that my brothers make an effort. I have a married brother whose wife is a teacher, and it's the same! In his house . . . no! . . . I don't like to say 'share'! Let's just say that in his house they do things together without any problem. I don't like to say he 'helps her' either, because it's not true. After all, he's at home. He does what he ought. Perhaps this is because my sister-in-law was right, able to assert herself from the very beginning. Because perhaps it's also the woman's fault. If at the beginning you start spoiling your husband and waiting on him, it will be much more difficult afterwards, when the children are there, to get him to accept that what happens in the house is his business too. Yes, I think that the woman must know what she wants. It's no good moaning and complaining and saying you are oppressed all the time. It's up to women to behave in such a way that things change, because men have no interest in things changing. As sons they were spoiled. Their mother and sisters were there to wait on them. It's up to women to make sure that things change.

M G: Does this change of attitude come because women are working?

O: Even in couples where the woman works, the problem is still there. I have women friends who are constantly complaining. When they get home, they have to look after everything. The husband does absolutely nothing! I remember a friend who had gone to see her sick mother. She was away for five days. When she got back she found all the washing up waiting for her piled up almost to the front door. He had done absolutely nothing!

M G: Do you think it was her fault?

O: Yes, of course! I think so. You have to know from the beginning what you want. When she is there I'm sure the husband doesn't ever have to do anything, so that it must seem quite absurd for him to do the washing up! Inconceivable! Even if the dishes pile up for a month! It's up to her to tell that it isn't. With my women friends, I say when they complain, 'It's your fault!' It's too easy to say all the time, 'Men are like this, they're like that.' Surely it's up to women to be clear about what they want. At work it's the same problem. Even for a woman in an executive job, it's not always easy to get herself respected and treated as equal to a male worker.

I realized from little, petty but significant things how men see women at work. For men, a woman's work is being a secretary! I don't say that to run down the job of secretary but because for men a secretary in some way 'services' the boss! She is at his beck and call. As soon as he needs something, he buzzes and she comes . . . just like the women at home! In a way the office is an extension of the house. The secretary is there to wait on the man. Whereas a woman officer is responsible for a particular job. She is not at a man's beck and call.

In a department near mine the manager's secretary went on leave. In this department there were only executives, including one woman. So the manager in question asked the woman to answer the telephone while the secretary was away. Of course, answering the telephone is nothing! But why ask a woman? A man who is passing by can answer the phone if he hears it ringing and take the message and pass it on to the boss. The fact that the woman was asked shocked me. Each time the telephone rang, this woman, who was an executive, I repeat, would come running . . . That's how I happened to notice it. I said to her, 'But your desk is farther from the telephone than Mr this or that . . .' She said, 'I don't know. He asked me to do it.' And she'd agreed! She didn't understand what I meant — it seemed quite normal to her.

One day I had come to the office, outside working hours, with a friend and her little daughter. One of my male colleagues met us, greeted us and stroked the little girl's hair. 'Ah! Here is a little future secretary!' What can you say?! Men always ask women to look after them. It's the dominant factor in relations between men and women in our country. It begins in childhood and now I realize that even at work women have this rather submissive attitude. Women serve the coffee. Everyone could quite easily help themselves from the thermos in the secretariat! But no! And the women put up with it. That is why I find them largely to blame for their own situation. Perhaps for girls who have not had much schooling or not read much, who've not had much chance to think for themselves, we can understand! But even those who have studied have the same attitudes.

M G: You know, listening to you, I thought of a recent survey by the women of the CNRS [National Centre for Scientific Research, in France] on the life-style and work relations of couples at the CNRS.[9] Even in an industrial country where women have been working for several generations, many of the issues you raise are still relevant. In Algeria, the weight of traditional models weighs very heavily on the minority of women who really want to see change.

O: Yes, but things *are* changing. Women complain now. They complain because they have become conscious of their condition. Women didn't used to complain before. But now they do, and they want a different life. But to get this other life women must put themselves out and stop complaining. For the men won't do anything at all. It's the women who must change things.

M G: Yes, but how?

O: There aren't any easy answers . . . For example I wanted to get a better idea of what the UNFA is, rather than criticizing without knowing. I went to a meeting to see what they were thinking and doing. I attracted attention because I said that there was no reason to have a UNFA section at work. I think that it aggravates the problem of the segregation of men and women. The existence of this section means that all the women's problems will be looked at there whereas there is an ATU [assembly of workers in the production unit] which is there to deal with the problems of workers, of either sex.

Going to a UNFA section to discuss women's problems, means 'feminizing' the problem too much. And then, since means are limited and the UNFA has no power, people will simply say, 'It is women who have women's problems . . . They always have the same problems!' The matter won't get discussed. Women's problems should be raised at an ATE (assembly of workers in the enterprise). I'm not in favour of separating women and men workers. And that's what I said at this meeting.

M G: What are these demands?

O: They're to do with problems of training, professional problems, career problems, promotion. And I'm not in favour of going and raising these at a UNFA section. The only role for UNFA in the enterprise is to 'consciousness-raise' . . . that's their word. One day I said to them, 'What is "consciousness-raising"?' When you get down to it what does it mean? They want to make women aware of their role in society . . . What are they going to do about it? It's not enough to talk!

But to come back to the problem of demands, the UNFA has no weight. The ATU is there for that. And I absolutely refuse to distinguish between the demands of male and female workers. Because men have similar problems.

Perhaps women *are* worse affected. But it is precisely by going to the ATU that you have some chance of getting heard in the right quarters.

M G: Did the women who attended these meetings feel disadvantaged compared to men at work?

O: Yes. At one meeting, there was a computer puncher who complained that promotion always went to men. She had several years' seniority and she was still in the same job. And men with equal training and equal seniority were getting promoted over her head. Others had problems with crèches. They said that the UNFA simply must do something. But it's unfortunate that in our country the problem of crèches has come to be seen as a women's problem, whereas ultimately it concerns both men and women. The women complained that, unlike the men, they did not get any training, or at least that they had no opportunity for courses to upgrade themselves. But it is very rarely that they ask for them. They keep themselves down! You have to fight to get something. What I criticize women for is for not trying, for simply waiting for something to happen and saying that they have nothing. But it is true that for training people often have to go abroad. When someone says, 'departure overseas for training', that at once sounds suspicious. At that UNFA meeting, there was a woman who had been abroad for a course and some women had said, 'It's either because she's got an inside track or because the woman . . . let's say flirts!' Yes, there was one woman who said that to another straight out. But training is not a privilege. It is a right that must be demanded!

Once, in my department, there were some women who were complaining all the time about their lack of professional training. I asked them what they thought about going abroad for a year to upgrade themselves. We could send three people. There were three women. This was the time for them to take advantage of what was being offered. One was married, two were unmarried. The one who was married had two children and it was impossible for her. But the other two . . . 'Oh, no! It'll be refused. It's not even worth asking. We'll be rejected!' They didn't put in the request.

M G: Perhaps they were thinking of getting married?

O: I don't know. It is true that they got married a year or a year and a half later. Perhaps it was that. But they didn't say so. Ultimately, marriage is still the most important thing for a woman. You get a qualification after studying and you don't try to go any further!

M G: I would like to go back a little to this question of co-education because I remember that in 1964, when the question of getting women to participate in political life was being discussed before the FLN congress — the first one after independence — some people said that segregation of the sexes had to be maintained, that women would not dare to speak, or work alongside men, that if there was mixing their fathers or their husbands would not let them be activists. There is a paradox in wanting women to participate in political and social life and maintaining structures which are designed precisely to prevent that. But it is also true that it is not an easy matter to come out from this exclusion and face the world of men. What do you think about it?

O: Yes, it is a problem. I was talking just now about this business of 'consciousness-raising' which is supposed to be the job of the UNFA. I said, 'Make women more aware? But all workers need to be aware of the problems of the business.' And it was then that they dragged up all the stories that are repeated ad nauseam about the liberation of women. The chairwoman said,

'Now I will let you make suggestions!' Hands went up and a woman said, 'I suggest that we produce a newspaper.' I said, 'An exclusively women's newspaper?' 'Yes, of course,' came the reply.

A second hand went up and said, 'I propose that we make a library.' I said, 'A women's library?' I began to feel that I was getting their backs up. A woman said to me, 'Why do you keep asking the same question? Women's, women's . . . We are women, we are talking of our problems. Why do you object?' I replied, 'But you don't realize what you are doing. You say that you have problems and you want to create a little separate women's world. You won't get anything that way. If you want to defend women join the ATU. At least it's not closed to women! And there you will be stronger because you will be with men who, ultimately, have power. That's the truth! It's still men who have power! But I find it absurd to make a women's library, or an exclusively women's newspaper. I don't agree.'

Despite that the women wanted to elect me to the UNFA section. I refused. My women friends treated me as if I were a coward. They said to me, 'In the end, it's easy. You can now say that the UNFA is no good but if you had stayed there you could have changed it.' In fact I don't think that's true. I could have done nothing on my own against a whole organization.

M G: But wouldn't the women have backed you?

O: I don't think I would have been supported because most of the women had ideas that seemed so way out. They refused to participate in the ATU as individuals. They said that a strong UNFA section was needed to influence the ATU. One woman on her own . . . No! They need an organization behind them so that they can stand as delegates of the UNFA instead of standing as women workers. Ultimately, it's their weakness that stops them. Women need to feel strong!

The UNFA leaders said that the sections in other enterprises were dynamic and effective. I asked them for facts. 'They organize excursions' . . . for women! There too I had said 'for women'! They looked at me sideways and someone replied, 'Yes, it's very nice. They have a car with a microphone and they were able to discuss their problems' . . . in the bus! Perhaps I am hard or cynical but I can't understand their attitude.

M G: It seems from listening to you that these women are of necessity involved in a form of mixing at work and that their only thought is to get out of it, and recreate a world of women and not to extend their contact with men and their power in a man's world.

O: No, Not at all! They complain that they have no power in that world. I say that they're doing nothing to change it . . . Quite the reverse! The only attempts that they make show that they want to deepen the chasm by retreating into purely women's activities. That is why I am often so hard.

M G: But weren't there some women who mobilized at the time of the discussion in the National Assembly on the Family Code in 1981?

O: Yes, but the UNFA clearly showed its colours. It was the last to mobilize!

There was a small group of us, about ten, who met in the canteen to discuss these things. We went together on the march on the Assembly and to important meetings. But it was still all very limited. As I was saying, there were only about ten of us at work who were interested and we were almost all executive staff. I didn't get the impression that the others were bothered. It didn't seem to affect them. Take the secretary. When the march on the Assembly took place, I took two hours off to go on it. I therefore warned my boss, who is a man. He's very good! I mean, he takes things the right way! But not the secretary. She didn't even show any curiosity about what was happening. It was the female executive staff and the women students who were concerned. They were the ones I could talk to.

M G: What most shocked women in the Family Code?

O: A provision that women could work only if their husbands first approved. This was what came up most in discussions. And then in the article on divorce it is stated that the husband can divorce if he wishes. All he has to do is pronounce the divorce and the judge must carry it out, with no possibility of recourse open to the wife. But the wife can ask for a divorce only in certain conditions . . . and they were listed in the text. Sick husband, etc. Ultimately, as soon as you set conditions, you can always play on words and when the wife asks, she will be told that she doesn't meet the requirement. These were the two points that raised the most problems. Polygamy doesn't concern young couples much nowadays.

I discussed divorce with a male colleague. We had been talking about the whole Code. When we got to this point, he said, 'If you give women the possibility of divorcing, they'll divorce on the slightest whim and be lost, alone in life with their children . . .'

M G: Yes, men don't have whims! Or shall we say that their whims are satisfied?

O: That's the difference! Women don't have the *right* to have whims. Look, I remember that one of our colleagues came with us on a demonstration. He wanted to show his solidarity with the women publicly. Yes, he was a brave man. Well, when we reached the place and met the cops, a policeman grabbed him and said to him, 'What are you doing here?' 'I'm supporting them!' 'You're crazy', said the policeman, 'it's a women's demonstration'. And he prevented him going any further! That made me think again about this problem of mixing. Even executive women sometimes turn against it. I don't know how to explain that. At the time of these UNFA meetings that I was telling you about, I discussed them with a very close (female) friend with whom I had always been in close agreement until then. We were going to these meetings together. But we no longer saw eye to eye. She did not think that women's problems should be discussed with men. She agreed that they should be talked about in a small section of the UNFA.

I was very affected by that. I saw myself as abnormal . . . or almost. I said to myself, 'Perhaps I'm the one who's wrong.' She didn't explain her reasons to me. She said to me, 'You know, you mustn't expect men to settle our problems. So we must meet among ourselves.' I replied, 'But it is men who have power! That's the reality. We can't do anything about it. What we can do is fight on their ground.'

It is true, it's the men who make decisions. You can't always be harping on the same great issues as the UNFA does. We must act. We've been independent for twenty years and for twenty years we've been hearing about the UNFA and for twenty years it's done nothing for women. What is needed is action.

But all the same it must be recognized that on occasion women have succeeded in mobilizing themselves in the UNFA. I know that the women in a particular firm once met together and drew up a statement in which they complained of their working conditions; not just the material ones, but the lack of respect. Yes, they asked for respect. They said that they were fed up with being treated in this way. It seems that heads of department allowed themselves certain liberties with their secretaries. The secretaries had dared to say as much. I thought that was very brave. They had sent this statement to those running the firm and to the FLN. It caused a big stir. They had dared to name names and demand sanctions. As the matter had become public, sanctions were taken. The UNFA had got going because it concerned attacks on decency. It seems that from that time women felt that men treated them with a new consideration. They could no longer take the liberties that they had before. I approved of all that.

But unfortunately, revenge was taken on the women. They were harassed afterwards and couldn't ask for anything again but they found that the protest, the statement that they had dared to write had had an impact. It had marked people. They had said openly that they would no longer tolerate being treated as women-objects . . . Perhaps they had gone a bit far in the language they used. But they had demanded respect and that is basic in relations between men and women.

You must have heard about what happened at Sidi bel Abbès in the SONELEC complex.[10] The Muslim Brothers had come to wait for the women at the bus terminal at five o'clock, armed with clubs. This was all in the name of the faith! They were put down by the police. After these events the Brothers cut off their beards so as not to be noticed. No more bearded people were to be seen!

M G: Muslim Brothers or not, in discussing women some allusion is almost always made to religion.

O:　　Certainly. But I've got nothing to say about religion. I didn't really have a religious education. It is only now that my father is getting old that he's beginning to say his prayers. I neither practise nor believe. But it isn't the men who worry me most about the Muslim Brothers. I wonder more about the Muslim Sisters and I say to myself, 'What do they expect from this movement?' Because I've talked with quite a few men who move among the Muslim Brothers and I know the way they think. They tell me that their ultimate objective is that women should disappear, and no longer have any active social life. I wonder what the Muslim Sisters think of that because many of them are working. It is because they go out that they have become Muslim Sisters. If not how would they have come across this propaganda? So what do they expect of this movement that is largely directed against them? If you listen to the Muslim Brothers, they never talk about work. Work and production are not mentioned. They always talk about women . . . It's an obsession.

One day during Ramadan last year, I was at the house of friends who live opposite the mosque. They use microphones for the sermon and prayers and broadcast them in the streets. Well, that day, the whole sermon was about women. And saying ridiculous things . . . 'You must not allow your womenfolk to go to the beach! It is against Islam that they should bare themselves in public . . .' Things like that in the mosque! I ask myself what women can expect from it. But do they realize? In a way they are intoxicated. They go along with it unawares! I mean that even those who 'get religion' as people say, I don't know whether they take a clear-cut stand on Islam. Whether they know what harm it will do them or not. Because it is said in Western countries that Islam is against women. In fact, Islam, pure Islam, is not! Islam is not against women, but it has now become distorted.

And it's like that not only in Algiers. In Blida, in the south too ... Look, at Medea[11] ... it's not possible for a man and a woman to go out together. Someone was telling me about X. Something happened in the mosque. Traditionally women don't go there even though, in theory, a small space is set aside for them. Then the Muslim Sisters had taken to coming every day to say their prayers. Now in X, women don't even go along the main street, my aunt who lives there has never even seen it. When you go there you arrange, even with the car, to go round it. And then, all of a sudden, Muslim Sisters are going there! There were scuffles and the police had to intervene because the Sisters began to perform their ablutions in a room which of course the men had never seen a woman enter. To perform their ablutions women, like men, have to bare their arms and wash their feet. As it happened, some men came in and found women there like that. The men were furious. They said, 'The mosque is becoming a brothel!' Shame! But there were some men who were in favour of women using the mosque. They fought one another.

M G: What memories do you have of your years at university?

O: Very good ones. In the late 1960s you could go to a café. Now that's no longer possible; the cafés are no longer mixed even in the university. We used to go to the library together.

M G: When you were outside the campus could relations with men, friendly or otherwise, continue?

O: For me, no. My family was very strict. When I came out of the university, that was it. I couldn't be seen with a boy in the street.

M G: Yet your family could accept you meeting boys on the campus?

O: Yes, but not outside. It wasn't right! A serious girl didn't do that sort of thing! I was studying, but for my family that was limited to the walls of the university. You had to cheat to have a few moments to yourself. It was the only way, and I did it. Look, I never even ate in the university restaurant. Girl friends who were in the university halls of residence had more freedom, but it was only an appearance. It was because they were away from their families. If their families had known that their daughters were walking in the street with boys, going to the cinema or café, that would have brought on a big argument. I remember a friend. One of her brothers came unexpectedly to see her from the country and got to know that she was acting with the rue Mogador group.[12] Her family rushed to save her and then beat her. She tried to get away through the window, but in the end they took her back with them. You know, the theatre has always had a bad reputation.

M G: But your mother? Was she as strict as the rest of the family?

O: Yes, but you know it's often like that. But I don't understand. Mothers should stand by daughters and this doesn't happen very often. Mothers are often harsher — I think they're afraid of their husbands; afraid of being held responsible if something goes wrong.

M G: Did you choose your husband?

O: Yes. But it was very difficult.

M G: Now that you are, unhappily, alone, are you freer?

O: Oh, not necessarily! There is a word we have to describe a woman who is alone, a widow, divorcée, spinster or whatever, any woman who can't boast of having a husband — *hajala*. And it's very pejorative. She is watched even more closely than the others because she might 'do anything'. Women find it difficult to live alone because people believe that they are more easily corrupted.

M G: Before we began the interview you told me you wanted to talk about accommodation.

O: I began with that because it is a real problem that worries me. Four years ago I asked for housing. I still haven't got it. And I know that one day I'm going to lose my temper at work. Some senior staff have got housing — but they are men. But can I blame my boss, who seems to be so nice, intelligent and understanding? Basically, he must think that for a woman it's not really urgent. Especially as I'm staying with my parents. But a male colleague was living in a two-room place and he found it too small. He was getting married and thought two rooms were too small for a young couple. I do think that with the housing crisis they could have made do. He knows that I've had a request for housing in for four years, but he said to me, 'Anyway, you've no problems because you're with your parents.' This means that if my request is just left lying around, it's because they think that compared to men I've no priority . . . compared to single men!

M G: Yes, I know the problem. I noticed that in 1979 the right to accommodation was among the demands made by the Congress of Working Women. But is it not the case that women alone get abuse from their neighbours as well?

O: For the neighbours a woman living alone is automatically loose-living. The day I made my request my boss first accepted it but then started to try and get me to withdraw it. 'You know, it's difficult for a woman alone. How will you manage? How will you be able to get along on your own with a child?' When I told him I'd be able to manage perfectly well, he turned the argument to safety, 'You won't be safe,' etc. Then — I don't know whether it was done deliberately — the places offered me were quite unsuitable for a single woman. It is alas true that a woman cannot live just anywhere; but housing has been given to men that I could quite well have lived in. But I haven't given up, I keep pushing my request.

M G: And your leisure activities? Now that your family no longer puts barriers in your way, perhaps society still imposes some. How do you get on?

O: I've got a lot of friends. We go out together at weekends either to the country or to each other's houses. They are all couples with children.

M G: Do you go to the cinema?

O: No, never. I was complaining with a female colleague about not being able to do anything. Like me she didn't have enough to do. And then one day, we said, 'Come on, let's go to the cinema instead of moaning.' That was in 1978 or 9. We agreed that we would organize ourselves to go once a week to see a film. I hadn't been to the cinema since 1968 or 9 when it was still possible. And so we went.

It was unbearable. We were never bothered directly. But all the young people screamed as soon as there was a slightly blue scene! It was intolerable! You couldn't concentrate on the film. We came out completely exhausted. We had gone to the Debussy.[13] Afterwards we went all the way down the rue Didouche saying, 'Yes, it's really unbearable, we won't go again.' Then when we reached the bus depot we thought that, well, at least we had seen a film and a week later we spoke on the telephone, 'Well! What do you think about it? Shall we go again?' And then in the end we just let it drop because ultimately it wasn't relaxing at all.

M G: Do you sometimes go to these tea rooms that are opening up now?

O: Yes! I went once with a woman friend after work. We were dying of thirst. But there was nowhere to sit down and we didn't want to stay because it was full of men looking for women to pick up. That's what happens when a place is mixed. The Princière used to be nice. Now it's always full to overflowing. You feel uneasy about staying there. We stopped going because it wasn't fun any more.

What can you do? It's difficult for a woman. We are so used to staying in the background. If you don't that means you're not a serious sort of person. Everything is 'serious, not serious'. The worst insult for a woman is to say that she is not serious!

M G: If you had a girl instead of a boy how would you manage?

O: I'm very glad I've got a boy . . . More and more so! It's easier! It's no good thinking, 'I won't bring up my daughter as I was brought up', the whole environment bears so heavily on you . . . I remember that once I'd been to visit a relative outside Algiers. My son was three years old. Her son who is about forty said to me, 'You came alone?' Then I said, 'No, I came with my son.' Then my aunt said, 'Yes, her son is a man!' She meant it. He was three years old, but he was a man!

Malika

M: My maternal grandfather was a postman. At the time, during the colonial period, in the 1930s, being a postman was something. Still today in T., when people talk about my grandmother, they say 'the postman's wife'. He was deeply involved in politics and, I think, although I'm not absolutely sure, that he joined the Algerian Communist Party and the Muslim Congress after '36.[14] T. was a communist municipality at the time and it had welcomed Spanish Republicans.

My father and mother went to school in T., up to *cours complémentaire* [old secondary modern school] and some of the teachers were Spanish refugees, including the famous M., a sort of aristocratic Marxist, whom everybody still talks about. Doctor M., a communist, was a friend of the family. My maternal great-grandparents came from one of the oldest Arab founding families of T. My aunts had all been to school. One of them who is now seventy years old had her primary school leaving certificate.

My mother herself passed the *brevet élémentaire* [school certificate]. Her teachers had pushed her to take the entrance exam for the Women's Teacher Training College at Orléansville.[15] She came out top. My grandfather wanted her to go on. He had eight children (five boys, three girls) and my mother was the last born. Her sisters were married but one had gone as far as the certificate (as I said) and the other to the *cours complémentaire*. My grandmother was against her continuing her education. She wanted my mother either to marry or learn to sew.

In any case, the eldest son said his piece and he said 'no'. He apparently felt guilty afterwards about this refusal. But he had to keep the side up. There was no question of sending his sister to Orléansville, even as a boarder. It's rather funny when I think about it because my oldest uncle came to Paris to finish his studies (because he was a marked man in Algeria as a nationalist) and married a Frenchwoman. When my father was arrested during the liberation war and my mother was forced to work in terrible conditions, she still regretted her lack of education. Her brothers had all done advanced studies. Two are doctors, one is a diplomat, one a civil servant and the last a teacher. Afterwards, when I wanted to leave home, my mother backed me, even though it hurt her. 'I wouldn't like my daughter to reproach me with what I still reproach my parents for.' She was always talking about it.

My father's family was of Turkish origin. My great-grandfather was a ruined big landowner. The family talk about this ruin as if they're proud of it! In the end my grandfather had to sell his land for a song to Frenchmen[16] and he ended up in the antiques business. It seems that when he was rich he lived like a prince. Sometimes he brought *muwachahet* (musicians) from Syria. He paid for their journey and the group came to T. where he organized festivities and they played Andalusian music. It must have been like in *The Music Room*,[17] which is also the story of a man's ruin. We still have a photo of him and his gold-embroidered horse saddle.

He had adopted an orphan, who was to become my paternal grandfather, to whom he gave his own daughter in marriage. A marriage of a brother and a sister in a way.[18] His wife, my grandmother, was, it seems, unbearable! Her father said, 'No man will be able to tolerate her'. For her, a woman, whatever her shortcomings, was always right! Her father thought that only a man with a lower social status than hers would accept her. So he gave her to his adopted son. Marrying an independent-minded daughter was a social problem — and independent-minded she was! She would get up early in the morning, go out without telling anybody and take her women neighbours with her. She would prepare food for her husband and then go out. Whether she ate or not didn't matter to her. She knew a lot about plants, flowers and all the traditional herbs and she would go into the fields to collect bunches of them. There were medicinal plants, plants suitable for cooking, plants for bathing. She used to take her bath under the verandah, letting out little cries of pleasure, she didn't care if people saw her!

My grandfather had a small business, which prospered for a while. He had built a very fine house in old T. He was, it seems, a man who worked very hard but even this man, with a reputation for being wise, was ruined too. Yet, even in hard times, he did everything to push his children to study.

My father went to the *medersa*.[19] It is very moving to hear him talk about his teachers. 'When my father fell ill, it was my teacher who looked after him. When I had to go to Orléansville, it was my teacher who gave me the money for the bus.' He was the fourth child, but he helped to support his brothers and helped them finish their courses. He came to Algiers to the *medersa* when he was about seventeen, and later enrolled in the law faculty. In the meanwhile he had almost been expelled from the *medersa* because he had founded a theatre group and was playing music. This theatre group was mixed and he had also tried to bring women into the Andalusian music orchestras. There were already Jewish women musicians, but bringing Arab women into orchestras alongside men, in the 1940s, was a revolution. The head of the *medersa*, an Arabized Kabyle, called him in and said to him kindly, 'If you want to stay here, you'd better stop these artistic activities.'

It was at the *medersa* that my father became friends with one of the brothers of the woman who was to become his wife, my mother. This friend, a convinced nationalist, had attempted — when he was called up during the Second World War — to organize nationalist demonstrations in the army. I think that he got away with it because the head of the *cours complémentaire* at T. happened to be among the officers there. He was transferred to the stretcher-bearers and was killed during the 1944 landings in the south of France in circumstances that aren't altogether clear. My father and uncle were also sympathetic to the ACP [Algerian Communist Party] and the Ulemas.

My parents were married traditionally; my mother didn't really know my father. They had glimpsed each other when my father came from Algiers for the holidays, that's all. Boys and girls didn't have the chance to meet each other — and it was not the done thing! My father's family made the request. My mother belonged to a well-known family whose daughters were much sought after. Several suitors had been rejected because they were not suitable. But my mother's father remembered that this one had been the close friend of his son killed in the war and that he had sent him a very moving letter when he died in 1944. So he was in favour of this marriage; however he asked the opinion of his eldest son, then a student in Paris, the one who a few years earlier had refused to let my mother continue her studies. He sent a telegram, 'Agreed. It's fine'. And so the marriage took place in 1948 and I was born in 1949.

So far as I know, the marriage was a very sober affair; in the area I come from, there is no dowry. Simply a symbolic twenty centimes. We are Maamria, belonging to Sidi Maamar's sect. He was a seventeenth-century saint, I think, who is credited with having introduced the true principles of Islam in the matter of marriage. We have a saying in Arabic which might be translated, 'You don't sell women like you sell cows.' As there is no dowry the girls' families are very demanding about the husband. Elsewhere the monetary value of the dowry makes it possible to assess the value of the girl. It becomes a cash down affair and today the dowry might be in millions (of dirham). With us, what are important are the qualities of the husband and his family.

When I was born my mother was twenty-one. My father was ten years older. He had been appointed an *adel* (one of the ranks in Muslim justice). We were living in a sort of detached house at El Biar.[20] We lived on one side of this house with my father's mother and one of my uncles, while on the other side there was a poor family from Algiers. The women made handicrafts and used to go and sell what they made in the *casbah*. Their old father was a widower and lived in one of the rooms with one of his daughters who was unmarried — his other daughter was married to a man much older than her, who was quite past it and wasn't much of a father. He lived alone with his horse away towards Bouzareah. This couple had many children, most of them married and two boys and two girls still at home. All the women worked very hard indeed and earned little — they hadn't even had electricity installed. For me, as a child, it was all quite charming, but for them, when I think about it now . . .

The whole family were Messalist [tr. supporter of Messali Hadj]. But the unmarried woman, Djamila, she must have been about forty, was a militant, a real activist. They all made a deep impression on me in my early childhood. I liked them a lot and was often in and out of their part of their house. When I wouldn't eat, my mother would put me with them and they would make me eat. I often used to go with Djamila when she went out to talk about Messali to other women. In the evenings, they would settle on the verandah together and compose *boqalas*.[21] Someone would shout into the night and Djamila would say, 'Listen! It's Messali's message! Ah, that means Algeria can liberate itself!' She always spoke about the liberation of Algeria with great passion. For me she was rather like a second mother, I used to follow her everywhere, into the poorest parts of the *casbah*, Clos-Salembier and Hussein Dey.[22] I would hear this name Messali all the time and yet I didn't know who he was. It was only afterwards that I understood.

Djamila didn't wear a veil. She went everywhere apparently without any qualms. When I got on a bus with her she would say, 'Speak to me in French'. This was no doubt so as not to be picked on, because in fact she was very aggressive, in an almost visceral way, against anything that was Pied-Noir, or colonial.

At the beginning of November 1954[23] I was playing on the terrace when I heard a great commotion. I ran to see. I saw Mahmoud, her nephew, talking about having been arrested (he had already been arrested in 1945). I think that the police commissioner had let him go home to get some clothes. His things were got ready and he embraced us all in a special way. I learnt much later that he had gone into hiding at Bab el Oued. A few years later Mahmoud and his brother died in the maquis. Djamila herself was later arrested and tortured. She died, mad, in the Hermitage, after independence. She is one of the countless women who fought and remained unrecognized.

My early childhood was divided between my outings with Djamila and the very different places that I was taken to by my father. I can see myself with him behind stage at the Algiers opera. Being interested in culture and the theatre was another way of being an activist. Every Friday there were theatrical shows for Muslims, as they used to call them, and my father was in charge of them. Touri and Bachtarzi were among them.[24] My father had written plays, and translated Sophocles' *Antigone* into dialect Arabic. *Barbarossa* had been banned and my father had been called in during the performance. This was a few years before 1954. I liked being with the actresses behind stage of the theatre among the scenery and the costumes. I met Wahiba, Kalthoum and Nachida who went away and now has a night-club in Boston. Of course we also knew Fadila Dziria and her group.[25]

My parents used to go to their Grand Maghreb circle where my father was also involved in cultural activities and they sometimes took me with them. It was unusual at that time to see couples going out together.

In 1951 my father travelled to the Middle East and was pleasantly surprised by the improved position of women in Lebanon. On his return he did everything to let my mother benefit from it. She would go with him to the evening classes he was attending to prepare for the baccalaureat that he took after I was born. At the beginning of their marriage he was the one who insisted my mother should wear a long veil, but now he wanted her to stop wearing one. But she only did so when my father was arrested in 1957 because she had to start working and had all the time to be moving about seeing lawyers and going to the prison. Shortly before the war he had bought a motor cycle and my mother would ride behind with her veil tightly tied up, sitting side-saddle with one or the other of the children between them. They had two daughters, including me, and a boy.

In the Algiers artistic circles that we moved in Fadila Dziria and her sister and her group of singers and dancers had enormous prestige. They were 'liberated' women and patriots who took part in the struggle. Awiwichet, one of the dancers, was arrested and tortured, she was thought dead. I remember her very well. She was a woman of unusual humanity who had brought up all her brothers and sisters on the money she earned by her singing and dancing. She had not married and lived with an actor who was arrested at the same time as she was during the battle of Algiers. I used to dance to imitate her and say that I too wanted to be a dancer. She would take me on her knee and say to me, 'My dear, you mustn't be like me. You must go to school.'

My father encouraged me to work hard in class. Sometimes he saw me going to the polytechnic and then he would say, 'When you are thirteen, you'll go into the maquis.' I was twelve in 1962, the war was ending with independence and my father had been arrested several times and spent three years altogether in prison. After having proposed to send me to the French-Muslim *lycée*, my parents had enrolled me in 1961 at Fromentin (which remained a French *lycée* after 1962 and was renamed Descartes). At this time, the ending of the war, there were some terrible times. It was the period of the OAS; Mouloud Feraoun's daughter and the daughter of one of the inspectors assassinated at the same time as him were with me at the *lycée*. During the 1961 putsch the daughters of settlers at the *lycée* had demonstrated and the students at the *lycée* Gauthier[26] had come up to join them.

How would I compare myself with the Pieds-Noirs and French girls? We valued our culture enormously and we were very proud of being Arabs and Algerians. Our class did Latin and Arabic. Most of the class were Kabyles, with a few Arabs, and a few daughters of settlers. The Algerian girls in my class were conscious of belonging to another world — the French school was alright, but our culture was something else. In other classes there were Algerian girls from more disadvantaged homes, mostly Kabyles, who did English and maths. There was always rivalry between us — we felt the social differences. I remember that they perhaps looked up to the French girls more, they didn't seem to have such a strong sense of their cultural identity as us. I thought I was the equal of the French girls and I don't remember having been envious of them. It's true that I accepted all the constraints as normal. When I went into the first form, my father had said, 'You are going in through the front door, try not to come out through the back door — you will be watched, don't think you'll be able to do anything you like!' I couldn't walk home alone from the *lycée*, nor go and see a friend without being taken in a car. Girls from less well-off families perhaps had more freedom of movement but then they were forced to marry very young. The well-off parents wanted education for their daughters before marriage but they were closely watched by their families.

I remember a friend, whose family came from the rural areas, who is now a lawyer. One day she arrived at the *lycée* all black and blue. Her father had beaten her because she had had to walk along the street with a boy. Nothing more. Girls from good families tended to exercise more self-discipline, as they say.

Throughout my secondary school years I lived in a closed world of home, school and the conservatoire where I was learning the piano. I used to dream of being at the university and living in a wholly Algerian environment. I envied my brother and my sister, both younger than me, who had been able to go to an Algerian *lycée*, El Mokrani, opened after independence. Well, when I did arrive at the University, it was a big shock — a really big shock! I was used to the *lycée* where co-education seemed natural to everybody, but at the university it was boys on one side, girls on the other. To the outsider looking at the student scene (even for professors), it looks like a mixed one. In reality there is a separation, there's no communication. It's like in the salons of good society where people think they are 'modern' because there are men and women in the same room but there's no real communication between them. That's the whole problem, that of communication between men and women and the perception that each group has of the other.

In my last years at the *lycée* I used to go to the cinema and I imagined the university with an atmosphere like you see in Truffaut's films. I imagined students as real intellectuals, with a revolutionary spirit. I day-dreamed, inspired by French films, of a university of Algiers imbued with the romanticism of Paris . . . or at least Paris as I imagined it! My uncles would come back from Paris and tell of their years of study. For me, going to university meant debates, research, contacts, real mixing and communication between boys and girls. I waited impatiently for my time to come. When I arrived at the university, all my dreams collapsed.

The girls' attitude towards the boys was unbelievable. All they wanted was to get married.

In the first year we read (because we studied with the profs, mostly aid people in the '60s) Sartre, Simone de Beauvoir, Malraux, Neruda and Hikmet. All day long we came into contact with liberal, progressive, revolutionary ideas and yet on the steps of the university the students behaved absolutely traditionally. I remember a girl with whom I had just done a presentation on women in novels about the Spanish Civil War. She spoke to me about her fiancé as we were going out, 'Oh, but I'm asking him to give me x millions (of dirhams) as a dowry!', a very large sum for the time, 1969.

The boys soon identified the girls who'd come from Descartes because we were more approachable, but they soon had them classified. The 'nice girls' were much courted so long as they didn't fall into the category of 'easy lays' or 'stuck-up' girls. They couldn't talk to girls normally: either they got tongue-tied or they treated us as easy lays. We simply weren't on the same wavelength. Some would say, 'If I get married, I want my mother to choose a serious girl for me, one without too much education.' These were the ones with a positive outlook. But there were also dreamers, ones who went around with Nazim Hikmet's *Les Romantiques* and Neruda's love poems in one hand and Che Guevara's writings in the other, and who chatted the girls up with poetry. But they were not attracted by just anybody. They preferred girls from good social backgrounds who impressed them by their femininity and manipulated them through the most classic methods of seduction. For most of the male students the main attraction of a girl was her physical beauty. Intelligence didn't matter much, or rather it did . . . it was disturbing.

I don't really know whether there were girls who had sexual relations with students because at that time I didn't quite know what to 'sleep with a boy' meant. It was almost impossible to have normal, easy-going relations with a male student without being treated as an 'easy lay'. Yet you can say that broadly, 'progress' was the Pied-Noir model of the sort of girl you could take home to meet your parents. The boys would come to wait for them at the end of classes, they would go and have a drink at the Princière, go to the cinema now and again and then the boy would escort the girl back to mummy and daddy early, keeping himself at a respectable distance. There was no question of taking her by the hand or the arm. Never! All those boys who were 'going steady' like that ended up marrying their 'little fiancée'.

I must have been the only one not to see myself getting married. I was so innocent at the time that I thought it natural in this milieu to talk of free love. I used to say, 'I am in favour of free love'. For me my models were Simone de Beauvoir and Elsa Triolet. And so I provoked great bursts of laughter. As I was also shy, I was called 'Madame de Sevigné'. So Madame de Sevigné is in favour of free love! What a laugh!

Liberation for girls meant being able to do what their mothers had not been able to do, that is behave like the Pieds–Noirs: go out with boys before getting married, but not too much . . .But there's been some progress since then. I think that young people are more at ease with each other.

The brightest female students were the ones who were the most put down. The boys feared them and the most misogynist ones were the most revolutionary . . . in politics, that goes without saying! They could not bear autonomous girls who didn't belong to the herd. And so they spread the classic insult: 'she sleeps around', 'she's working for the police', 'she's unbalanced' vis-à-vis the West! She was not 'for real'.

I remember a girl from Oran who was going out with a professor of medicine, an aid man at Algiers. What really upset people was that she was quite open about the relationship and made no attempt to hide it. I can remember another girl who was very beautiful and clever. She came from a family of activists who had given a great deal for independence. She was a self-confessed feminist. She was one of the first to take out a cigarette on the steps of the university. She inspired fear, and she was one of their favourite targets. Ten years later, their insults still dog her, in Paris.

The fact that most women kept quiet encouraged misogyny, coupled with envy, among the boys.

I was not one of the sort of girls who were noticed. I kept myself to myself and I wondered whether I had got into a mad world or whether it wasn't I who was going mad. My only breaths of fresh air were the cinema and the rue Mogador theatre group. In the end boys and girls simply didn't speak to each other. The only pleasure was work, and I threw myself into it. There were a few of us who met to study together, including two boys who likewise felt that they were marginalized. But for almost all the girls that I had known at the *lycée* work had been pushed into the background. Everything centred on marriage.

My parents used to say to me that since my last year at school I was no longer the same. It was true. I had begun to think seriously, and ask myself questions. I began to stand up to my parents. Before, I had been very conformist, very religious — an almost mystical little girl. I used to say my prayers regularly. Then I lost my faith. That was an important break. I closeted myself in the library and devoured books that I tried to understand. I discovered Marx and psychoanalysis. Later at the university, I clung to these books, saying to myself, 'No, no, I'm not mad, there are people who think the same as I do!' My reading gave me the idea of going away. I said, 'I shall leave, I can't go on living here'. I wanted to make my life and my ideas compatible. In Algiers, that was impossible.

By then it was less a question of studying than of going away. I said to my parents, 'Either I leave, or I kill myself!' Beirut or Paris! In my family some were for and some against. My father was against, my mother for. An uncle said, 'Let her go. She needs some air!' In the end they held a family meeting and found me a husband, a member of my maternal family, young, good-looking and dynamic who had just come back from the USSR. They begged me to stay and promised me the earth — including being able to continue my studies. I had just got my first degree. I said 'no'. After him, there was a doctor and then an architect. Husbands came in droves!

I'll skip the rows, the tears and the sleepless nights; I found myself saying to myself more and more often, 'Either I go or it's all over' and I said as much to my parents. I applied for a scholarship and, after a few hiccoughs, went to Paris. My family was against my going right up to the last minute. When I got this scholarship, my father almost started crying but he realized that it really was the end. I had an old aunt who used to say to me secretly, 'Don't oppose them like that, my dear. Pretend to be listening to them but carry on getting ready to go. If I can give you some advice, go away, and even marry a foreigner. It's good to mix the races!' And in front of the family she would talk like all the rest.

Ultimately, I think I've been very privileged and that this privilege, that of having been brought up by parents who got on well together, in a family that was very open to the world, has paradoxically been a handicap ... Going up to university was a shock, yes, because it involved meeting young Algerians who had not been brought up in the same way as me. For me, going to the library, to the cinema now and again, was not progress. But I had been expecting intellectual debates, discussions and all sorts of things that can only happen if there is a certain equality of relations between men and women. Instead of that there was fear, aggressiveness, cold-blooded calculation and seduction. That's not exactly designed to promote intellectual cooperation! I found myself without any bearings, I couldn't understand anything and I felt like an outsider. My ideal of a woman was my mother, always my father's help-mate. She fought for him when he was arrested but she also fought with him and that was not common. She was a quite implacable fighter. And although my parents had a traditional marriage, they were a real couple with a deep mutual understanding, both in terms of affection and intellect. It's very unusual among our people where husband and wife are often strangers to one another. My mother used to say, 'If I'd known I'd have brought you all up differently.' What she meant was, 'I would have opened your eyes to society as it really is.' But how could anyone have foreseen society after independence?

Algiers–Paris, 1982

Draft Law on the Status of Persons in Algeria

Extracts

Art. 1. Marriage is a legal contract between a man and a woman, with the purpose of procreation and founding a family based on affection and goodness.

Art. 3. The age for contracting a valid marriage is eighteen years for men and sixteen for women. A judge may however grant an age dispensation for reason of public interest or in case of necessity.

Art. 4. No one may contract a marriage with more than one wife except by way of a derogation which will not be given to a person who is deemed incapable of ensuring equity in the provision of accommodation and maintenance or without a lawful motive or if the wife opposes it.

Art. 6. Marriage is contracted by the consent of the future spouses, the marriage guardian and two witnesses, together with the payment of a dowry.

Art. 8. The responsibility for giving away the woman lies with the marriage guardian who is either the father or the latter's executor, or a close relative, in succession according to the rules of succession.

Art. 27. Marriage between a Muslim woman and a non-Muslim man is prohibited.

Art. 32. The husband is responsible for:

1. providing for the maintenance of his wife so far as he is able and in accordance with her condition, except when it is established that she has abandoned the conjugal home.

2. equitably sharing his time if he has several wives and providing separate accommodation for each one.

Art. 33. The husband cannot forbid his wife:

1. to visit her parents, or to receive them in accordance with use and custom.

2. to dispose of her goods in complete freedom.

3. to work outside the conjugal home if she has inserted a clause to this effect in the marriage contract, if she was working before the marriage or if she worked before the marriage with his formal or tacit consent.

Art. 34. The wife is responsible for:

1. obeying her husband and granting him every respect as head of the family.

2. feeding her children if she is able to do so and bringing them up.

3. respecting the parents and relatives of her husband.

Art. 43. Divorce is the dissolution of the marriage contract; it lies within the sole power of the husband and is only established by due legal process after a conciliation procedure.

Art. 44. If the husband still desires a divorce after the attempted conciliation, the judge shall pronounce the divorce; his judgement is final and he shall grant the wife the right to accommodation and compensation if he decides that the husband has misused his power.

Art. 45. The wife is permitted to ask for a divorce for the following reasons:

1. for failure to pay the board allowance pronounced by a court unless the wife had known of the poverty of her husband at the time of the marriage subject to articles 67, 68 and 69 of the present law.

2. for a disability preventing the fulfilment of the purpose of marriage.

3. for wrongs legally considered as an infraction by the husband of the provisions of Article 33.

4. for refusal of the spouse to share the wife's bed for more than four months.

5. for condemnation of the husband to a penalty involving loss of rights that deprives him of his freedom.

6. for absence of more than one year without a valid excuse or without a maintenance allowance.

Art. 51. Custody consists in the maintenance and upbringing of the child in the religion of his father as well as the protection of his physical or moral wellbeing.

Art. 53. Custody ceases, for the male child, when he reaches the age of ten years, for the daughter when she reaches the age of marriage.

Art. 57. If the person to whom custody is entrusted chooses a domicile in a locality other than that in which the father of the child being looked after resides thus making it impossible for him to go there for the purpose of exercising his supervision of the child's situation and to return home the same day, he shall be deprived of his custody.

Art. 110. It is forbidden to give an adopted child the patronymic of the person who has adopted him.

N.B. Several proposals on personal status have been drafted since independence. But none has yet come to fruition. The extracts quoted above come from the latest draft. It was against this one that a number of women protested when it was put before the Algerian National Assembly. It was then withdrawn. This draft was again being discussed early in 1983 and will probably be put before the Assembly again.

Notes

1. See Tayeb Kennouche, Mustapha Haddab and Idir Khenniche. *Les Jeunes ruraux et l'école, mythes et réalités*, preface by A. Benchenhou (CREA, Algiers, 1982).
2. B.F. Hoselitz, *Tradition and Economic Growth*, quoted by T. Kennouche, p. 5.
3. See Monique Gadant, 'Les Femmes, la famille et la nationalité algérienne', *Peuples Méditerranéens*, No. 15, April–June 1981.
4. Ibid.
5. *Khali*, maternal uncle; *khalt khali*, maternal aunt of the maternal uncle; *bent khali*, daughter of the maternal uncle (cousin); *khalt khalti*, maternal aunt of the maternal aunt (great-aunt); *ammi*, paternal uncle; *amt ammi*, paternal aunt of the paternal uncle; *bent ammi*, daughter of the paternal uncle (cousin); *amt amti*, paternal aunt of the paternal aunt (great-aunt).
6. *Adjouza* and *sheikh* are words which describe the pair of grandparents, but in the sense of 'old ones'. In English we often talk of the 'old man' or the 'old woman', but the word *adjouza* has a rather pejorative connotation and is used to describe any woman who no longer excites desire (it is used sometimes to describe a young woman who has been repudiated). On the other hand the word *sheikh* is wholly positive; it means the wise man, the pious man, the scholar . . . These words are commonly used without people thinking about their connotation.
7. 'Make gold' means buying jewelry, a form of traditional saving.
8. In fact, with a population growth rate of 3.2% — one of the highest in the world — the reproduction rate has not slowed down with the younger generation. 61% of women have their first pregnancy between the ages of 15 and 19, 16% between 20 and 24, 3% between 25 and 29. 50% of women have their third or fourth pregnancy between 20 and 24, and 50% of women have their sixth pregnancy between 25 and 29.
9. *La Recherche des femmes: enquête, reflexions sur les femmes chercheurs au CNRS* (published by the Syndicat national des chercheurs scientifiques, FEN, Paris, 1981).
10. SONELEC, the National Electricity Corporation. The complex which is mentioned here depends on it and makes radio and television sets. It employs about 1,200 women who have repeatedly been attacked on arriving for and leaving work by Muslim Brothers . . . or others. The pretext for this campaign was that a few years ago the company had taken on one or two unmarried mothers.

11. Blida is 40 km from Algiers, Medea 100 km.

12. This group did not last long. It had been formed by young students or activists, boys and girls and had put on a series of sketches on the emancipation of women in 1968–9 which was much talked about.

13. Although the cinemas were given Arab names, this is still the name given to this cinema in the centre of Algiers which is at present reputed to be the only one in Algiers to which women can go alone.

14. In 1936–7 the ACP (Algerian Communist Party), the Ulemas and the *Fédération des élus* [tr: a grouping of elected office-holders] formed an alliance under the name Muslim Congress.

15. After independence Orléansville was renamed El Asnam and after the October 1981 earthquake, Chlef.

16. This ruin was one of thousands and was the result of colonial policy which succeeded in 'legally' taking over most of the good land belonging to Algerian owners.

17. An Indian film by Satyajit Ray that deals with the ruin of a landowner, a great music-lover, and the rise of *nouveaux riches* with no culture.

18. The marriage between a daughter and an adopted son is possible since adoption is forbidden by Muslim law and is simply a question of 'taking in' (*kalafa*). Marriage is therefore possible. Since endogamous marriage is preferred, it is almost an ideal union.

19. The *medersa*, strictly a school, was a sort of bilingual Muslim *lycée* that functioned in the colonial period, in which future officials, especially lawyers, needed by the colonial system were trained. The *medersas* took part in the Arab cultural revival.

20. An outlying suburb of Algiers.

21. A divining ritual in which poetry plays a large part.

22. Outlying parts of Algiers.

23. The liberation war began on 1 November 1954.

24. M. Bachtarzi, a man of the theatre and singer. Touri was an actor.

25. Fadila Dziria was a famous and very popular singer. She died in 1976.

26. Boys' *lycée* in the centre of Algiers; after independence it became an Algerian *lycée*. The *lycée* Descartes is the *lycée* of the French Maison Culturelle.

Spain, 1936: Free Women

A Feminist, Proletarian and Anarchist Movement

Pepita Carpena

It took more than forty years and the death of Franco for civil marriage, divorce and the right to contraception (to mention only rights that affect women directly) to be established in Spain in the face of the strong opposition of the Church whose age-old influence still remains enormous. But securing the right to abortion looks likely to be more difficult. A draft reform of the Criminal Code, including some decriminalization of abortion — which is still considered by Spanish law as a criminal act liable to imprisonment[1] — is soon to be put before the Cortes by the Spanish socialist government. Although the proposals on abortion are very limited, allowing the termination of pregnancy only in carefully defined cases such as risk to the life and health of the mother, malformation of the foetus or duly confirmed rape — this 'permissiveness' has raised hackles. Already, in the name of 'respect for life', the Catholic hierarchy, backed by most doctors and paramedical associations, has denounced this timid proposal. Feminist groups, right-to-abortion collectives and the parties of the far left[2] have mobilized against the proposals which they see as unacceptable and contrary to the right of women to dispose of their own bodies. Demonstrations, petitions, statements for or against abortion have followed one another and the polemics fill the columns of the Spanish press.

Feminist organizations criticize the government proposals because they mean that thousands of women who continue to have secret abortions in Spain (according to estimates, there are 300,000 to 400,000 illegal abortions a year) and abroad are acting illegally. They feel that the proposals do not go far enough and are too restrictive, showing no consideration for the rights of women. In its manifesto, the Coordination of Feminist Organizations of the Spanish State asserts that the struggle for the right to abortion 'is only one more part of a free sexuality', adding, 'We, women, demand the power to decide whether we wish to be mothers or not, when and how many times.'[3]

Yet the right to abortion would not be something new in Spain. The Second Spanish Republic (1931–9) which had given women the right to vote[4] and had established civil marriage and divorce during the short-lived participation of the anarchists in government (1936–7) also, on the initiative of Federica Montseny (then Minister of Health) legalized *de facto* marriage (after a couple had been living together for ten months), information on birth control and abortion.[5]

We thought that it would be interesting to talk to a woman who had been both witness and participant at this time. So we attended a debate on 'Women in Social Struggles' organized in Barcelona in January 1983 by the National Labour Confederation (CNT) at its congress, at which Federica Montseny herself was to give a lecture.[6] During her talk, Federica Montseny went over her own position and her agreement with most of the present demands of the women's liberation movements, all included in the programme of the confederalist and anarchist movement to which she belongs. She added that she was not a feminist because, being active in one organization, she felt no need to be active in another.[7] For her there was no specifically women's question, but only a general problem: the liberation of the human person.[8]

In the discussion that followed this lecture, Pepita Carpena rose to talk about the specific problems of women in the anarchist movement and about the organization of Free Women that existed at the time of the civil war (unfortunately very little known in France and England). Pepita Carpena left Spain, like half a million of her fellow-citizens, in 1939 at the time of Franco's victory. Formerly a dressmaker, she is now in retirement. A militant anarchist in Spain and in France where she now lives, she continues to maintain very close political and family links with the land of her birth.

Even though it is impossible in a single interview to give a complete picture of the woman problem in Spain, the choice of an anarchist militant may appear rather peculiar and very unrepresentative to the uninformed reader. But Spanish anarchism is an old working-class tradition and it produced the CNT (the great anarcho-syndicalist confederation) which had between 1,500,000 and 3,000,000 members at the beginning of the Civil War. In this sense, Pepita Carpena, a worker (feminists come predominantly from the middle classes) and an anarchist, is an example of a traditional extremist. It is very difficult to assess the present-day impact of this movement after forty years of dictatorship and a repression that has been imposed on almost three successive generations of the Spanish people. We have simply been able to observe that in Barcelona the CNT still had sufficient prestige to arouse the interest of a large number of people who came to the various activities (debates, slide-shows, exhibitions) that it had organized.[9]

The condition of women has always been a concern of anarchism — at least since it parted company with Proudhon who considered women to be inferior. Anarchists would like sexual freedom for men and women.[10] They support the education of women because it is impossible to conceive of sexual freedom in the absence of complete equality, at all levels, between men and women. Since they also believe that the emancipation of men must go hand in hand with that of women, they demand the economic independence of women.[11]

But, in reality and in attitude, even within the anarchist movement, this equality often remains theoretical and 'machismo' is still very widespread in this country which is both Latin and Mediterranean. The sexual question, like the problem of equal rights for women, gave rise in the 1930s to debates in the anarchist press and polemics within the anarchist organizations and all these discussions helped to make anarchist women conscious of their condition. They observed in their everyday life the frequent gap between the great anarchist principle of the equality of the sexes and the activist (and also professional and family) practices of their companions.[12] The fact that great female figures like Teresa Claramunt, a textile worker, and Federica Montseny, an intellectual, were able to make their mark within the Spanish anarchist movement was altogether exceptional. This movement never accepted the idea — and Federica Montseny shared this point of view — that a women's problem could exist, even less a feminist anarchist organization. Whence the problems that Free Women was to face: it was a movement that, even though it was born out of anarchism and claimed allegiance to it, was never to succeed in getting itself wholly accepted.

The Free Women movement is, in comparison with feminine organizations in general, peculiar in more than one way. It marked a radical break from the women's organizations that had preceded it in Spain, which might be described as 'bourgeois feminism'. They saw no other goal than to prepare ordinary women for their roles as wives, mothers and child-rearers by improving their knowledge; these organizations never questioned either the social structures or the traditional roles of women, the prejudices towards them or their dependent condition. Free Women, on the contrary, saw itself as a political movement ideologically linked to anarchism and called these structures into question. It addressed itself to ordinary women and tried to make them become conscious of themselves as women and as producers and to win them over to anarchist ideas. Free Women wanted 'to emancipate women from the triple slavery to which in general they have been and are subjected: the slavery of ignorance, slavery as women and slavery as producers'.[13]

The aim of Free Women was never to emancipate women in general but working-class women in particular. It was not a question of waging war against men but of preparing themselves to wage the social war alongside them; this meant forming conscious individuals who would be able to take a full part in the revolutionary struggle. The founders of Free Women conceived of their movement as a sort of training school for professional, social and political life. It was necessary 'to save women from dictatorship, from mediocrity; a cultural and constructive work to win the war and make the revolution'.[14] And this, in the Spain of the time, amounted to a complete questioning of the roles assigned to women.

Free Women first announced its existence in a review[15] launched in Madrid in April 1936 (three months before the revolution) by three women: Lucia Sanchez Saornil, Mercedes Comoposada and Ampara Poch y Gascon, respectively journalists and a doctor. From this beginning, and in spite of the existing severe climate of repression (banned workers' organizations carried on their work secretly; activists were imprisoned) and the civil war which broke out shortly afterwards, Free Women grew rapidly and before long had 30,000 members, drawn almost entirely from the working class.[16] It had a federal organization functioning on the anarchist model of the self-management and autonomy of the various groups. Free Women, unlike any of the women's organizations which were formed shortly after at the instance of parties paraded and manipulated by male political leadership, was wholly self-reliant.

Free Women first attacked problems of education and went on a crusade against illiteracy among women. In its institute, as in the groups that had sprung up, elementary teaching was given; vocational courses were also organized, training nurses, infant-care specialists and secretaries. Libraries were set up, information and propaganda campaigns started. Free Women established day nurseries for the children of refugees, abandoned children and also for the children of working mothers. It started free creches in factories and working-class areas and organized refectories for adults. A Free Women column armed with sewing-machines, washing-machines and pressing-machines was sent to the front.

Such activities might appear to be at odds with the initial objectives of Free Women. In fact, the circumstances of the war demanded the participation of women in the common effort and Free Women could not but support this effort to bring about a victory which would make a more just society possible. These activities, carried on outside the home, in a collective framework, contributed to bringing women into social life and giving a political purpose to their actions. It should also be said that, generally speaking, the war had obliged most women to go to work, to replace men on the farms as well as in the factories; some of them had even signed on and were taking part in military operations with (and on the same footing as) men, notably in the anarchist militias. (This once again confirms the truth of the saying that wars and revolutions have often been fertile ground for women to assert themselves.)

In a less traditional context, Free Women had organized female labour sections and even a women's trade union in the transport and food services in Madrid and Barcelona. It also took action against prostitution (not against prostitutes), an action that may appear rather peripheral but which is an indication of the principles of the movement. How could Free Women advocate freedom of women and free love (Free Women strongly condemned marriage) and accept the existence of prostitution? To fight against what at the time was a major social problem, Free Women undertook a parallel propaganda campaign to dissuade men from resorting to prostitutes and founded, for prostitutes who wanted to give up their profession, rehabilitation centres. These offered medico-psychiatric research and treatment and psychological and moral treatment to encourage a sense of responsibility in those on the course. Vocational guidance and training were given, together with moral and material assistance whenever it was needed, even after the women became independent of the centres.[17] History does not tell whether the action embarked on by Free Women hung fire, but, as Pepita Carpena says, 'We wanted to do in three years work what would have taken twenty. It simply wasn't possible.'

ERMI-CNRS, Paris, March 1983

Pepita Carpena and the Free Women movement

The women in the CNT organized themselves into Free Women in April 1936. These women were feminists before the word was invented. They had joined the CNT but had become conscious of their role as women and of the need for a women's organization. At that time men were generally very 'macho'. Male friends in the CNT willingly accepted that women join the union. But the problem for feminists in the CNT arose when they came into contact with activists. The women realized that these men who were anarchists outside the home were rather less so inside it. It was not deliberate; but as men they had been brought up like that and were unconscious of it.

I joined the CNT when I was very young, fourteen years old. So when the war broke out, I was sixteen and a member of the CNT and the Anarchist Youth. I had no problem with the comrades until they needed to give the lie to the Communist women. Instead of doing it as an anarchist organization where there was no distinction between the sexes, they decided it should be the women who gave the lie to the Communist women. Now, on the one hand, they had no need to 'feminise' the problem which, in this particular case, concerned both men and women, and set up a women's section within the organization. On the other hand, if it was a problem which concerned women particularly, they were quite simply forgetting that there was Free Women. So I told them that I didn't agree with what they were doing. And to win me to their side, they were finally stupid enough to appoint me local secretary of this women's section in Barcelona. I said to them, 'Do you think that because you appoint me secretary, I'm going to accept your proposal? I'm against it. I'm sorry, but I'm going to join Free Women. If I haven't joined up to now, it was because I thought that there was no distinction between the sexes among the anarchists, but you are now proving just the opposite.'

And I joined Free Women almost on the spur of the moment. It was with them that I became conscious of the fact that women in Spain had even less freedom than those in other countries. But, well . . . in every country it's more or less the same. But we had the burden of traditions, of eight centuries of Arab occupation, and it was very difficult to get out of men's heads the idea that women must stay in the home and be used only for making children and being a 'companion'. There was a very widespread idea among the anarchists and men in the CNT. They believed they could take any woman and 'train' her. 'O, my companion is not a member of the CNT, but I feel certain I'll be able to make her into one.' But what right had the man to say that? The lover he had chosen had the right to be, or not to be, in the CNT. The male has the right to try and guide his woman, but if she has her own ideas of what she does and does not want, he cannot make demands. There were tremendous problems. Some men had Catholic women who wanted to baptize their children and some thought they had the right, as anarchists, to oppose this. But others didn't agree. Problems of this sort were numerous at this time and I don't think that the men in the CNT ever noticed this contradiction. They were very proud to be able to say, 'I've a fantastic companion'. In their eyes, because she had accepted an activist lover, she had accepted all the sacrifices that that involved. But did they bother about their partner's problems? She was nothing except in relation to them, she had no existence herself.

When I joined Free Women, I was in the propaganda section and I was on tour mainly in Catalonia. I went round with companions in the Anarchist Youth and the CNT in the same car. There was enormous enthusiasm among women who came to our meetings in large numbers. We used to talk to them about their lives, and their condition as women. It had a fantastic impact. And I must say that it was only the anarchists who raised these issues.

I was very active. I had joined the CNT when I was very young. I was tailoring men's and women's clothes, not in a factory (at the time there weren't any in Spain) but in a workshop. In 1935–6 we had succeeded in getting a lot of women to join the Union. I was on the battlefield twenty-four hours a day. In the end my father protested. I said to him, 'Dad, I'm in an organization that is fighting for the workers and I'm fighting alongside it. These are things you didn't tell me about' (because my father belonged to a union, but that was all) . . . I said to him, 'I'm doing what you should have done so that the workers' conditions wouldn't be like this. So, if you like, come with me. I shan't stop you!' Of course, he was afraid that I was sleeping around. So I said to him, 'Come with me and you'll see what I'm doing.' He came and when he saw all the work I was doing with these women he said, 'What am I doing here? I'll leave you to get on with it.' After that I had no more problems . . . at least with him, for I still had to fight.

Free Women, unlike the bourgeois feminists, linked the social and political struggle with feminism and fought against machismo even among anarchists. It was all very well for them to say that men and women were all the same, were equals; machismo still existed. Men were quite happy to have a woman who understood them, as activists; but they were not happy for her to be an activist. They still thought that most women were incapable. They thought a lot of Federica Montseny because she was cultured; but what of the rest? The men thought women knew nothing about economic and social problems.

As for those who had activist wives, well, they were there to take in new arrivals, to get the food and act as hostesses. Activists were often in prison. The lot of men in the CNT was three years in prison, two years' freedom, four years in prison, three years' freedom; so they needed to have someone there for when hard times struck. If their women too were activists then they too would be liable to arrest. Activists could not start a family — the risks of imprisonment were too great. The men in the CNT saw no further than giving women a social conscience. The anarcho-syndicalists did not go beyond that. They wanted women to become conscious of their situation as working women and of the necessity of joining a trade union. Among the anarchists, we went more deeply into the problems of women as activists and talked about sexual freedom. In the journal *Mulieres Libres* (Free Women), all the questions of social issues and the emancipation of women were touched on. We even dealt with sexuality. We were trail-blazers. We talked about the role of a woman with an activist companion, the role of women who were activists and those who were not. We discussed the religion of children — there were atheist comrades who had Catholic wives. Spain is Catholic. If a man or woman believes in God but is not baptised and does not go to communion, it's serious. And anarchist men, to compound the problem, fell quickly into the role of head of the family ... whereas for an anarchist militant there should be no head of the family! I felt that a militant should not take a Catholic wife unless he was going to give her some say.

In the same way I thought that boys and girls should be brought up with equal freedom. In my family, my brother who was two years younger than me was free. But not me. I had to fight to be free. Freedom isn't given, it has to be taken. It's like the state, it gives nothing, it has to be taken. Well, for most men it hurts to see a woman who wants her freedom. Today, it's true, I see men who are beginning to understand, there are couples who are getting used to it. I'm talking about Spain. Because in Spain, men didn't used to do the shopping. Now yes, they do, but not all of them. Even Spaniards who moved to France wouldn't lift a shopping bag. It was a dishonour to pick up a shopping bag and do the shopping. Men in France were more willing even though they were still the head of the family. And in spite of everything, you must not forget that the Spanish revolution had established the right to abortion, and that it was Federica Montseny who had established it. The anarchist movement had worked hard to spread the idea that everyone is free to dispose of his or her own body and that women could consequently have abortions.

But I don't agree with all feminists. I want to be a woman. I don't want to dress like a man, nor become a boss to give the workers some stick. But I want to be free, I want to be myself, be free to do what I like with my body and my life. Being a woman has to be carefully defined. Because if being a feminist means fighting for the top jobs that men have and being more competitive than them, I'm not interested. If I have a lover, I don't want to impose my view on him; but neither do I want him to impose his on me. We would have to discuss what we do together. If we are both militants and something has to be done which stops us going out together, then we must take it in turns to do the washing up or look after the children. But I don't want anything to do with a man who makes me have children and then stops me having an abortion. This freedom of abortion (in France) is something that we owe to the feminists. On that I agree with them. But on other points, I don't. I've a woman friend who is an activist in France in the women's movement; she invited me to go to a meeting once, saying, 'Come, but on your own, because we don't want any men.' I refused to go.

A man once said to me, 'Oh women! Liberate yourselves quickly, so that we can be liberated too! We suffer constraints as well.' I said to him, 'Yes, but the liberation that you want is not the same as the liberation that we want.' It's true that men are under constraint. The state weighs on them, they are got at from all sides, they are not free.

When I talk about women's liberation, I get no reaction from working women. Now, I've retired, but I used to work in a tailor's workshop. There were about thirty women there. When I talked about women's liberation, they didn't understand what I was talking about.

When I was new in the CNT and the Anarchist Youth, we were steeped in the ideas of the French Revolution, Rousseau and Zola. When we got to France, we thought we were reaching the land of freedom, but — it hurts me to say it — we were treated like cattle. In the middle of February 1939, in the freezing cold, men were parked in camps, at St. Cyprien, Barcarès, etc. It is true that it was in war-time, and there were 500,000 people on the frontier and it was difficult. We had to adapt, and I adapted, I had children who are French. But, all the same ... when I think of the attitudes of Frenchmen at that time . . . When I crossed the frontier, there were gendarmes at Perpignan and they spoke Catalan. That's how we were able to understand them. When he noted my identity, one of the gendarmes said, 'Sign.' As I went to sign, his colleague said to him, 'It's not worth asking her to sign, you know perfectly well that all Spaniards are illiterate.' It's true that the Spanish people lacked culture, but it was not their fault. It was the fault of their rulers who had never done anything for them. And if I compare the Spanish people at that time with the French people, I feel that the Spaniards were more aware than the French. It is true too that in France I came across a liberalism that did not exist in Spain. I found in France a liberal bourgeoisie that did not exist in Spain, where the petty bourgeois behaved like capitalists. The university-educated people were different too, the French ones mixed more with the people than the Spanish ones did. But in the working class, even today in France, I have the impression that things have not changed much in the relations between men and women. Men impose their will on women.

It is for that reason ultimately that feminists are right to continue to press their demands because even with a socialist government information does not circulate. An effort needs to be made. When I speak to working women about these problems they wonder how I come to know so much. They don't even know about family planning. I've been retired for seven years now but when I was working I used to explain to them and say that if I was well informed it was because I was already a political activist when I was in Spain and that I continued to be one in France. So I got to know things. But they didn't know their rights. Even now they think that the man is the boss.

It is absolutely vital that information circulate among working women because bourgeois women are informed and it's easy for them to be liberated . . . They have economic freedom and all sorts of advantages. That's not the case for working women. There are still not enough creches here. During the revolution in Spain we raised all these problems, creches, housing, women's liberation. We argued for them passionately because we wanted to do in three years what would have taken twenty. Of course, it wasn't possible. But all the same, some things did get done, and I'm proud to have lived through the Spanish Revolution because in three years of revolution I lived twenty years of my life.

When I remember this period from the time I joined the CNT in 1934 . . . I was fourteen years old. In the beginning, when I joined, I joined the Metallurgy Union (although I worked as a tailor) because all my friends were mechanics. It is there that I met a chap who later became my lover. We were both militants. Out of all that group of young people, we were the closest couple. But he died during the war.

The men in the CNT tried to mix with young people at dances. There were some who didn't go to dances because they didn't like dancing, they were very austere. No sex, no drinking or smoking. They took everything seriously. I didn't agree with that because after all I am a woman and I like to please. But, well . . . the great value of the CNT was that it said to us, 'Now you've left school, you have to become aware of your situation. Come with us to the Anarchist Youth, we've got schools.' These were evening classes. I had left school when I was twelve, and I knew how to read and write, but I used to go to these classes to learn about things that interested me. I owe my culture to them. We became self-taught. The CNT pushed us to learn, to improve ourselves.

Before the revolution the CNT was banned. It was just luck that I didn't go to prison. We functioned despite the ban. We used to collect membership fees in bars and anywhere. We met people and said to them, 'Is your membership card up to date?'

In the end you can only say what you feel, but everybody must agree what the revolution in Spain really was. The FAI and the CNT made it. And the communists? There weren't any. It was Franco who made the most communists.

Young people say that we are rehashing the past. So I talk about it as little as possible because what interests me is the future, even if my future is behind rather than in front of me! And I am closer to the young people, which causes problems for me with the old; I always try not to blame the young. They make mistakes, but that's because of lack of experience as militants. They're arrogant? That's quite natural. I was arrogant at their age and I still am, even at the age of sixty-three! You mustn't set the old against the young because we all need each other, and I'm happy when the young rebel says 'shit', even when it's to me. That's even happened in my family. I had arguments with my youngest daughter (and with the others). My eldest daughter lived in Paris for a few years and she belonged to Daniel Cohn-Bendit's group in 1968. Before that she had been with me in Marseilles and we did anarchist camps. In these camps we preached, quite logically, sexual freedom. Only we, the parents, were still using the Ogino method. At the time I was using it. (That's how I had my children!) And I said, 'Up with sexual freedom!' But not with just anybody. If I'm to be forced to bear a child that I don't want, I don't want to have just anybody's child. I want a child that is wanted. If you sleep with a man without taking any precautions and you find yourself pregnant, what happens? We discussed this with young people. I didn't mean, 'I don't want my daughter to have sex', but the young people didn't understand. They thought I was being dictatorial, whereas all I was saying was be careful. My lover was even more reactionary. He used to say, 'If you come back with a child, who's going to support it? It won't be you, it'll be us!' It was true though. It was the parents who bore the consequences of sexual freedom. There was a certain degree of fecklessness among young people. Young anarchists were all in favour of freedom — especially the men because that suited them fine. And that should have been discussed too — who does sexual freedom suit? It was not that Spaniards were authoritarian, as Daniel Cohn-Bendit used to say, but that the Spaniards were in an economically difficult situation and they thought, 'If my daughter comes back with a child, what are we going to do with it?' It was material rather than moral questions that worried them. Spaniards were not authoritarian or narrow-minded people. You take liberty if you can afford to be free. That's all that I wanted my daughters to understand.

The youngest, she is now thirty-one, had a lot of problems with me. When I say that she had psychoanalysis I've said it all. All her problems were apparently my fault! It's true in a way, but at the beginning, when the conflict between us erupted, she made me suffer a lot because she said things about me that were unjustified because I'd brought her up with every possible freedom. In May 1968 she was only fifteen. She went off and she was away for a long time. She was in a commune in Marseilles and I said nothing. But we eventually clashed and she began to say, 'Freud says that all my problems are my mother's fault.' The years went by without our being able to talk to each other because she felt that her shortcomings were my fault . . . Not the father, always the mother! But I think that it's a little of the father and a little of the mother . . . Happily in the end we were able to talk it over between us and she explained to me what she felt. She said, 'You have a strong personality, you overpower me.' In other words, she concluded from her analysis that my strong personality should have been effaced so that she could come out on top. That's perhaps true, but I must admit I didn't altogether agree. But I said, 'Listen, V., if my strong personality bothered you, I'm sorry but that's the way I am. I never took my mother to task, never. I had very serious problems and I found myself alone, with no family, my lover had died in Spain. I married a Frenchman, agreed. But when I found myself in difficult situations, even though my education had left something to be desired, my mother had too many problems for me to be going to her and saying, "It's your fault". You're clever enough to understand, but what can I do about it? Explain to me. If you can't express your personality because I have a strong personality, must I then efface mself? I'm sorry, but I won't efface myself because I too have the right to live. Perhaps if you had talked to me at the time about what was going wrong, I would have acted differently, but now it's too late.'

But our relationship improved because we had been able to talk about it and I learned something. I often say to her, 'All that I know had remained almost useless and thanks to you I am beginning again to learn and to know the young.' All in all, I am happy that this disagreement happened because I began to question myself again. With the other daughters, I had problems because, when they were very young, I went away and they were brought up by my lover (a Frenchman) and not by their own father. They criticized me for not making them believe that he was their father. I told them that I had never wanted to cheat in my life and that, consequently, I had preferred to make everything clear. I want to be myself, not to use trickery. From this point of view I don't want to be a woman.

But with my daughters we were constantly questioning things. That's unusual among Spanish comrades. Usually they and their children lead completely separate lives and there are some things they don't like talking about. Homosexuality, for example. They often have violent reactions to that. As far as I'm concerned everyone can do what they like with their own body. Some people don't agree; but they are not being asked to agree, simply to be tolerant. I have a brother of fifty-two who now tells me that because of me we talked about everything with our parents. It's true. I remember that I took out a subscription to a naturist journal and my parents were shocked . . . so there were discussions! It makes me laugh now, but at the time I had to struggle to get them to understand that nudity was quite natural.

I wanted to give my daughters maximum freedom. I think the young were right in 68. More freedom was needed, even in France, the land of freedom. But despite that there are problems. My youngest daughter gets around a lot, and it sometimes happens at work, or at the university, that people will say to her, 'Ah! You're Pepita's daughter!' She said to me, 'Do you realize? Even my friends know who you are!' She couldn't bear it. I am what I am. She can't cope with having a famous mother. It's the same with men; they like a woman to be free, as long as she's not their mother or wife. Children like other mothers to be headstrong — not theirs. Yet I am maternal. But how contradictory my daughter can be! She criticizes me for having mothered her too much. Why? She says, 'It's because in my analysis . . .' And I reply, 'Oh shut up, I've had it up to here with psychoanalysts.' Because when I'm with her and all her friends, who are psychologists, sociologists, I say, 'OK, I know nothing, but I've had it up to here! You distort everything. You can't say a word without it being interpreted ... Because she said this ... because that comes from ...' I like talking to people but not if at every opportunity they're going to reinterpret everything you say. I've noticed that in those circles couples don't really get on. It's true that today young people are in a difficult situation. If social security did not exist, there would be a revolution; you go to the social security, they pay your rent, etc. But governments of the right, like those of the left, know perfectly well that wealth has to be redistributed. The socialists are going to impose a wealth tax, but that's insignificant. Wealth will have to be redistributed. Wealth ... it's being able to live, to have a decent life. Everyone is entitled to be able to lead a decent life.

Barcelona, January 1983

Notes

1. During a trial in Barcelona in 1983, the Procurator General had asked for a sentence of ten years' imprisonment with hard labour for a woman who admitted that in 1968, when she was suffering from a serious heart complaint, she had agreed to surgery to terminate a pregnancy that she thought put her life in danger (see *El Pais*, 19 February 1983, p. 23).
2. The 'traditional' parties of the left are satisfied to support the government draft proposals, no doubt more for electoral than ideological reasons, the latest opinion polls in Spain having given the following results: 69% of Spaniards agree with therapeutic abortion, 50% with abortion in cases of rape, 65% in the case of malformation of the foetus, and only 27% agree with abortion on demand (*El Pais*, 3 February 1983).
3. See *El Pais*, 12 February 1983, p. 16.
4. The right to vote was retained by Franco.
5. When I was looking for some references to legislation on divorce and abortion during the Spanish Second Republic, I first consulted a dozen works, of various tendencies, dealing with the period without success: I found nothing on the role of women during the Spanish Revolution. Although I'm a rather luke-warm feminist, I found this gap shocking. I didn't find much either about the agricultural collectivizations or on the collectivizations in the factories; yet these were among the most interesting achievements of the Spanish Revolution. It's as if this revolution was made up only of military operations and political manoeuvres. There is one exception: Ronald Fraser, *Recuerdalo tu y recuerdalo a otros. Historia oral de la guerra civil espanola* (Barcelona, Critica, 'Temas hispanicos' series, 1979).
6. CNT-AIT (International Association of Workers, IAW): Spanish anarcho-syndical organization.
7. Remarks taken from a lecture on 11 January 1983, noted by N.B.
8. For more details about Federica Montseny and her stand on feminism, as well as for this short presentation, see the work by Mary Nash, *Femmes Libres. Espagne 1936–1939* (Claix, La Pensée Sauvage, 1977, 'L'Envers de l'histoire' series, pp. 203 and appendices). This is an anthology of publications by Free Women, mainly on women's issues.
9. Another indication that this influence has left its mark at least in attitudes might be seen in the repeated failure in Spain of the Communist Party as a mass party.
10. This demand for 'free love', like the direct action that they are believed to advocate in all places and at all times, for a long time contributed to the 'reputation' of anarchist militants, the two things being easily treated as licence and disorder: anarchy in the popular sense of the word.

11. In the report of the CNT Congress held in Saragossa in 1936 it is stated: 'Given that the first action of the anarchist revolution will be to ensure the economic independence of human beings, with no distinction of sex, the existing economic interdependence between men and women will disappear. This means that the two sexes will be equal in rights and duties.' Quoted by Mary Nash, op. cit., pp. 5–6, note 6.

12. Companion: translation of *companero*, the word anarchists use among themselves.

13. Mary Nash, op. cit., pp. 68–9.

14. Ibid., p. 87.

15. The journal *Mulieres Libres* published thirteen issues in Spain. It was a general journal of thought, in which the debate was not limited to women's issues; it was a weapon for anarchist propaganda and published information on the movement. Alongside the journal, Free Women also published a number of popularizing pamphlets, aimed at a less informed public, dealing with such matters as child development and education.

16. It goes without saying that this movement was only active in regions under republican control.

17. Op. cit., pp. 164–5.

The Inner Revolution of a Khomeyni Activist

Abdolrahmane Mahdjoube

This interview took place in the autumn of 1980. At that time, Sakiné, a girl of sixteen, was a servant in a well-off Iranian family north of Tehran. Since then she has found a job in the public services and has continued to study. The revolution brought about an improvement in living conditions for her and her father, who is a contract labourer and was given a permanent post after the revolution. He lives in the ministry building where he is the watchman-gardener. Each receives the guaranteed monthly minimum wage of 2,500 toumans a month.

In so far as Sakiné is opposed to the power of her father and asserts the right of a woman to be a political being, her point of view is shared by (young) Islamic and non-Islamic women revolutionaries. However, Sakiné differed from other young Muslim women of her age when, at the end of 1980, she still supported Khomeyni and so allied herself with that sector of the working class that has benefited, in one way or another, from the new regime and closed ranks around it. Her reasoning is on two levels. On the one hand, it might be called 'reactive', since it relates to a specific situation at a specific time. For example, she praises Khalkhali,[1] whose firmness she compares favourably with the weakness and indecisiveness of the Bazargan[2] provisional government. On the other hand, she reasons at a deep level, where the notions of good and evil, just and unjust are structured; and here Sakiné calls on a body of images which express the idea she has of Islam. In it are to be found the key concepts of the 'dispossessed' (*mostaz'af*), 'the powerful'. (*mostakbar*), the 'guide' (*rahbar*), 'martyr', idolatry (*tarhoute*), 'material' (*maddiyate*), 'inner revolution'. Sakiné derives from these concepts an idea of ideal Islamic society and her judgements on actual society are inspired by it.

A simplified diagram of these linkages can be drawn by opposing the concepts to one another as positive and negative.

The references to Islam are constant and unravelling the meaning of the word 'Islam' is the basic problem in understanding Sakiné's viewpoint and the image she has of social relations.

Islam here is essentially the religion of the dispossessed, the poor, the people that sacrifice their life for it. If religion helps the dispossessed, if the poor recognize themselves in it, it is because this religion identifies itself with them and with their struggle. Islam is the religion through which there

59

Good	Evil
Islam	Idolatry
The people	
The dispossessed	The powerful
The poor	
The guide	The Shah
(Khomeyni)	
The spiritual	The material
Equality	Luxury
	Inequality
Islamic government	Superpower
	Imperialism
Veiled women	Unveiled women

will be no more dispossessed: in it is incarnated the demand for equality.

The devotion of the poor (economically speaking) to Islam must be rewarded with the establishment of a just society. This task is opposed by the powerful *mostakbar* who live at the expense of the dispossessed and enrich themselves with the people's mites. It is the rich who have the power in America and the Shah's court was a reflection of this. Such power is illegitimate because it is founded on the appropriation of what should go to the poor. But the *mostaz'af* have Islam and its dignitaries on their side. They have for them the Mahdi, the Imam of the Age, whose appearance will put an end to injustice and overthrow the superpowers which prop up the powerful. In Sakiné's mind, the dispossessed are always poor, though the rich are not always powerful. There are virtuous rich people who, she says, 'spend in the path of righteousness' and are not among the powerful. The practice of charity puts the rich on the side of good. The moral criterion is thus essential and consequently limits the condemnation of 'injustice'.

To put an end to the rule of the powerful (and of idolatry) Islam needs a Guide. This is one who goes in the path of Islam and in whom the believers recognize themselves. So Khomeyni was promoted Guide not because he belongs to the clergy but because of his adherence to authentic Islam, the religion of the dispossessed. In other words, Khomeyni is the Guide because he is a popular leader and not because he is a Shi'ite patriarch. The greatness of the Guide is the reflection of the greatness of the people who have conferred on him the dignity of representing them and he gives them his voice: here the expression *vox populi vox Dei* is to be taken literally. The Guide is the expression and the guarantor of unity.

Sakiné is very jealous of this unity, but when she speaks of it, she is not thinking about national unity but the unity of the *mostaz'af*. The role of the Guide is to perfect this unity, to turn the mosaic of the dispossessed into an organized whole, a reflection of the oneness of the word. The Guide is the catalyst of the people when he transforms them into a nation of militants.

The struggle that he is waging is at once a religious, moral and political struggle. He fought idolatry incarnated by the Shah, the lackey of the United States who drew his legitimacy from America and not from Muslims. The Shah was the antithesis of the Guide who draws his legitimacy from the people of believers. The Shah was the most perfect example of idolatry; he was anti-Islamic because anti-popular and not the reverse. Similarly, a person who dies in the service of the people is a martyr, even if he is ungodly. It is not piety that determines belonging to Islam but membership of the community. The martyrs are the dispossessed; they are not afraid to give their lives for religion but in return Islam must work to improve their lot. True Islam is the one that supplies the dispossessed with a Guide and not the one which endows the believers with a 'church' or a 'clergy'.

The difference between the popular Shi'ism of a Sakiné and the clerical religion of the religious stands out starkly here. For popular Shi'ism, Islam is a representation of the world that takes the side of the dispossessed; for the religious Islam involves a set of social relations that legitimates the clerical hierarchy. They are antagonistic approaches. One is conservative, the other seeks to turn into a ruling class a stratum that claims to be the sole reference point in the establishment of an 'Islamic' society.

It is in the name of this belonging to the community that demands militancy and self-sacrifice (even unto death) that Sakiné criticizes her father and defends her right to disobey him by opposing his conception of relations between the sexes. In Sakiné's view, the repressive control that he exercises over her is the mark of a narrow and egoistical interpretation of Islam, whence his refusal to allow her to become a militant: he is incapable of 'inner revolution'. The revolution is at once a social upheaval and a moral conversion. Sakiné incarnates the new religious fervour of young people in which the demands of the revolution take precedence over every other consideration, particularly family demands. Mixing of the sexes is justified in the service of the revolution: it is tolerated by Islam if this meeting takes place with mutual respect and is intended for the service of the community.

Of course, Sakiné's religious fervour stands in contrast to hidebound archaism and the freezing of social relations in terms of pure and impure. But she displays her intolerance and her taste for authority — characteristics of conformity with the social class to which she belongs — in her attitude to the wearing of the veil and respect for fasting.

She condemns the modernism of the 'educated'. Sakiné's diatribes against the towns express a desire to retain her roots. For her, 'deruralizing' oneself is equivalent to becoming a 'de-Islamized' woman. The classical argument that sees the village as the great outsider from industrial 'progress', kept in 'backwardness' and 'traditionalism' is here turned on its head. The village was in advance of the town, because it was already fighting for Islam. At the same time, according to Sakiné, it was to punish it that the old regime kept the village in the background. Unveiling is the work of the towns, of the old regime, of idolatry. For Sakiné, the unveiled woman is a woman who is culturally extraverted and economically powerful.

Veiling or unveiling are signs of the membership of certain social classes and are a compromise (or refusal to compromise) with an illegitimate regime. The unveiling advocated by the Shah was in fact a violence exercised against the people by an anti-people government. Here we see the categories pure and impure being politicized.

But then is it the case that Sakiné's argument is a coherent rejection (politically) of social inequalities? By her reference to 'good rich people', Sakiné shows that this is not so and we shall see as we read that at many points she swings between an interpretation of Islam that underpins a certain conception of the class struggle and another one that justifies inequality if the powerful agree to fulfil their duties according to the implicit code of *do et des*.

Interview with Sakiné

Q: This revolution took place under the leadership of Mr Khomeyni. Why, in your view, did he become the representative of the Imam?[3]
R: Everything Mr Khomeyni has done is good and wise. His conduct and his way of thinking conform with the conduct, character and manner of acting of our imams. That is why the people have confidence in him (*rhabouleshe dare*). Not only our people but those who imitate him in Islamic countries all over the world, have recognized him and find him superior to the others, even to Mr Borujerdi,[4] and think that it is quite right to imitate him.
Q: What, in your view, is the essence of what Mr Khomeyni says?
R: The essence of what he says is that we should be wholly Islamic — and not simply in words. He insists, much more than people think, on Islam and not on material things. Many say that everybody should have plenty of everything, but he asserts that, however we live, we must give ourselves only to Islam and pay no heed to anything else, to the comments of others, to plots and to the superpowers. All that is as dust for him. Islam, Islam, nothing but Islam. Man must have a Guide. Since the time God created him, man has always had a Guide and the Guides have been sent so that man should remain pure, that he should live and die completely pure, so that he should have a good end in the other world. He must choose the Guide whom God has sent him, a Guide who can make him worthy in this world and in the other, so that he directs his path in the way of Allah; otherwise man might opt for the wrong way and, as people say, there are two categories of people: those who are happy in this world and unhappy in the next and those who suffer in this world and are blessed to the end of time, happy and worthy. Human beings are so created. Everything depends on the way of living that a man has chosen, everything depends on the world he believes in. The reasonable man chooses his Guide, his way, follows the Guide that he has taken for himself and listens to what he says. Islam has a Guide, the Koran proclaims it so. If we are Islamic, we must listen with an attentive ear to our Guide, and not only listen to him but act in accordance with what he says. Action is the important thing. These days people only listen (discreetly); but we must act in the way the Guide wants. Only deeds show whether you are listening to the Guide or not. The Guide speaks with completely

pure intentions, he acts according to his duty and the people must conform in their deeds to the wishes of the Guide.

Q: In your view, who are the dispossessed (*mostaz'af*)?

R: The dispossessed are the bottom rung of society. The dispossessed in developed societies like America or Europe do perhaps have the standard of living of our middle class, but I still call them dispossessed. Why? Because in those countries there is nobody lower. In our country, those who are poor, the real dispossessed, have a low economic, moral and cultural level. When a person is not self-sufficient, when he does not have the means that all of God's creatures should have, he is dispossessed and must be helped to attain a minimum of decency.

Q: And who are the powerful (*mostakbar*)?

R: The powerful are those who are rich beyond measure, who only use wealth for themselves and act only for their own interests. The powerful seize what belongs to the people and pocket everything. Yet there are rich people, and even very rich people, who spend their money well. These cannot be called powerful. But those who think only of their own interests and the interests of those about them, they can be called powerful. They take their money from the pockets of the dispossessed.

Q: What does Mr Khomeyni say about the dispossessed (*mostaz'af*)?

R: Mr Khomeyni says that we must look after the dispossessed, he says that there must not be any, that everybody must be equal (*dar yéke sathe*). It was the dispossessed who made the revolution. And it is really true what Mr Khomeyni says, that it is the dispossessed who saved Islam in all the towns, in all the villages. In the time of idolatry the villages made a greater effort than the towns to preserve Islam. I myself am a countrywoman. I've been in Tehran for four years and I spent three or four years in Karadje.[5] In all, that makes seven or eight years that I've been in towns and even now as soon as someone sees me in the street they say to me, 'Aren't you suffocating under that scarf (*rusari*) and that *chador*?'[6] I reply, 'No.' They say to me, 'In Tehran it is the custom to wear the *chador* but not the scarf.' But I wear the *chador* and the scarf together because I do not want to expose my hair to people who are my 'non-intimates.'[7] When I was small, my father would never allow me to take off the scarf or the *chador*: similarly, in our village, my father absolutely insists that my sister, who is seven, wears the scarf and the *chador*. That's what religion requires. It's laid down by God.

During Ramadan, all the Islamic rituals were carried out precisely in the countryside, whereas in the towns, the young men soon let themselves be influenced and the girls, as soon as they arrived, took off the *chador* and the scarf and not even their parents could reform them.

The countryside, although behind in everything, was ahead for Islam and, on this issue, showed no weakness in the time of idolatry when terror prevailed. It was the dispossessed who prevented the disappearance of Islam and they will certainly continue to do so as long as they are able to. The martyrs that we have given were all dispossessed people. The lower down the social scale, the greater the number of martyrs. Why? Because the faith of the dispossessed was so strong that they were not afraid to sacrifice their life for Islam. For these people, the dispossessed, unnecessary expenses, like good food, the latest fashion, gourmet meals are pointless: they ask for Islam, Islam before all else.

It is quite right to call these peasants who are behind in everything dispossessed. They were deliberately left in this state of underdevelopment because they believed more strongly than anyone else in Islam and the notables in the old regime knew quite well that it was they who would prevent Islam from perishing and would overthrow the idolatrous (*tarhoute*) government. That's why the old regime didn't help the development of the countryside. The dispossesed are the lowest stratum of society, but they saved Islam and, by the grace of God, will continue to do so. So long as the world is the world, it is these classes that will save Islam. It is these people, who have nothing, who offer themselves body and soul for Islam. The powerful, on the other hand, are those who do wrong to the dispossessed and to Islam.

Q: Who, in your view, is a martyr?

R: A martyr is one who in his soul and mind seeks to help Islam and fights against the enemies of Islam. Such a person is a martyr, however he dies, whether on the battle-field or elsewhere. When he makes his vow, the martyr must respect it and his deeds must be in conformity with it. Remaining in the service of Islam, of God, of the Koran, and of the people, this person will give his life for Islam. Such a person will have his peace in paradise, however he dies, because he has chosen the way that Allah has indicated and that all the prophets and our imams have designated. If someone dies on the battle-field, even if he is ungodly, since he is a human being and God created him, he too is a martyr.

Q: Who was the Shah?

R: The Shah's father was a soldier whom the British put on the throne because they realized that he knew how to wage war, that he was very cruel and could put down revolts. Because of his cruelty, the British thought that by putting the kingdom in his hands he could protect their interests in Iran and this is exactly what happened. After him came his son. Once the British had left, it was the Americans' turn and America helped and supported him up to his death.

Who can be in any doubt that this Shah, this idolator (*tarhoute*), this enemy, this bloodthirsty individual, was nothing less than Yazid[8] and Moavie?[9] He didn't have a single good quality and, in my opinion, he did nothing good at all for this people, only for his master America and the big men in the superpowers. He did nothing for the people and everything for his own interests.

These unveiled (women) in our country don't agree with that. If at that time Reza Khan hadn't taken the veil off those women, we wouldn't be where we are now. He's the one who did that. Before Reza Khan and the ban on wearing the veil, no one could even glimpse a woman's hair, no 'outsider'. No one had ever heard of a woman without a veil and this man wrenched the veil from women's heads! He spread oppression and corruption. He dragged the country into the mire. He did nothing good for the future of the country, nothing for the people.

Q: What, in your opinion, is the most important thing that Mr Khomeyni talks about?

R: The most important thing is Islam. He tells us to take the way of Islam. As long as we do that, everything will be fine. He also tells us what to do to follow the path of Islam and shows us how to help those who haven't found this path. As Islam and its holy book demand, the people must maintain its unity, this oneness of the word[10] which Allah gave us, as a gift so that Mohammed and the disciples of the Doctrine do good according to it and do not act in a hundred different ways. As soon as we are dispersed into several groups, Islam is weakened. Our doctrine is one and those who have created separate groups, who are supporters of the East or the West,[11] are counter-revolutionaries. Those people want to create a different society. According to them, our Islam is 1,400 years old and is out of date: we should make progress. But if we look to the Koran and God, we shall reach the good society and we shall make progress in all fields. If our country has not progressed, it is because these disgusting people, these traitors to the people and the Koran didn't let our country go on as God has commanded. If from the beginnings of Islam,[12] when Mohammed was named Prophet by God, things had gone properly, our situation would have improved day by day and today, instead of being inferior, we should be superior to every country in the world. It needs a little patience to reach perfection by following the commands of the Koran.

Q: Do you take part in the Friday prayer?

R: Yes.

Q: What do you see there?

R: When I go there is an enormous crowd and you see new things all the time. I talk to all sorts of people. The other day, in a taxi, a woman asked me if, in this heat, I wasn't suffocating under the scarf and the *chador*. I said, 'No, I'm used to it and if you wore them you too would get used to them.' I got out at Valiyé Asr square and walked. Halfway there, I had a discussion with this woman who said to me, 'You think Oveissi[13] is good, for you and those like you only he is good. You deserve to have Oveissi govern you.' I also talked to a girl who was a supporter of Pichgam[14] whose leader is Mr Peyman[15] and she told me that she didn't know much about Islam. I said, 'How is it that you know so much about Pichgam but not about Islam?' She replied that people had made an idol of Imam Khomeyni and that she didn't accept that, that we were almost back to the ways of the old regime that had made an idol of the Shah. There are many discussions like that at Friday prayer.

A girl was selling the paper *Ommate* and I said, 'You who are wearing an Islamic veil, don't you know that Mr Peyman is the editor of this newspaper?' As for the Mudjahidini Khalq,[16] I've had discussions with them; they are ignorant and don't know it. As someone said on the radio, they indoctrinate young people under eighteen and hide behind them, they understand nothing about Islam. In my village, my sister is in the ninth class (equivalent to fourth form in England), and her friend asked her to join the Mujahidin. Why? Because every day she talks to her about them in class. Most of those people are like that, but what I am sure of is that Islam doesn't say what the Mudjahidin say. Those people don't have an Islamic view, they are Marxists.

Q: What is Marxism?

R: I don't know really. It is an 'impure mixture'.[17]

Q: Do you feel the same as your father about Islam?

R: No, we don't think the same. We see Islam differently. I've not yet really discussed it with my father but I've come to the conclusion that he neither can nor will discuss it because his viewpoint doesn't correspond to Islam. His words are right but his deeds aren't. Take me, his own daughter; Islam never says that a father should behave as he does towards me. My father says that according to Islam a man should not speak to a woman, and that it is a sin for a woman to speak to a 'stranger'. But if Islam says that, why did my father make me work in a house where there was a man who was a 'non-intimate' (the head of the house) and why did he prevent me taking lessons and learning the Koran? He wouldn't tolerate his daughter taking (evening) classes whereas Islam is all in favour of it. He laughed at me and my six sisters. I don't know why. His thoughts are Islamic but his deeds aren't.

Q: What do you think of Mr Khalkhali?

R: Mr Khalkhali acts for the benefit of the people and the country. When a country loses its young people, there's no one to defend it and that country will be lost. This is what the government of idolatry was doing. Of ten young people who entered the university, perhaps not one came out safe and sound, all became drug addicts. Khalkhali saves young people like that.

Mr Khalkhali is very strict; everything about him is Islamic and is in the image of Mr Khomeyni, but Mr Khomeyni, thanks be to God, is eighty years old. If Mr Khomeyni was the same age as Mr Khalkhali they would be the same. Mr Khalkhali follows in Mr Khomeyni's footsteps. Everything Mr Khalkhali does he does with great strictness, unlike those who are now in power. Our country must be governed like that. Mr Khalkhali is someone very good and, in my opinion, is pleasing both to God and the Koran. Wasn't it the same in the beginning of Islam? How strict people were then! Now that the country is Islamic, it ought to be the same ... Mr Khalkhali's strictness helps the people, his actions have benefited it, as has his struggle against drug traffickers, and the exemplary punishment he inflicts on those who publicly break the fast in this month of Ramadan. It's very good. I think that offenders should be punished severely. The day before yesterday, I telephoned the Committee to inform them that some people were not respecting the fast. I said, 'It's Ramadan now. Since our country is Islamic, should people behave like that?' They said, 'We'll be there in a few minutes.' and they thanked me. Immediately afterwards, people from the Committee arrived and picked up those people. I forgot to tell them to come every day to check this area — the taxi-drivers wash their cars and eat in front of everybody.

Q: It is said that this revolution is anti-imperialist. What do you think of that?

R: Imperialism is exploiting us and keeping the whole world under its domination. It wants everyone to be its lackeys. America wants the land and people of Iran to belong to it. The Islamic Republic, on the other hand, is friendly to all governments that are free and independent (of imperialism) and that are in favour of justice. It is a form of government that the people wanted and that it has created for itself. This government is the friend of freedom and the enemy of imperialism, communism and all the rest. Countries like America never give any freedom to the dispossessed and favour only the powerful.

Q: Could you explain what you mean by that?

R: Those in the government, who support the Shah or Western governments, live at the expense of the dispossessed and fill their pockets with the people's mites. They are against the poor whom they only use to enrich themselves ...

Q: What do you think of your father?

R: My father isn't a revolutionary. I call someone revolutionary who has had what I call an inner revolution. If someone says, 'Ah! It would be nice to go to the community prayer on Friday! If only this or that wasn't stopping me, I would certainly go,' he isn't a true revolutionary. A true revolutionary goes. A revolutionary boy or girl runs away from his or her father's house at night if the father opposes him or her going to fight on the battle-field. The next day he or she writes to him to tell him. Someone who has had an inner revolution is not afraid of being got at by his father.

My father claims to be revolutionary and every evening he goes to the mosque. I said, 'Why are you so self-satisfied? Why does your daughter have to respect you so much and you not respect her at all? I have duties towards you but I'm not the only one to have duties. You too, you have duties towards me.' He only intervenes when the good name or the interests of the family are threatened. He takes me under his protection so that my name is not spread about in a bad way in the family but he doesn't help me, he doesn't leave me free so that I can become somebody, he doesn't let me go to the Holy War for Reconstruction.[18] Why? Because in the family it would be said that he had a daughter with loose morals. He says, 'It's not worth your going to the Holy War because you mustn't go alone and I'd have to go with you.' Well, that's not an inner revolution. When you have an inner revolution, you must go with completely pure intentions, and since I'm his daughter and I have pure intentions, he should allow me to go. Those who are taking part in the Holy War are not people who will corrupt you, those times are over. They're not people who will take advantage of you.

Q: Why should you wear the veil?

R: It is the mark of female modesty (*effate*). The greatness of a woman is in her veil; an unveiled woman has no value for Islam. God created woman with her 'modesty', with her veil, so that she can become perfect. In an Islamic country everyone must follow the government in the way it does things and anyone who doesn't conform should leave the country. The veil doesn't harm anyone and if you don't wear it, some men might follow you in the street.

Our culture was evil. It was idolatry that made people believe that veiled women were sluts, corrupt people and madwomen, that they committed a thousand filthy deeds beneath their veil and that prostitutes were made to wear the veil. But now, no man follows us in the street because today all veils are Islamic. The veiled prostitutes are very few and even if there are any men no longer dare to follow them in the street.

My father has seven daughters and one son. We used to live in our little village near Damrhan; later we moved to Karadje and we stayed there for three or four years. My father was a gardener there and found it hard to work because he has pains in his kidneys. When he was young, he did too much work with a spade and he can't do heavy work any more. When he went to Damrhan he had kidney pains after two or three days working with the spade and had to rest. My mother had said to my maternal uncle, 'Since you're working in Tehran, in the civil service, find a decent job for Sakiné if you can.' My uncle then sent me a note and a few months later he asked me to come to Tehran, supposedly to work in an office. I arrived in Tehran just before the Nowruz festival (beginning of spring). He took me to a gentleman who he told me was a director in a ministry and would get me a job in the ministry if I worked for him for a year or two. He wasn't lying and I saw with my own eyes that he had found jobs for several of his former maids in the ministry. I was fifteen or sixteen and I had no experience. Seeing that my wages were low and that I was beginning to get varicose veins, my father put me with another family where I was paid more. Then, there was a flood in our village and our house was seriously damaged. To repair it, I gave my father all I'd earned.

I've been working now for four or five years. I've got varicose veins in my legs and I will have to wear medical stockings for the rest of my life. There are other things wrong with me too; but one's mental attitude is the most important thing and that has changed since the revolution. Before, I was completely ignorant and yet I still didn't like this work. I knew I was unworthy and I was ashamed of myself in front of other people. After the revolution, I felt no more shame, I simply asked myself why I should be doing this sort of work. I had to look for another job, take a course in weapons use in the mosques and go on with my studies. That year I went to enrol for evening classes but Mr Abbas (the head of the house) didn't let me go. This revolution had such a great impact on me that I didn't want to work there any more and I found the way they treated me unfair. Why? Because if you harm someone who wants to serve the revolution, you are harming the revolution itself. Can someone call himself human and claim to be part of humanity when he prevents another from serving the revolution? Recently, I've really been paying attention to my state of mind and I've at last come to understand that the reason why there are so many problems in my relationship with my father is because this revolution has really turned me inside out. Day and night it worried me all the time. I thought about it, and I ended up almost mentally ill that I should be in that house and be unable to get away from it, and that my father should not let me go away. Once, I tried to go to the Imam Khomeyni Aid Committee to find work and a room. They took down my details and sent me to the Martyrs' Foundation for a room. There I was told that they only looked after the families of martyrs and I went back to the Aid Committee. There I was told that Mr Karroubi, its director, was going to give me a room.

Q: What do you think of the (American embassy) hostages affair?

R: The hostages were in fact spies, spies who were taken as hostages: in exchange for freeing them, we have just demands. We agree with everything that the Guide says about the matter: our Guide is the voice of our people, just like the President of the Republic and the Prime Minister. We approve of everything they say and they speak the truth ... Is it sensible that in an Islamic country, another country, because it is a superpower, should be able, for its own interests, to transform its embassy into a nest of spies? They sucked the people's blood ... They spied for their government and their government sucked our people's blood; they took from our people everything they had. They left them nothing, everything was under their rod. Savak was run by the CIA.

Q: What is America?

R: America is nothing; America is hollow but it doesn't want to admit it; it sees only the material things, it takes no account of things spiritual and yet that's what's important; it says it is Christian, but as Imam Khomeyni says, did Christ ever behave like that? Wherever its interests are threatened, it does everything to protect them because it is powerful; America and Russia have divided the world in two so as to dominate it better; they have drowned themselves in things material, they wallow in the mire. An Islamic man has no time for that, he pays no attention to material things, but only to things spiritual; that is the true Islam. In fact, when you have the spiritual, you also have the material, you are a real man in every sense of the word, you are a complete man. You become a complete man when you take no account of material things, of money, wealth and possessions. What's the good of all that when you don't need it? You work for your daily needs, everyone should have provisions enough for a year so that when he goes on the pilgrimage to Mecca his family has enough to live on — God certainly doesn't ask you to lose sight of your future. But how these people suck the people's blood! Now America has oil itself but it still takes away Iran's oil and the oil of other countries and they keep theirs in reserve ... We now live in an age when no one country can dominate another. Every ruling order has its time, its law, its span. It is established, then it becomes stabilized and it ends by declining and disappearing. Everything, except Islam; that has endured for fourteen hundred years and it is still there when everything else has disappeared. Those traitors who submit to America and become its lackeys are so shabby, so dirty and evil. It really makes me pity them. Hostage, American spy — what does it matter?

Many Americans are discontented; but in the intoxicated atmosphere in which they live they don't know why. Even in America, many students are on the same side as the Iranian students, who are Muslims. Even in some of the European countries there have been demonstrations in support of them ... All over the world, everything [good] that's done is done by the young; it's the young who are fighting for the freedom of the people and not the others; in our Islamic country it's the young and the religious people but in non-Islamic countries it's the young who rise up first.

Our people have chosen their own way, they know what they are doing, they have complete confidence in their Guide, their president and prime minister. As for the students of the Way of the Imam, they've done the best thing in the world; they have taken the nest of spies by storm and closed its doors; I am very grateful to them and I thank them for it. They have done something great, they have truly Islamic vision. America has done us no good; if it wants to have diplomatic relations with us, it must understand that every country has its own way of organizing itself, its laws, its President, its Guide; no one must interfere in our affairs, just as we don't interfere in other people's. America is trying to deceive countries so that they fall under its yoke, so that it dominates them and they become its lackeys, so that it can continue to extract petroleum and carry it away. That's the source of our misfortune and the war against Iraq has the same origins. Without America, Iraq would never have dared to attack us; it's because it has America's backing that it did so. When a country becomes a superpower, power paralyses it, just as a person gets puffed up with pride when he reaches the peak of power. According to the rights of man, humanity ought to enjoy comfort, it ought to be free and no one should be dispossessed; that is precisely what Islam seeks. Americans don't act this way because they think only of themselves; they have put themselves totally outside the spiritual realm and think only of material things, and that's exactly what the devil does; he thinks only of himself. There are two superpowers, one in the East, the other in the West. They are face to face and have divided the world in two.

Q: What do you mean by superpower?

R: A country that has more power than any other. The superpowers are in a favourable economic situation. That's because they have sucked the blood of other peoples, stolen their industry and economy. That's how they became superpowers. With the petroleum we have, our Iran should have been like a paradise. We should never have lacked for anything and we should not have had poor people. There should be no more dispossessed or homeless people in Iran. A countryman like Reza Khan, who was illiterate, an ordinary soldier, made himself the lackey of the superpowers so as to attain power without thinking that he also had duties towards the people. He forgot that he had an obligation to provide them with a degree of comfort; he only wanted to become

Shah and have flatterers. Later it was his son's turn.

Without other countries under their lash, these superpowers cannot exist. If every country were to defend itself there would be no superpowers; it is even possible that after our revolution the Iraqi regime might be overthrown like the one in Egypt. We are no longer as we were; the people are more aware now. Until now, Islam didn't exist in any country; if Islam — the real Islam — is established in Iran, it will be able to spread from here to other countries. If our revolution triumphs, there will be nobody any more to be the lackey of the superpowers.

Mr Khomeyni says that the country must be Islamic, that Islam must spread to other countries, that the dispossessed must free themselves, that the powerful must be wiped out and the oppressed shake off the yoke of domination. Saddam Hussain[19] says no, he is acting like Yazid. He is making himself the lackey of America and has the support of Russia. He's worse than Hitler. Hitler the Nazi was the most bloodthirsty man in the world before Saddam . . . Yes, Saddam's worse than Hitler.

I have come to a conclusion. In this world, from the time Islam saw the light of day, it began in blood; and it's still the same today. As soon as anyone wanted to talk about Islam, he was silenced. When people wanted to spread Islam, its enemies fought and prevented it from triumphing. Now it's the same. Even if the present crisis blows over, we shall have others with other countries such as Turkey. It's American imperialism that will do this, until the Mahdi[20] appears. We are waiting for him. I hope with all my heart that he appears soon . . . or if not, may God who is capable of everything, the creator of the universe and of men, rid us of the two superpowers. I hope that the Imam Mahdi will arrive and set the world to rights. The world will then be near its end, the dispossessed will be freed, the oppressed will be released from their chains and they will surely have a choice place in paradise. It is because the superpowers are oppressing the dispossessed so much that the Imam Mahdi is going to appear. I am waiting for the arrival of the Mahdi, that is all I think about.

Tehran 1980

Notes

1. Khalkhali: a revolutionary judge famous for his expeditious judgements.
2. Bazargan: Prime Minister of the first government of the Revolution, a liberal in every sense of the word, who thought that the revolution was completed with the departure of the Shah.
3. The representative of the Imam: one of Khomeyni's titles, since he is deemed to be the representative of the Imam of the Age, the twelfth, during his occultation. He is also called 'Iman Khomeyni' or Mr Khomeyni.
4. Ayatollah Borujerdi was the most famous Shi'ite patriarch before Khomeyni; he died during the Shah's reign just before the old regime's agrarian reform.
5. Karadje: a medium-sized town 50 km from Tehran, now a suburb of the capital.
6. *Chador*: long veil, often black, that covers a woman's body completely.
7. Non-intimate (*na-mahram*): all who must not see an unveiled woman (especially her hair), that is all men except her husband and the intimate family circle.
8. Yazid: an Umayyad caliph during whose reign the Imam Husain, the third Shi'ite imam, met his death in a very unequal battle. Shi'ite Muslims celebrate the martyrdom of

Husain, the Great Martyr, on the days of Tassua and Ashura. In the Shi'ite consciousness, Yazid is more a symbol of absolute Evil than an actual historical figure; the Husain-Yazid pair corresponds to the Manichaean dichotomy absolute Good–absolute Evil.

9. Moavie: father of Yazid who fraudulently had Ali, the first Shi'ite imam, deposed from the Caliphate, and took his place. He became the lesser symbol of Evil, both for his behaviour towards Ali and because of having been the father of Yazid, the incarnation of absolute Evil.

10. Oneness of the word (*vahdaté kalamé*): an expression used by Khomeyni, which means that there must be unity of the Muslim community, a unity founded on the oneness of the Word, of god and of the Koran.

11. 'Neither of the East, nor of the West, Islamic Republic': a slogan that indicates the rejection of both Western-style capitalism and Russian-style socialism; in his speeches, Khomeyni castigates the supporters of the East, i.e. the Marxists, as well as the supporters of the West.

12. 'The origin of Islam' (*sadré eslam*): an expression often used by Khomeyni which refers less to a specific historical event (the historical time of the beginnings of Islam) than to a Golden Age, to the Archetype in relation to which all history is judged and that no history is able to reproduce in its splendour: the mythical time of the Prophet of Islam.

13. Oveissi: a general in the Shah's army who gave orders to fire on demonstrators in 1963, leading to thousands of deaths.

14. Pichgam: a group of secondary school students claiming to belong to the Fedayin Khalq, one of the largest guerrilla organizations, Marxist in tendency. Sakiné wrongly identifies this group with another, that of Djama.

15. Peyman is not the leader of Pichgam but the editor of the newspaper *Ommate*, supporters of the 'Imam's line'.

16. Mudjahidini Khalq or Fighters of the People, claiming to be the spiritual heirs of Ali Shariati, Muslims much attracted by an Islamic reading of Marxism.

17. Impure mixture (*eltérhati*); this could be translated as 'syncretic', but this would miss the religious connotation; among other things, it is the expression which the clergy applies to other groups that claim to be Islamic, showing that among them there is a mixture of Islam and Marxism; this latter being impure, it taints their religion which cannot lay claim to Islamic 'purity'.

18. The Holy War for Reconstruction was launched to improve living conditions in the countryside by such work as electrification and the building of roads and public baths.

19. Saddam-Yazid is a nickname for Saddam Hussain, the president of the Republic of Iraq, who is blamed for behaving like Yazid and not, as his name suggests, like Husain.

20. Mahdi is the twelfth Shi'ite imam; for Shi'ites his reappearance will mark the end of the world and the disappearance of ungodliness and injustice.

Palestinian Women in Palestine

Didar Fawry

The testimonies in this chapter were collected in October and November 1982 and are part of a field survey to test and complement materials from direct sources that I was gathering for a study of the conditions of working Palestinian women in Palestine. This was begun well before the Israeli invasion of Lebanon and the transfer of the Palestinian political leadership to Tunis.

While I was engaged in research on the problems of development in the Arab world, I had become aware of statistical reports on production and the Palestinian working population in Israel and in the territories occupied by Israel in 1967, the West Bank of the Jordan and Gaza. These reports led me to conclude that a socio-economic process was producing situations comparable to those of colonialism proper. These were the dependence of the Palestinian labour force on Israeli business, sub-contracting reserved for the owning classes, the blocking of technicians from management positions, a systematic expropriation and repression and, at the same time, the opening up of employment to part-timers and women. In other words, a deliberate policy was transforming the population into a cheap reserve labour force for Israeli business and encouraging the well-off and the heads of family who rejected working as construction labourers to emigrate.

On the other hand, a preliminary field survey helped me to detect a fundamental political process: the displacement of the motive force of Palestinian history back into Palestine, the external political leadership acting above all as the symbol of the armed resistance of the Palestinian people and of the international recognition of its cause.

In 1975–6, mass demonstrations took place in occupied Palestine,[1] supported by the Palestinian minority — the so-called 'Arab' minority — in Israel who were, at the same time, making their own demands. On 30 March 1976, as a sign of protest against the decision to expropriate Arab lands in Galilee, a strike, called by the Committee for the Defence of Arab Lands, ended in the first violent clash between the Palestinian minority in Israel and the authorities.[2] In the occupied territories strikes were launched as a mark of solidarity and, since then, 30 March has been marked each year by demonstrations and strikes, on both sides of the 'green line'. The Palestinians inside Palestine have begun to appear as an organized socio-political force.

Elements in the Palestine National Front[3] linked with the PLO won in the April 1976 municipal elections in occupied Palestine and the majority of votes at the last two elections in Arab towns and villages in Israel has gone to representatives of the Khadash.[4]

The displacement of the motive force towards the homeland is to be seen fundamentally in the territorial definition of the Palestinian project: the statements of the chairman of the PLO that from this time on the goal of liberation and national independence will be limited only to the territories occupied in 1967, in accordance with the resolutions adopted by the international community.[5]

Palestinian women inside Palestine have begun to speak out: they have begun to take part in organized demonstrations and meetings, even in military-style operations;[6] some have begun to write and win an international audience;[7] finally, they have begun to organize on the basis of new concepts foreign to the subservient ideology that used to permeate the women's associations in the region.

The Committees of Working Women established in occupied Palestine (the first was set up in Ramallah in 1978) affect women at work and women in the house, in the university and in the factory, in the towns and in the villages. Women claim rights in every field: the right to self-determination, autonomy, the right to better wages, the right to equality between the sexes. They have also undertaken profit-making cooperative work: workshops producing Palestinian handicrafts are functioning in a number of villages and their works are occasionally put on show. The women's movement has succeeded in laying the bases for coordinating activities at the national level: in 1981, the Union of Committees of Working Palestinian Women in the West Bank and the Gaza Strip was formed in Jerusalem.

Among the projects of the cultural section of the Union that were outlined to me are debates on the situation of women in the independent Arab states,[8] the study of the rights of working women and the learning of foreign languages, including English and Hebrew. All of these show that the leadership intends to fight against sexual discrimination within their own community, against the exploitation of Palestinian women by the occupy-ing power and against chauvinistic attitudes. But they are very short of personnel and money and they have to face opposition and repression from many quarters; from men, particularly the Muslim Brothers and from traditionalist women too, including those who are active in other women's organizations.

The statistics underline the level of sexual discrimination which women in the Union have to combat. Most wage-earning women work in the primary sector,[9] in occupations like farming which are seasonal and outside any control.[10] The excessive infant female mortality shown in the tables by age-group and sex[11] can only be explained by extreme discrimination against baby girls.[12]

The leaders of the Union are subjected to all kinds of harassment[13] and, through the Village Leagues that it has set up, the occupying power prevents any outside financial assistance arriving to open creches and nurseries that would enable working women to be less dependent on older women or at least reduce their overwork (given the scale of emigration of family heads in the 25–64 age groups).[14]

The situation of Palestinian women in Israel is at once similar and different. It is similar because, like their sisters in the occupied territories, Palestinian women in Israel are doubly penalized: whether they are employed in the least-skilled sectors and receive the lowest wages, or whether they look after all the everyday problems of their families on their own when the men come home only at the end of the week, in either case they have to obey patriarchal traditions within the family and the village in the name of the preservation of socio-cultural identity. In Israel all development projects are in the Jewish areas. Arab towns and Arab quarters in the mixed towns were left in a run-down, even a half-demolished state following the 1948 war, while Arab villages are no more than dormitory villages for workers who return there in the evening or at the end of the week. The Palestinian community in Israel is completely marginalized.

The 'traditionalism/modernity' approach, which maintains that for change to occur there must first be a mental and spiritual transformation in the Arab community, must therefore be rejected. This is widely held in Israel, for it provides a justification for keeping the institutional framework of Israeli society intact, and more particularly the system of ethnic-religious segregation.[15] But half the 'Arab' population in Israel is today urbanized and half the rural population live in large villages. Arab wage-earning women in Israel are poorly represented in the primary sector and well represented in the tertiary sector, above all in public and community services, a sign that working women have a more favourable socio-economic situation here than in the occupied territories where the opposite situation obtains.

But if casual labour continues to be the lot of even skilled working-class women (even if for work demanding the same levels of skill, their Jewish fellow-workers receive a monthly salary) there is still a single central union organization for both communities and working women have the right to join a union at their work-place. This is not the case for Palestinian women in the occupied territories who work in Israel. Palestinian women in Israel have the right, despite harassment and even dismissal from their jobs, to be active[16] in the political formations and associations of their choice; in the occupied territories, they run up against the restrictions decreed under the emergency laws.

But it is still true today that the right to exist has not been recognized for the Palestinian national minority in Israel.[17] The issue provokes debates not just among communists, but also among feminists. The feminist movement in Israel invited a group of Palestinian women from Israel to participate as such — and not as 'Arabs' (as they are officially described in Israel) — in the Fifth National Conference of the movement which was held in Beit Aba Kushi, Haifa, on 8 and 9 October 1982. They spoke at two workshops, one devoted to the situation of Palestinian women in Israel and the other to the problem of women and war. It was a great event and the debate was passionate.

There were no joint final communiques and the Palestinian women did not take part in the march through the streets of Haifa on the evening of the first day of the conference. They agreed with the feminists' slogans against rape and for the protection of battered women but they had demanded, and not secured, that slogans be added calling for equality between the Jewish and Palestinian communities in Israel and the right to the self-determination of Palestinian women in the occupied territories.

Even so, the fact that the feminist movement in Israel had recognized the Palestinian community was enough to spark off venomous criticism from a well-known woman journalist who attacked the feminists for having provided a platform for 'representatives of the terrorist Palestinian organization, the PLO'. On the other hand the English-language newspaper of the Labour Party, the *Jerusalem Post*, allowed the publication of a report by one of the participants who favoured the establishment of working links with Palestinian women and denounced the 'stereotyped views' that hindered dialogue.[18]

Palestinian and Jewish women in Israel found themselves united in a common struggle against the war.[19] The Palestinians were in the forefront of the first demonstrations which took place after the Sabra and Chatila massacres, particularly the ones at al-Nasira on 20 September which lasted until 23 September when the police stepped in violently to put an end to them.[20]

While there is no equivalent in the Palestinian community in Israel of the internationally known women writers (such as Raymonda Tawil and Sahar Khelifa) in occupied Palestine, the observer is struck by the rapid growth in the number of women in the areas of professional activity open to them, and also by their politicization. In 1971 a woman stood and was elected as mayor of a village in Galilee — Kafr Yassif — whose inhabitants are Muslim, Druze and Christian Arabs. But progress is still slow. At the meeting held in al-Nasira to mark the 40th day of mourning for the victims of the Sabra and Chatila massacres, it was a Jewish woman, a member of the Khadash, who spoke publicly, despite the role played by women in the demonstrations in the Arab 'capital' of Israel.

This situation is reflected in Michel Khulaifi's film *Memoire Fertile*,[21] the first film made by a Palestinian. It discusses the problems of Palestinian women inside Palestine. It was filmed on the spot and is remarkable in several ways, particularly because it shows with great sensitivity and without exaggeration, the horrors of oppression; it provokes discussion about the reality of women's lives. It presents two different stories. In Israel, a Palestinian woman who is a widow of a former landowner in the Nazareth region refuses to sell her land despite the fact she has no right to work it because it is included in a Jewish development zone; in order to bring up her son and daughter she worked, and still works, as a labourer, in a clothing firm. In occupied Palestine we learn about the life of Sahar

Khalifa, an intellectual in the prime of life, a teacher and a writer, who is divorced and lives alone with her children. Different generations, different social realities, different perspectives; but similar oppression.

Yet in 1982, the idea of a Palestinian woman in Israel clinging to her piece of land is beginning to be a little out of date. Women who struggle, even mature and illiterate women, like the remarkable figure in Taibeh, Najila Abu-Ras, demand their economic and social rights within the Na'mat trade union organization,[22] or else, if they are young, organized or not, they prepare for a career and claim rights as women and as Palestinians, like their sisters in the occupied territories.

The testimonies were collected from activist women who have not before been able to make their voices heard. It was pointless to seek testimonies from women able to express themselves in writing, or from women who have no impact on their environment. The first piece, by Samira Khoury, the main Palestinian leader of the Women's Democratic Movement in Israel, a mixed organization linked to the Rakah, is reproduced virtually complete. The story of her family recounts the different fates of different members, depending on their careers. It evidences the policy of harassment of the Palestinians by the Israeli Establishment. The discussion stresses the continuity of the traditional Arab family and the place occupied by the father and the husband's mother, as well as the obsession with lost land. The narrator, a woman of about fifty, is modest, generous and impassioned, the product of an experience that has combined militancy at work with the life of a mother. She has pulled herself up by personal effort, being careful not to let herself be overtaken by the new conditions of the struggle, she is without the least trace of chauvinism, a fighter in the midst of a society which has seized up for lack of development. The main interview was in English;* her replies to new questions I asked her during the month that I followed her about in her numerous activities are added.

Zuheira's testimony is part of a series of interviews that I had with Palestinian women in Israel. It gives a glimpse of the strength and persistence of archaic customs in the Palestinian Christian community of al-Nasira which deny women any right to a separate existence. Such customs are also to be found in the Jewish community. The Rabbinate has taken over legal responsibility for matters relating to marriage and divorce and relegated women to the status of minors or mentally defective beings. Zuheira is a young woman, although she has a daughter of seventeen and a son of fourteen. Although she is very upset by the personal struggle she is waging, she is nevertheless planning to resume her studies to acquire a profession; she attends women's meetings and demonstrations and drives a clapped-out Renault 4CV that she acquired when times were better and that has to be pushed to start it. She lives in the Jewish town, in a tiny studio flat, in a small quarter where the landlords are willing to let to Palestinians. She asked to give an interview when she learned that I was preparing a study of

---

* It has been retranslated from the French. (tr.)

working Palestinian women. Now that Zuheira has left her husband, Samira is helping her to adapt to her new life, convinced that she has the necessary energy and intelligence to succeed.

The last testimony, which is very short, shows the rigidity of customs in a well-off, urbanized and French-culture milieu. The girl works and is an activist. One of the sons married the girl of his choice who is divorced with a child and, although the family is Roman Catholic, the marriage took place in the Orthodox church because the Catholic church does not recognize divorce.

Paris, February 1983

Samira Khoury, office of the Women's Democratic Movement, Tel-Aviv, October 1982

I am the eldest of a large family: ten children in 1948, including a single son, then a very young boy. This perhaps explains my unusual role for a girl within her family in our society. My father ended up giving me the nick-name 'Samir'.

We used to live in Nazareth with my father and mother and my grandparents. Only my father was working when the UN partition plan to divide Palestine into two states was drawn up in 1947. He had a shoe-maker's shop and earned enough to give us a reasonably decent life despite the large number of children. At that time there weren't that many shoe-makers in this Arab town.

My younger sister was already married. I had fought to continue my studies, supported by my mother. I was then finishing the last year at the Girls' Teacher Training School, in the Orthodox Jewish quarter of Me'a Shearin (the 100 doors) in Jerusalem, where I was a boarder. It was a free government school where the best pupils chosen from all over the country were trained for teaching. Most of the teachers were British. The conflict between the two communities — Jewish and Arab — worsened after the partition decision. Arab society, dominated by the great traditional families, was opposed to partition. But it can be said that they were indirectly aided by the Zionist leaders, or at least so I believe, since nothing was done to iron out the dispute. The Zionists and the British let them get on with it.

The atmosphere in the school was so unbearable that the teachers left for Britain and we were sent home, firmly believing, however, that we would soon be back. Some of us even left our personal boxes at the school. On my return to Nazareth I soon received offers to teach at elementary schools in various places near where I lived. I chose Acre.

During the first months, I made the journey from Acre to Nazareth and back every day. I would take the bus at 5.30 a.m. with Arab workmen who were going to the refinery or further on to other factories. I was the only girl making the journey. The refinery is still functioning but there are fewer Arabs working there now.

During the school year, I succeeded in persuading my father to allow me to live with a female relative of my mother's in Acre. I was receiving a salary of £25 a month, and this enabled me to look after myself and help my father.

When the 1948 conflict broke out we were forced to close the school and turn it into an asylum for the refugees who were flocking in from Haifa by boat, train and road. I was responsible for meeting those arriving at the port. The refugees were like those we see arriving today from Lebanon: women in nightdresses and bare-footed, with small children clinging to them ... This was how I came to know that many families who had not wanted to flee had been encouraged to do so, always with the assurance that the conflict would only last a few weeks and that they would then be able to return to their homes.

A few days later, the head of the school told me that the families were going to be distributed among the various villages and that it would be better if I went back to my parents, because of the uncertain situation. And indeed, the very day I left, Acre was surrounded by the Israelis. On 9 July it was Nazareth's turn.

Like Tiberias, Jaffa, Haifa, etc., Nazareth would have been part of the Palestinian state if one had been created.

In Nazareth, very few families left in 1948. And even then, it was not whole families, only a few members; it was a special case.

In Nazareth, the Communist Party — which was then called '*usbat al-taharur al-watani* (National Liberation League) was working secretly and already publishing the newspaper that is now called *al-Ittihad*. The Party was very active among the workers and artisans. I can remember having pamphlets printed clandestinely by the League from the time I was in secondary school, in Nazareth and later in Jerusalem and Acre.

When Nazareth was surrounded, I was eighteen and I was not yet a member of the Party; but my father's sister's husband, who worked in the refinery, would often call me in to read him the *Ittihad*. This was how I came to read Marxist writings and books, sometimes in Arabic but more often in English — secretly, of course.

I cannot say that I was brought up in a religious atmosphere. My family would take us to church every Sunday, and on holy days. But we would also go to the mosque with other members of the family who were Muslims. I remember all that simply as so many festivals without any meaning. I had no problems when I became a Marxist.

From the beginning of the conflict, and when Nazareth was surrounded in 1948, the Communist Party called on the population not to leave their homes, warning them against the final loss of their possessions. They even posted units at all the gates of the town to dissuade those who wanted to leave. They also sent comrades to our house. They succeeded in getting the people of Nazareth to stay put.

My mother was very afraid. She was afraid that her daughters would be raped. She was afraid for her only son. But I was opposed to leaving. My younger sister and her husband, who came from Transjordan and had some land there wanted to go because the man could no longer earn a living in Nazareth. But I would not let them take my little brother. In the event of danger I intended to hide my whole family in my uncle's (my father's sister's husband) cellar, but he was killed in the street as he was going home.

When Nazareth was surrounded, things changed. At the beginning of the school year, all the men and women who had been teaching were able to resume work. I had a post in Nazareth. My sister, the third child, aged sixteen, got a job as a trainee in the photo laboratory with my backing. I became a member of the Party and the teachers' union. At the end of the year, I was dismissed because of my views, as were five hundred teachers, men and women. Only those who left the union kept their jobs.

It was then that I had my first serious argument with my father. I would not give way. And I proved to him that without giving up my views, I could earn my living. I started giving private lessons at home. I earned more than I had done as a regular teacher. But my father explained to me that he was not opposed to my militant activities for financial reasons but because he feared that I would be imprisoned and tortured. We were then (and we remained so until 1966) under military administration.

I held out and my father gave way. He stopped working as a shoe-maker in the early 1950s. Competition with manufactured products was becoming too strong. He began to rear pigs and chickens on the little piece of land attached to our house. My sister also had to leave the photograph laboratory which was not doing much business.

All the girls in the family, as well as a young aunt who had been in teaching, turned to trades which, at the time, offered possibilities of work; my sister and my aunt became welfare workers and three other sisters became nurses. One of my sisters learned sewing and works with a tailor. Another works as a technician in an architectural firm. One of them, finally (my parents had two other children, after 1948, a boy and a girl) studied medicine in Bulgaria. She left in 1968. Since her return she has been working in a clinic in Nazareth. Apart from my sister, who had married very young and lives in Jordan, all the women in my family are working in Arab Nazareth.

For my brothers, things turned out differently. Israeli universities are more willing to accept foreigners than Israeli Arab citizens. My sister was able to study medicine only because she won a scholarship to Bulgaria.

My brother (the one born before 1948) was passionately interested in electronics. Once he had completed secondary school, he entered the Technicum (where technicians are trained). Being unable to find a job as a technician, or to enrol in the Technion (where engineers are trained), he studied on his own, thanks to the help of a professor at the Technion. He passed the exams, in front of fourteen examiners who were amazed by his results but awarded him only a higher technician's diploma.

He then looked for work, still with the help of this professor. He made 38 applications and received 38 rejections. On the advice of his professor he joined a ship as electronic technician. But he had to go to Tokyo to sign on. He made voyages to Australia, South Africa, Holland, England and America. But never to Haifa. After a year he renewed his contract, because his job applications in Israel were still rejected.

Finally, he passed his electronic engineering exams in Holland and has been working there for fourteen years.

It was the same with my younger brother. He was able to complete his course as an agricultural expert thanks to a Bulgarian scholarship. When he came back to Israel, he couldn't find a job as an engineer. With his brother's help, he is now finishing his doctorate in Belgium and will certainly not come back. I had to intervene with my parents on my brother's behalf. What else could I do?

I had before me the example of the husband of one of my sisters, who had become a mechanical engineer through a scholarship offered by a socialist country, and who, finding no work, finally opened a workshop making iron fittings for the construction industry.

On the other hand, my son, who also did higher studies in a socialist country (in Leningrad), found work in Nazareth on his return because he had studied as a doctor. My two daughters are also completing their courses in Leningrad, one to be a doctor and the other a psychologist. I know that they will be able to find work in Nazareth when they come back.

I married a comrade in the party. Like me and his sister he was in teaching. Both of them had been dismissed for their political opinions. His sister became a nurse. Their parents owned and worked a piece of land inherited from their grandfather who was a priest (whence the name Khoury). The land was confiscated after 1948 and they've never been able to get the least bit of it back. It's a lovely piece of land. I showed it to you this morning.

After his dismissal, my husband worked at first as a book-keeper in an ice factory. But he very soon decided to become a professional party man. At his death he was Party Secretary for the Nazareth region. The old and sick lady you saw in my house is his mother. Looking after her gives me problems when my daughters are studying in the USSR but we don't send our old people to old people's homes. One of my godsons lives with me and we take it in turns to stay with her.

I've always been active in women's organizations. In Jerusalem I was a member of the Union of Arab Women when I was in the Teachers Training School. When I returned to Nazareth, during the war, we had to look after refugees. There were 10,000 refugees in a town with a population of 12 or 14,000. They had come from the neighbouring villages surrounded by the army; their lands had been confiscated. In the beginning we put them up in churches and mosques. I showed you the old refugee camps this morning at Safouriyeh, Tabariyeh, Ma'loul, Umm Q'bai, Mjedel . . . After working for thirty-five years they have managed to build themselves their own individual stone houses. They have come together just opposite their old village. It must be terrible for them to see their lands transformed for others. I don't think they'll ever forget. Even the younger generations.

Jewish Nazareth (or upper Nazareth) was built on our lands and those of neighbouring villages, in all 14,000 *dunums*, 7,000 of which belonged to al-Nasira. In 1948, we numbered 12 or 14,000 and we had 14,500 *dunums*. Today, there are 45,000 of us and we have 7,500 *dunums*. In Nazareth-Elit, there are 26,000 inhabitants and they have twice as much land.

Our conditions were so deplorable in the time of the military administration that we got ourselves organized. Women were not even conscious of their rights then.

Our first organization, Jam'iyyat al-Nahda (Renaissance Association) was set up by Communist women militants, in 1948. There were only eight of us. We grew in numbers and we even formed links with the villages and with other organizations and groups in Acre and Haifa and with Jewish women's groups. In 1951, we decided at a congress to unite with Jewish Communist women. Thus the Union of Democratic Women (Jewish and Arab) of Israel was born. But we were all members of the ICP. When we succeeded in extending our membership to include groups not in the party, we replaced the word 'Union' with 'Movement'. In recent years, we have grown still further. Perhaps we will decide to drop the word 'democratic'. We'll see where we are when preparing for our next congress, which will take place on 8 March.

We hope very much to grow larger. And above all to get the young interested. We were right to participate in the feminist movement's seminar that you attended at Beit Aba Khushi. It is the first time that Palestinian women in Israel have been invited to speak as Palestinian women. For us it is an important event and the debates were useful. I learned a lot and I had the chance to push the debate further during the breaks. I hope the contact will be maintained. If we didn't take part in the feminist demonstration organized at the end of the Haifa seminar, it was because we did not succeed in getting our own slogans adopted by the Women's Democratic Movement. We refuse to demonstrate solely on feminist slogans, against rape and so on. If we don't add slogans for real equality between citizens, we don't feel our views have been represented.

We have links with all the peace movements but we are more directly involved at present in the *Gisr lil-salam* movement, which is fighting for peace and understanding between the Jewish and Arab communities in Israel. It was set up in 1975. It meets every month, sometimes more often, sometimes less, depending on circumstances. Last month the meeting was held in Herzliya, near Tel-Aviv. This month, you saw that the meeting was held in the Arab village of Taibeh (Nethanya) where the mayor explained the situation to us. You saw that there were nearly a hundred of us, men and women, Arabs and Jews. At that meeting you met that woman from Taibeh who, although illiterate, is very active in the Na'mat union organization in her village.

The Front (Khadash) has its own union section but we encourage women, especially the young ones, to enrol in the Na'mat branch in Nazareth.

The YWCA is interesting, but in Nazareth the branch has only some twenty members. We have links with other philanthropic organizations, the *jam'iyat-al-khariyya al mesihiyya* (Christian Charity Organization), which is very old, and the new Muslim charity organization. A few young women in the *Abna' al-balad* organization take part in our activities although they criticize our political viewpoint.

The most important thing is to fight together; it is the whole of Israeli society that will pay the price for the growing fascism of the system and the use of violence and corruption. You followed the affair of the murder of Elham Shahberi, the young nineteen-year-old girl, killed at point-blank range by Riyad Kana'an, a traitor from the same village, as she was demonstrating with the inhabitants of Dabbouriyeh. He had come back after having infiltrated a Palestinian organization in Jordan and later living in the Chatila camp. You came with a group from our organization to present condolences to the family.

Even the young Israeli militia, who are generally still at secondary school, have learned how to behave brutally to the Arab workers. They force their way into the huts where these workers are cooped up for the night as if in a prison, to search them. The most worrying thing is that the bosses exploit them at will. Every society has its sadists, you know. If they're allowed to get away with it and we keep quiet to avoid a scandal, then tell me, what's the difference between here and South Africa?

I don't think there's any need to distinguish between types of struggle. The struggle for women's liberation is not distinct from the rest and I don't see any contradiction either between the assertion of our national identity — Palestinian and Arab — and women's liberation. But I prefer to let the young people answer you on this point.

Zuheira, thirty-seven years old, Nazareth-Elit, 6 October 1982

I was married to a man over forty whom I didn't know, before completing my secondary school. The marriage had been arranged by my parents. He is a wealthy businessman from al-Nasira, very hide-bound, very authoritarian, very violent. He gave me everything I asked him for. He even let me have a car and allowed me to drive it. But he didn't let me go out alone, even to go shopping. Nor did he allow me to go to women's meetings. So I went secretly, when he was at work. If he found out he used to beat me for hiding it from him.

One day, I decided to leave with my two children. I went back to my mother. Everyone I knew intervened to sort things out and my husband asked me to come back to the house. In the end I agreed. You know that, with us, a woman who asks for a separation from her husband is ostracized by society. And my husband was threatening to take the children.

Then I went through two years of hell. My husband wanted to make me pay for having dared to want to leave him. He went so far as to lock me in when he went to work and my children were at school. He used to beat me for nothing. The most terrible thing was when he began to beat the children too to make me suffer. We lived in terror of his moods. When he came back late, he used to find us hiding together in one room.

After two years of this life, I fled with the two children and went to my mother's again. In spite of what I have told you about his behaviour, there was pressure on me to return. The whole family, even very educated women friends, intervened and told me that if I went about it in the right way and didn't annoy him, he would calm down and stop beating me. And that at least I could have a decent life, whereas if I refused to go back to him, I would only be a burden for my mother. They couldn't understand that my husband was vengeful and that I had ended up hating him.

This time I held out. But when I began to do the necessary work to be legally separated from my husband and get a grant to bring up the children and pay for their education, my mother too began to harass me all the time. She must have been thinking that if she made my life unbearable I'd go back to my husband. I decided to go and live on my own with the children. I took this accommodation in the Jewish town to get away. But all the same I chose this quarter because the landlords make no difficulties about letting to Palestinians. I feel I'm at home. Friends have given me what we need to sleep, eat and work. Until I can get a grant for the children, I earn my living making artificial flowers.

Do you know what my mother has done now to force me to go back to my husband? She made a complaint to the police accusing me of prostitution. Have you ever heard of a mother behaving like that to her own daughter? Is she a mother? She told them that it was to ply this profession that I had left her house and that the children should be taken away from me. Fortunately, my sister-in-law, who is highly educated and who knows how to get her way with my mother, got her to withdraw her complaint. She's promised to withdraw it tomorrow. Meanwhile, I'm on tenterhooks.

When I get the grant, I shall take up my studies again. Samira has even got a scholarship for me so that I can specialize as a nurse for the handicapped.

Mrs Y., wife of a well-known doctor in a town on the West Bank, about forty, a practising Catholic, mother of a daughter, who supports the Union of Working Women's Committees, late October 1982. The interview took place in French.

I have always lived in town. I went to school with the Sisters. I come from a well-off family, as does my husband. Indeed, we are related. It was our parents who decided on our marriage.

I have never worked. In our families, the girls didn't work. I have three children, now all grown up, two boys, both married, and my daughter, who is not yet married and who is teaching in the university.

I didn't stand in the way of my daughter completing her studies and even of her doing a course in the United States. Nor did I oppose her working. As you can see I've even set aside a corner of the flat which is hers, with everything she needs to work, listen to records and entertain her woman friends. But before I used to be very strict about what was and was not done. It's because of my son that I changed. It was very hard. The eldest one posed no problems. He married as both of us wanted. But the younger one fell in love with a woman who was divorced and had a child. She was working to bring up her child. He went out with her for two years and then let us know, through third parties, that he wanted to marry her.

For a long time I absolutely refused to agree and everyone said I was right. Everybody criticized her for having got a divorce. I wouldn't even let my son talk to me about her. At first I had hoped that he would stop loving her. But nothing changed his mind. Then I began to be afraid. I love my son dearly and today more and more young people are marrying without their parents' consent. Inevitably, they end up not talking to each other.

One evening, and I know that I must give thanks to the Virgin Mary for it, I awoke my husband and told him that I was going to agree to receive this woman in my home. I let my son know that he could ask me to invite her to dinner.

Afterwards, everything fell into place. But it was very hard. Do you realize what I had to put up with? The marriage had to take place in the Orthodox Church because there is no divorce for Catholics, she's still considered to be married to her first husband. But the priest agreed and he told me not to get upset about it, that the fact of getting married in another church would not change our beliefs.

Now I am very happy. She is very nice and the child sees itself as one of the family. They don't live with us but we see each other almost every day. Now that she is married to my son, people of course don't criticize her any more; they sing her praises.

I thank the Virgin Mary for having helped me. It was very hard. I spent sleepless nights. Now, after this ordeal, I accept quite willingly that my daughter should work. I only feel that she works too much. She's going to make herself ill.

Notes

1. The term is used here to describe the territories on the West Bank of the Jordan and in the Gaza Strip occupied by Israel in 1967, that is the Palestinian lands — although substantially diminished — of the 'Arab State' proposed in the UN plan for the partition of British-mandated Palestine in 1947. A third of all the Palestinians in the Middle Eastern Arab area live in these lands and have expressed themselves overwhelmingly in favour of an independent Palestinian state led by the PLO.

2. There were six dead and several wounded.

3. Set up in 1973 in the occupied territories. It published its programme of 'resistance in all areas', resistance to the Israeli occupation, resistance to the plan for a return to the old Jordanian entity. Initially it was activated by the West Bank branch of the Jordanian Communist Party which has today become the Palestinian Communist Party.

4. Or Democratic Front for Peace and Equality, formed in 1977, with the support of the Rakah (Israeli Communist Party) and left-wing groups (Charlie Bitton's Black Panthers, University Teachers Union, Students Union, Union of Businessmen, etc.).

5. UN resolutions.

6. According to press reports, 1,229 Palestinian women were arrested between June 1967 and mid-1979 for such activities (see *Palestinian Political Women — prisoners and detainees in Israeli prisons*, pamphlet published by the Women's International League for Peace and Freedom, Lebanese section, 1975, and *al-Fajr*, 2–8 August 1981).

7. Such as Raymonda Hawa-Tawil (see *My Home, My Prison*) and Sahar Khalifa, who has written a series of works, including *Wild Thorns*. Both works have been translated into English recently and are published by Zed Books and Al Saqi Books respectively. Raymonda Tawil is a journalist (owner of the Palestinian Press Agency in East Jerusalem). She has recently founded a newspaper which she edits (an Arabic-language weekly, *Al-'Awda*, literally 'the return'). Sahar Khalifa is a professor at Bir-Zeit university.

8. A debate reflected in a pamphlet published by the Union on the occasion of International Women's Day, 8 March 1982, entitled *Tariq al-mar'a* (literally, 'the voice of women').

9. 23,400 out of 30,300 in 1978. The rest are divided between services (8,300) and industry (4,000).

10. This refers to the fact that Israeli farmers settle Palestinian families on their lands for the farming season. The settlement is illegal and thus not recorded. The farmers behave as if these families were part of their property, whence the name 'continuation of domestic slavery' given to it in Israel itself.

11. See *PLO Statistical Document*, 1980, table on p. 53 (drawn from official Israeli statistics).

12. Biologically, boys, being more fragile, are more likely to die in early infancy. The phenomenon of excessive female mortality is also to be found in Algeria and elsewhere in the underdeveloped countries.

13. Bans on movement outside the town, closure of clubs that display works from the Union's workshops, etc.

14. See *PLO Statistical Document*, op. cit.

15. Legally, Israel is the 'Sovereign state of the Jewish people' and not of its citizens, i.e., the nation is not Israeli but Jewish. This domination by an élite population ('of Jewish religion, race or origin' as defined in the Charter of the Jewish National Fund recognized by Israeli law) has become so much a part of the natural order that the discriminatory content implied, for example, in the title of the 'programme for the Judaisation of Galilee' raised no reservations in the press at all. Yet, before the Second World War, Zionist leaders had warned against the perversion of the Zionist ideology, which was based in theory on a socialist-oriented bi-nationalism. See Elia T. Zureik, *The Palestinians in Israel: A Study in Internal Colonialism*, (Routledge and Kegan Paul, London, 1979).

16. The Palestinians in Israel have from time to time attempted to create a specifically Arab political organization (Arab Popular Front, al-Ard, etc.) but have failed to secure

legal registration because of the application of a law dating from the Ottoman period outlawing the formation of a nationalist party.

17. It is called 'Arab' and is divided into religious communities (Muslim, Roman Catholic, Orthodox Christian, Druze, etc.); its cultural and ethnic specificity and its religious specificities are recognized, but not its nationality.

18. In its edition of 3 November 1982.

19. Notably in the *Gesher leshalom* organization (*Gisr lil-salam* in Arabic, literally 'bridge for peace').

20. The demonstrations in Nazareth took place before the great demonstration in Tel Aviv involving 400,000 people.

21. A Palestinian Christian from al-Nasira, born in 1950, he gained his diploma as a producer at the INSAS in Brussels. In November 1980 his film won the 'prize for a first work for its new vision of the reality experienced in occupied Palestinian territory' and the 'international critics' prize for its aesthetic beauty' (Carthage festival).

22. Women's organization linked to the Histradut, Israel's central union organization.

Choosing the Revolution

Mai Sayeh

The Union of Palestinian Women was created in 1965 shortly after the creation of the Palestine Liberation Organization. Its aim is to bring together Palestinian women wherever they are and it attempts to establish branches in every district in both the Occupied Territories and the refugee camps in Jordan, Lebanon and Syria. The Union tries to help women to solve the problems posed by the education of children. It has a social role and organizes child-rearing and sewing courses in the Centres in the districts, as well as literacy and political education courses. Except in the Occupied Territories women learn how to use weapons and, as far as possible, play a military and political role. But the participation of women in the Resistance does pose problems and our organization does not always play the role envisaged for it; each time the PLO is attacked somewhere, as for example recently in Lebanon, there is a falling off of support. Many women are alone: a woman who loses her husband loses her source of financial support and sometimes even her meagre possessions and her house, and finds herself in a situation where her first concern is to survive with her children and secure food for them. You must add to that the fact that Palestinian society is part and parcel of Arab–Islamic society, although many Palestinians are Christians, and that the place assigned to women in it has repercussions on the availability of Palestinian women for political organization and changes in their way of life in general. Of course, our political struggle, for us women, gives us a greater possibility of liberating ourselves than that given to other women in Arab countries at present; but we feel that the liberation of women will only come about within the framework of a socialist society, an authentically socialist one, since the fate of women is bound up with that of society as a whole. We Palestinians are fighting for a non-sectarian and democratic society. It will create the conditions for liberation from all chains, for men as well as for women. We want it to be possible for all Palestinian citizens to live there, Muslims, Christians and Jews.

I was born in Gaza. In Gaza, we have always been Palestinians, unlike those who were dispersed and had to migrate to Jordan, Syria and Lebanon. In Gaza we have always remained Palestinians and the struggle has never ceased. As we were under Egyptian administration we had to get our papers from the Egyptian Ministry of Defence.[1] Besides that, look at the geographical situation of Gaza: on the one side Israel, on another the sea and on the others the desert. We were cut off from other Arab peoples and we remained Palestinians.

Palestine was already alive in me when I was very small and I can still remember the struggles we had to wage at that time. After partition I can remember that there were some Palestinians who wanted to harvest their crops on lands that had been taken away from them and who were killed by the Israelis. I knew the brigades that attempted to defend Gaza in 1956 when the Israelis invaded our land and I can remember Mohammed . . . who set up the first defence brigades and was killed two years later. All that was before the formation of Fatah.

I left Gaza to do my university studies in Cairo in the early 1950s. In Cairo I had more freedom than in Gaza. All girls are subject to tradition; if it's not the family, it's society that imposes restrictions, so that there's no question of going out at night; a girl can't be free as she'd like to be. Relations between boys and girls must respect these restrictions. At that time, however, the situation of women in Egypt was very different from what prevailed in other Arab countries. The women's struggle in Egypt had a historical precedent, which is not the case elsewhere. The Nasserist revolution had given women greater freedom.

At that time, my sympathies lay with various political parties. The Arab world was seething with revolutionary ferment. There was the Communist Party, the Ba'ath, the Nasserist Youth. I got to know these various tendencies first in Gaza and then later in Cairo. In Cairo I married a Palestinian militant who had Jordanian nationality and I left Gaza and Cairo to live with my husband in Amman. There I was active with the Palestinian women and we were able to do some good political work, since in Jordan, at least in the towns, a sizable proportion of the population is Palestinian.

During the 1960s I had my four children. Then came 1970, the Rogers plan,[2] which we Palestinians were against, and Black September.[3] It was at this period in my life that I began to be more and more involved in the Resistance. I remember that I organized demonstrations of several hundred women against the Rogers plan in the streets of Amman. Complications followed from this in my family life. My husband was a militant but he wanted me to stay at home and look after the children. Yet, in my family, as in most families, family solidarity helped: my mother and my maternal aunt were always there to look after the children both in Jordan and later in Lebanon. However, my husband wanted me to look after them myself and give up being an activist, or at least be less involved. Obviously, I didn't like that solution. He therefore decided to put our four children in a boarding school in Beirut and we finally had to get divorced.

It is true that men agree in principle that women should be activists; but there comes a time when they feel that women should withdraw. Deep down, they think that it is up to them to make the revolution and not to women and that consequently it is the man's job to decide how far the women's involvement should go. The men always want us to struggle as they decide but they won't accept that we should choose how we fight. In September 1970, I chose the revolution and I've always put this participation in the struggle before all else.

Certainly my life is not like that of many other Palestinian women. Many of them adapt, bend to the customs of the country where they live and, depending on the country, have more or less freedom. But if a Palestinian woman becomes committed in the struggle, she escapes from these restrictions.

In 1970-71 the situation was very difficult for Palestinians in Jordan. That's perhaps why families were less opposed to the political involvement of women than elsewhere and often had no objection to women spending a fortnight in camps undergoing military training, alongside men. In the camps, I remember, the men even brought us things to eat and drink. It is true that in those years the whole Palestinian community in Jordan was involved in the repression and the problems raised by traditions were pushed into the background. The Jordanian people too were concerned and their struggle against oppression linked up with our struggle against Zionism.

Lebanese society is very different from Jordanian society. In Jordan, a woman is put on a pedestal and people are very tradition-bound. In Lebanon the freer situation of women is partly the result of their living in a consumer society. After Black September, I had to leave Jordan and moved to Beirut. In Lebanon, the participation of women in the revolution was a topic of endless discussion. To participate or not? What is it permissible for women to do and what not, in relation to the revolution and to social life? However, our problem is not to pose the question of women's liberation as such but to pose it in the context of women's participation in the revolution, for only a revolutionary transformation of society can change morality. The expression 'women's liberation' is not a term we can use in the circumstances in which we live since our problem is not the same as that of European feminists. We are living at a time of revolutionary struggle and we are determined to assert the need for the presence of women. We say, 'It is not possible to envisage the liberation of society if we accept that one half of it should remain in the home.' In future men and women must have equal rights. We are discussing that at the Palestine National Council and we are trying to discuss it in all the branches of the Union of Women, in every country where there are Palestinians.

It is also being discussed in the Executive Committee for which we did a series of studies on the condition of women (in the home, as revolutionaries, as working women) and on the condition of children, in the spring of 1982.

The laws concerning women are an important question for us. These are the laws of the various Arab countries in which they are living and we Palestinians have no say in the making of those laws. The PLO has no power to alter these laws in Lebanon, in Syria and in Jordan. There is thus an internal contradiction within the Palestinian Revolution. It asks people to give their lives and their time, but it has nothing to offer them in return in the here and now. We need some land, a state where we can make the laws. But a few months ago we prepared a document for submission to the National Council (which I referred to above) which contains the broad outlines of the demands of the Union of Women. Perhaps the next Council will discuss it, but, unfortunately, it's rather unlikely because of the present situation. There are so many acute, burning issues . . . Faced with what is happening now, with Sabra and Chatila, with the dispersal of all the revolutionaries, the dispersal of our people and the questions people are asking themselves, 'How can we live, how can we find housing, how can we get some food?'. . . 'How many martyrs are there, how many orphan children or children who are hungry, how many to be educated?' make the problems of women seem rather unimportant. One of the most difficult tasks is the number of orphanages that we need to build after each massacre. In 1948 there were three, in 1967 one more, in 1978 another one in Beirut, for after Tell el Zaatar in 1976 there were so many orphans and now, after Beirut, we shall no doubt have to open two or three more. We have little choice but to agree there are more immediate problems to be solved.

But women are not inactive and there are many areas where they are taking on great responsibilities. At the last National Council for example, there was a Health Committee, and a Cultural and Social Affairs Committee, all composed of women, with a few men to give a hand as experts. Through this sort of responsibility, women are gradually raising the question of their equality with men and the issue is beginning to be discussed in the various PLO bodies. Women on the National Council raised precisely this question at one of the latest meetings. The men said, 'But you are equal!' We replied, laughing, 'Look at this Council: there are 350 members, of whom 31 are women . . . only 31 women! The day when half the members of the National Council are women, then we shall be able to talk about equal rights.' Of course we are conscious that achieving this equality is difficult and can only be done step by step. Palestinian women can become an example for women in other Arab countries . . . although the position of women is beginning to change everywhere.

Up to now, Palestinian women have been present everywhere, as liaison agents, as fighters; but last summer the role of women increased because of the very fact that the invasion of Lebanon was a barbarian and fascist act. Women participated in military actions to defend the towns and refugee camps. In Beirut the Union of Women felt that it had to take an active part in the defence of the city. That attack was the cruellest anyone has seen since the Second World War; it had to be resisted, morale had to be kept up, popular resistance had to be maintained. The people were suffering enormously. They were afraid but they had to eat and drink and be effectively protected. The problem was to find food and water. The Union of Women assessed the situation at the beginning of the attack and decided to take over looking after those problems. It was only after taking this decision that they went to the PLO leadership in Beirut and informed them of it. We had already taken on these responsibilities during the attacks on south Lebanon in 1976 and 1978 and we said that we'd do it again.

The most important thing was milk for the children, then taking care of them when they were ill or wounded and finding blankets and giving food to adults too, arranging for the transport of the wounded to hospitals and making these hospitals function as well as possible. The water supply had to be protected. In 1976 we had located the artesian wells in Beirut. That summer, when the water was cut off by the Israeli army, people remembered the artesian wells. There are many in this region. The women got themselves organized with the youth and students and we toured round the houses where we knew there were artesian wells and we found many more by looking for them. With a collective of doctors we analysed the water and then we told people where to go.

The experiences of 1976 and 1978 stood us in good stead in 1982. A National Committee of six members of the Lebanese National Movement and six members of the Palestinian Resistance (including Umm Jihad and myself) had the cooperation of the PLO and the Union of Palestinian Women. We set up Centres in each district, which was divided into seven 'regions' each of which we divided into rectangles. This was done in Beirut, Borj el Brajneh and the surrounding camps. The women moved from one Centre to another to organize help and distribute aid since the population itself was very afraid of the raids and scared to move about. We thought that it was up to us women to do that.

The people of West Beirut were living anywhere where they thought they were safe, such as in cinemas. In the La Concorde cinema a hundred families were crowded in one on top of the other. The health conditions were very bad. I remember that one night rats invaded a shelter where refugees were living and ate the tips of the noses of one family.

We used cars that their owners, especially young people, made available to us; we hired lorries and we tried to divide the population between buildings where there was still space and to find shelters for them. The Union of Women took responsibility for keeping the buildings clean. We tried to make sure that shelters were always in a state to receive people in the best conditions. The PLO gave £100 a head. If a family had five members, it received £500. After a certain time, food became short and was becoming dearer and dearer and we couldn't give people any more money. We appealed for international assistance. The Red Cross gave us help but distributed it directly to the Centres because the Lebanese government didn't want it going through the hands of the Lebanese National Movement or the Palestinian Resistance. The Israelis refused to allow it to move from east to west through the Museum crossing-point. Food became very scarce, especially bread and milk. With the help of Fatah we were able to get flour and kerosene and we opened ovens with the cooperation of the population. Many people were afraid of running short.

The water eventually became polluted and we feared epidemics. Cases of typhoid and dysentery had already appeared. People were piling up rubbish; not knowing what to do with it they let it rot in the streets. So we formed teams to move around Beirut with loudspeakers to explain to people that rubbish absolutely had to be burned to avoid an epidemic.

In the end the water supply was reconnected. Unfortunately the ovens led to very long queues that were very much exposed to bombardments. We did not succeed in solving this particular problem before the end of the siege. Each new day brought a new problem to be solved. We had many wounded and we lacked doctors.

When the fighters were evacuated many women cadres were able to get away by car through the Kataeb sector and the mountains, accompanied by their children. Some were recognized by the enemy and arrested. There were many arrests. Those who were well known left by ship. I left Beirut on 4 September on a boat leaving for Tartous in Syria. Now I don't know where I'm going to go ... Tunis? ... Damascus? ...

Paris, December 1982

Notes

1. After the partition plan of 1947 the Gaza Strip was placed under Egyptian administration. Egypt's nationalization of the Suez Canal (July 1956) led to the Israeli invasion of Sinai and Gaza which were occupied for several months. Gaza became 'occupied territory' after the Arab–Israeli war of 1967.

2. Named after the American Secretary of State William Rogers who drew it up; it envisaged a negotiated solution to the Arab–Israeli conflict. The Egyptian head of state, Gamal Abdel Nasser, accepted the plan and signed it on 23 July 1970.

3. In 1970 the Palestinian refugees in Jordan were cruelly put down by King Hussain and his army.

Women's Emancipation after the Ataturk Period

Gaye Petek-Salom and Pinar Hukum

We will try here to discuss the evolution of what we see as some of the fundamental stages of the emancipation of Turkish women. We shall be looking at two aspects: the stages and the main theoretical features of this emancipation and what is happening in practice to Turkish women from ordinary backgrounds. We shall illustrate our discussion with the replies of a few Turkish women, wives of migrants in France to whom we gave a questionnaire about emancipation. We make no pretence to a comprehensive sample: but we have tried to make it socially and geographically representative. We have for this reason chosen ten women from differing social origins (illiterate peasants, women from small towns and villages in the provinces, daughters of teachers and white-collar workers), geographical origins (western Turkey, Black Sea, central Anatolia, south-west, south-east) and ethnic group membership and religious allegiance (two are Kurds and Turkish Shi'ite, or Alawites; the others are Sunnis). Four of them were questioned in the presence of their husbands and the interviews took place at their homes.

We have deliberately excluded from the questionnaire Turkish women from the urban bourgeoisie and women intellectuals who are far from being at all representative in the social landscape of Turkey, 60% of whose population is of rural origin.

Turkish women before the Republic

Some old documents and accounts by European travellers tell us that Turkish women used to enjoy great influence within the family and had equal customary rights within marriage. They were subject to few restrictions and their status did not subordinate them to the patriarchal order; they were rather 'made responsible' by virtue of the very fact that the men, warriors, were often away from home and they then exercised control over the family. The account of a French traveller who was a member of a scientific mission in the late 19th Century and studied the nomadic Turkish tribes who had not been touched by Islamization, informs us that the Turkish women is often alone. When she is with her husband, she has precedence over him, she goes in first, takes the place of honour, is the first to smoke, the first to drink: in the street, she walks in front of her husband.[1]

Pre-Hittite archaeological remains, as well as studies of the Uighur Turks and the Oghuz tribes, confirm this picture.

The beginnings of the Islamization of the Turks date from about the 10th Century and continued until the 15th Century. While Islam recognizes that women have certain rights it also asserts the supremacy of man over woman and that the latter is necessarily subject to the Koranic law that establishes this authority. Turkish women thus came to be slaves to male domination (father, husband, or brother). They were secluded in the home, restricted to being no more than a shadow. Ottoman society made them into submissive wives, concubines and objects of pleasure, destined for the whims of their husbands and masters who secluded them in harems. The harems of the Ottoman sultans were typical; the life of women there was regulated by more or less repressive edicts, stating when they could go out, setting out the places where they could go and the clothes they had to wear (even detailing how transparent the veil covering the face should be). But women in the Ottoman period were endowed with real power in the home and a degree of authority within the harem. It is surprising to read from the pen of a European who lived for several years in the last century in Turkey that,

> basically, the condition and role of a wife, I mean the lawful wife, among the Muslims, are not essentially different from what they are in the various European societies. Owing her husband a simple duty of obedience, without him being able to maltreat her, she rules in the home.

And he adds that 'the authority of the lawful wife is exercised unchecked in the harem'.[2] This 'journalist' of the time describes the women at Constantinople as wearing very little within the harem, going out during the day on foot or in a barouche, wearing a sort of *chador* (*feradjé*) and with the face covered with a muslin veil (*yasmak*), abandoning themselves luxuriously to *keyf* (resulting in a sort of passive, hedonistic state). But there is little evidence about women in Anatolia. We only know that they were always active and dynamic in economic life, working on the land, sharing men's tasks; they were moreover less affected than some women by the restrictions of Islam dealing with clothes. They only covered the face in front of strangers and after work.

It is rather odd that Islam was something progressive for Arab women to whom it gave new rights (such as a ban on killing new-born female babies, the limitation of polygamy) whereas it brought the Turkish women only obscurantism and seclusion.

But Islam among the Turks proceeded from a Byzantine heritage, and among the Ottomans from the influence of Persian culture. It made a Turkish woman into a hidden being, her sole existence whatever the man felt like giving her. Under the Ottomans, the father of a daughter announced her birth by saying that God had given him a 'hidden one' a 'veiled one' an 'invited guest', a being of passage who would leave the home to marry.

We asked the immigrant women whom we questioned what they saw as the image of women in Islam. Their definitions can be summarized as follows:

'Too covered and too closed.'
'Not too open, reserved.'
'Must not go out, shake hands, she must cover herself.'
'Covered with a *chador*, she must not be seen.'
'Speak in a measured manner, be a believer, must cover her face and legs.'
'Very closed, must not speak to men, must be cut off from the world.'

When asked about their personal interpretation, they gave varying responses.

'We are Muslims but we are neither too covered nor too closed. We go out bare-armed in the village but with a headscarf. In my village everybody is uncovered, the *chador* no longer exists, and that's as it should be.'
'It is natural that religion should not allow women to be too uncovered. But I don't respect everything; not the face, I only cover my head.'
'It's fine. When I go back to Turkey on holiday, I put the *chador* on again, I have it in my case. Here, it's because of the others that I don't wear it. Everybody looks at you and laughs; they tell me that we're not in the village here. Every time I go out like that, with just the headscarf, I feel I'm committing a sin, denying God. I make my daughters cover their heads in Turkey, but here they won't do it.'
'Here we are more uncovered but we have bad dreams about it. Deep down we are ashamed. But it's because we haven't become used to it. I wish I had been educated more freely.'
'For the woman who practises, all that is fine but . . . for others too it's fine not to practise.'
'Women are dominated by men, I don't agree.'
'I don't agree with women being secluded; religion won't feed me.'

In the 19th Century the few women who began to emancipate themselves came from the Ottoman bourgeoisie. In 1869 the first feminist journal, *Le Progrès*, began to appear. The first working women were midwives. In 1873, the first school-teacher was appointed and in 1883. the first school headmistress.

At the turn of the century, with the fall of Sultan Abdulhamid, during the period of the *Mesrutiyet* (Constitutional Monarch) and the Young Turks, feminist associations appeared. In 1908 Red and White was launched, an organization for promoting the education and schooling of women, and then later the Evolution of Women, another organization of which the novelist Halide Edip was an active member. In 1910, Mrs K. Ihsan, the secretary of the Association of Ottoman Women, was the first woman to dare to have her photograph published in the press. All these women were members of the property owning classes and the intelligentsia. Some began to go out wearing very light transparent veils or even no veil at all. In 1912 there were some who 'displayed' their faces during a reception in a foreign embassy.

The most active organization was, in 1913, the Association for the Defence of the Rights of Women. In 1915 a decree authorized the suppression of the veil and the *chador* during working hours in the public service and Ziya Gokalp[3] called in his university lectures for equal rights for women in the areas of marriage, divorce and inheritance.

In 1917 the Ottoman Family Code was promulgated; it marked the beginning of monogamy since a woman secured the right to stipulate on her marriage contract her refusal to let her husband marry a second wife. She could ask for a divorce on the grounds of breach of this promise.

At the time of the war of independence, industry took on a lot of ordinary women who worked in the armament factories with their faces uncovered. Various public bodies, including hospitals, opened their doors to female labour. The decadence of the Ottoman Empire and the war accelerated the liberation of women. The great poetess Nazim Hikmet celebrates Turkish women in her 'Epic of the Independence War' (poems written between 1941 and 1945) in these lines:

> And the women,
> our women,
> with their terrible and holy hands
>   their small finely chiselled chins,
>   their enormous eyes,
>
> our mothers,
>   our wives,
>   our beloveds,
> they who die as though they had never lived,
> and whose place in the home comes after that of the ox,
>   comes after that of the ox
> they who rear us, for whom we are thrown into prison,
>
> they who toil at seedtime,
>   who prick the tobacco,
>   who cut the wood,
> they who go to the market,
> they who hitch up the plough,
> they whom we have in the stables,
> by the glow of knives stuck in the ground,
> with their heavy and supple thighs,
>   and their cymbals,
>   the women,
>   our women.[4]

The entry of Greek troops in 1919, followed by French and Italian ones, gave Turkish women a leading role in the struggle for independence. Many young women, 'Mother Courages' celebrated by Nazim Hikmet (in her collection of poems entitled *Kuvayi Milliye*) participated in the *Kuvayi Milliye* (National Front) set up by Mustafa Kemal in Anatolia.

On 19 March 1919 the first classes for women in the philosophy faculty opened in Istanbul and in 1921 the first mixed university courses where girls went unveiled. In 1922 the first woman doctor opened her surgery in Istanbul.

In 1919 the Organization for the National Defence of Anatolian Women (*Anadolu Kadinlarinin Mudafaai Milliye Teskilati*) was set up at Sivas, followed by the opening of branches in other towns. In 1920 the branch at Nigde had 1,090 members. The lot of women was debated in parliament. On 3 February 1923, Mustafa Kemal praised the courage of Anatolian women during the fighting and called for equality in education and freedom; but the parliamentary majority blocked the proposals. The following month, he declared at a meeting, 'Our women, who live in conditions that are much less easy than those of men, fought alongside them and sometimes surpassed them in courage. It's proof of their equality.'

The majority of women whom we questioned about what they knew of Turkish women before the Republic said that they knew nothing about it. One said, 'she had no freedom'; another, 'her conditions were more difficult. She was used as an object' and 'they were the slaves of men.' None of them could tell us about these fighting women nor about the liberation of women in the towns. Their mothers or grandmothers had told them nothing about it. Given this empty memory we wonder about the slight impact of these early feminist movements. Those associations and journals were the work of women from the intellectual élite of the Ottoman aristocracy and their struggle did not overcome the social barriers of a society made up of antagonistic classes ignorant of one another. We must stress that these movements and associations proclaimed the bourgeois and petty-bourgeois image of woman as good mother, good wife and good housewife.

Turkish women after the secularization of the state

On 29 October 1923 the Republic was proclaimed, and the history of Turkish women was to be transformed by Mustafa Kemal Ataturk. The principle of secularism adopted by the new republic was of course in opposition to the Islamic tenets whose impact it reduced. For Ataturk the evolution of women was part and parcel of his work to modernize and secularize Turkey. In his mind, modernization meant Westernization and the image of women must follow this path.

As early as 1923 the chief of police in Istanbul decided to remove the curtains that separated men and women in public transport. This decision led to a wide-ranging debate in parliament in the context of a debate on the idea of an Islamic republic. What are the limits that a republic should impose on itself in a country of Islamic origin? But for Ataturk, secularism came before everything and he inaugurated a series of reforms which were to lead to giant steps forward in the evolution of the status of women.

In March 1924, with the abolition of the Caliphate and the law on the unification of education (*Tevhidi Tedrisat Kanunu*), the religious schools were brought under the aegis of the Ministry of National Education and the equality of the sexes in education was established.

No law was passed abolishing the veil but there were instructions by Kemal Ataturk to ban it and many proclamations and speeches designed to encourage its disappearance. Thus in 1935, in a speech at Inebolu, Ataturk expressed his surprise at seeing women covering their faces and said,

> I imagine that with this high temperature that must be uncomfortable. Gentleman, comrades, it is our egoism that causes the wearing of the veil, because we are very punctilious about our honour, but, dear comrades, our women too can feel and think. They must be able to show their faces to the world and be able to see the whole world.[5]

The first step towards the legal recognition of certain rights to women was the adoption of the Swiss Civil Code in 1926.

Before this Civil Code such practices as polygamy, marriage of girls at nine and repudiation by the husband without need to give reasons were standard. The new Civil Code which came into force on 4 October 1926 declared:

- monogamy;
- the right to divorce by either party;
- the sharing of parental authority;
- the surviving parent to retain custody of children in the event of the death of one parent;
- custody of the children to be decided by the judge in the event of divorce;
- equality in inheritance and succession (before, women had between one-quarter and one-eighth);
- marriage to be celebrated in the presence of the bride (before it could be done by proxy);
- equality of status as witnesses in court (before, the evidence of two women was equal to that of one man);
- the legal marriage age set at seventeen for women and eighteen for men (after Ataturk's death this was lowered to fifteen and seventeen);
- Koranic marriages no longer to be recognized. Any imam who celebrated a Koranic marriage without checking whether the civil marriage had been performed became liable to prosecution.

Many of these rules were watered down by the Democratic Party in the 1950s and the Justice Party and the National Salvation Party in the 1960s.

Despite the progress that it signified, the Civil Code laid down that the man was the head of the family; the patriarchal principle remained and a wife still needed her husband's permission to work. And the texts still said that it was among her functions 'to manage the house' and 'look after the home and the children'. There was also a contradiction between the Civil Code and the Constitution,[6] the former remaining more traditionalist.

We asked the immigrant women what they saw Mustafa Kemal as having changed and what he had done for women and what they thought of the 'Westernized' woman that Ataturk approved of. Very few replied to the first question; they could only say, 'No one ever explained it to me'. 'He liberated Turkey but I have no education and so I don't know what he said about women.' Others mentioned only the suppression of the veil; one said, 'He unveiled women, he modernized the language, and people said he was going to suppress the Koran.' Another said, 'He said that men and women should be equal. But that was for educated women. In the east, nothing really changed and it's still the same, the woman is still a dog's body.'

The teacher's daughter, who comes from a rural background but was active in a women's organization in the provinces before coming to France, said, 'He changed little. Only superficial things. Afterwards things reverted to what they had been before.'

Another one admitted that she didn't know whether it was Ataturk or someone else who liberalized the status of women.

Most of the women responded positively to the second question and approved of what Ataturk wanted to do in improving the status of women. 'We won't make progress in a *chador*. But only those who really want to advance; and anyway, women aren't given the means to know things and open their eyes.' 'It was all very well, but it only affected women in the towns. In the villages things stayed the same. It's a question of class.' 'Of course he was right, a human being is a human being.'

But another one said, 'He wasn't right, he was going against God. If he wanted us to be like Europeans, that was all right. But no one thinks of the other world, although we'll spend much more time there than here.'

The words of these few women are instructive. They confirm our belief that the Kemalist reforms were only superficial. They did nothing to alter the class inequalities in Turkish society. Since the socio-economic infrastructure had not been changed, these reforms were simply stuck on to a contradictory reality. Ataturk died too soon and the political parties that came after him went back on his ideas on many points and particularly on the status of women. Rural women in Anatolia still marry today against their will, have no equality in inheritance and remain the object of anachronistic horse-trading through the age-old custom of the dowry. The reality for Anatolian women is the scarf on their heads and even, in some villages, the *chador*. We are a long way here from Ataturk's idea of an emancipated woman. It is paradoxical that Turkish women should still today be alone amongst the women of the Middle East in enjoying virtual legal equality with men and that in practice they should be light years away from fully enjoying it.

In 1975, on the occasion of International Women's Year, a women's congress was organized by 27 associations. It drew up an impressive list of inequalities and spelled out women's demands. The 'lack of harmony between law and custom is frequently noted in Turkey. Custom often leads to changes in the law, but here the opposite is the case. Custom has never been able to catch up with law.

To the question of whether there is equality between men and women we obtained the following answers.

'I couldn't judge. You have to be educated to answer that.'
'Life is lived in common, so we should be equal.'
'No, women are not equal. Women are made for domestic life. Men ensure outside life. It's like that, and so it must stay.'
'Yes, women have equal rights' (This woman's husband contradicted her by asserting that this is not true in reality).
'There has to be equality.'
'Now, yes, they are equal.'
'There is a little more equality than before but not for peasants and working women.'
'Equality exists only for the rich.'

The political role of Turkish women

In 1930, by an amendment to the constitution, Ataturk gave women the right to vote and stand in local elections. This gesture demonstrated the depth of his determination to emancipate Turkish women; they got the right to vote well before most European women.

On 8 December 1934 all adult women were entitled to vote in the parliamentary elections and all men and women over 30 could stand for election. The number of women in Parliament was 24.5% at the beginning, 2% in 1946, 0.6% in 1950, and 1.8% in 1965.

We attempted to find out whether the immigrant women we met had used their right to vote, whether they had done so under male influence (father, husband) and what they thought of this right. We got a measure of agreement in responses in favour of the right to vote, but there were slight differences in responses about how it was used.

'I voted twice; it's good. Everyone votes for himself, and I was not influenced.'
'I voted with my parents, as they had advised me to do.'
'It's not very important. But if you have the right you must use it. I followed my father's guidance.'
'It's very important. I decided for myself, but if my husband hadn't gone to vote, I wouldn't have gone either.'
'It's right. I voted the way my whole family voted, except once. Anyway, you can say you agree and at the ballot box vote as you want to.'
'My husband being in France I always voted alone.'
'It's a very important law. It must be used at all costs. But in the villages the men sometimes say "your vote doesn't count, stay at home, we'll go".'
'I was too young to vote. But I would have done so as I wanted. If I work I have my own ideas.'

To the question whether they would vote for a woman candidate for the position of minister or president, the women questioned unanimously responded 'yes'. Some of them said that with 'equal education' they would

prefer a woman because 'she would understand better'. One made it a
condition that she be 'modest in her behaviour and believe in God'.
Another said that it was still her policies and programme that would count
in her eyes.

Women and work

Turkish women, especially peasant women in Anatolia, have for centuries
always had an important role in production. Women form 47% of the
working population. But this active role in the agricultural sector is not
recognized. Yet when men left to work in other countries, it was always the
women who carried on with the harvest and weaving and so on. In 1969, out
of 1,000 people working in the agricultural sector, 497 were women. 88% of
working women were in agriculture, 4% in industry, 8% in other sectors.

Women in the small towns or villages are almost always less active than
those in the countryside. They are very sedentary, dependent on the status
and wishes of their husbands. There, only the wife of an emigrant is
respected and can work in the absence of her husband without being the
butt of harsh criticism. The situation of rural women who are 'internal
migrants', living in the outlying districts of shanty-towns around the large
cities, is rather special. These women want to work in industry and they
share a large part of the responsibility in the family. However, only 30%
succeed in finding work, usually household jobs in buildings where their
husbands are working as caretakers. In regions bordering on the large
metropolitan areas, the number of wage-earning women is increasing all
the time.

Table 1 *Women as a proportion of the work-force in Turkey*

	Agriculture	Industry	Services
1950:			
Total number of wage-earners	389,937	350,095	379,693
Women	133,353	42,011	35,959
1960:			
Total number of wage-earners	9,737,489	884,659	676,838
Women	5,031,008	143,889	75,334[7]
1971:			
Total number of wage-earners	10,482,966	1,243,567	1,886,002
Women	5,256,484	204,111	264,105[8]

But the most striking figures relate to emigration. In 1960 in West Germany only 173 Turkish women were wage-earners; in 1975 there were a total of 143,611 in Western Europe.

There is considerable participation by women in the white-collar sector, especially in the public services — but not of course at the higher levels: in 1938, 12,716 women were working in the public services; in 1970, 123,812.[9] 24% of employees in the banking sector were women; and 27.6% in public education. In 1973 these two figures rose to 35%. Overall, however, 93% lack any real skill and the problem of women's work will become more and more serious as Turkey industrializes. In the towns the number of wage-earning women is lower than it should be in comparison with women working in the rural areas. There are only 16.5% of wage-earning women in Istanbul. It can also be observed that the woman town-dweller works of necessity for an extra income but in reality she would prefer to stay at home (there have been several surveys in Turkey on this point).

It is interesting to see that the women we questioned, who were all of rural origin, responded positively to the question of whether women were better off at work or in the house:

'If I could work here, I wouldn't hesitate. I'm so bored and I have nothing to do.'
'If I didn't have four children, I would certainly work.'
Two are working in France in the clothing industry and are happy doing so. Yet they didn't work in Turkey.
'I would have preferred working in a factory.'
'If you work you don't get depressed.'
Only one woman said that 'work means promiscuity with men. A woman's place is in the home.'

Women and education

Of all Islamic countries, Turkey is the one with the most university-educated women. But whereas the percentages of boys and girls in primary school is equal, at the secondary level the proportion of women is 1:3 and in higher education 1:5. Girls from rural backgrounds are only 11.7% of the number of female students and 2.6% of the total. But when we look at the figures of daughters and women of the bourgeoisie and the intellectual 'caste' the high level of education achieved by women is surprising.

The most popular faculties are law and medicine: in 1965–70, 25% of doctors were women; in 1970–5, 28% of lawyers were women.

One out of five lawyers is a woman (in the large cities, one lawyer in four is a woman). One doctor in six is a woman whereas in a country such as the USA only 3% of lawyers and 15% of doctors are women.

Access to higher education is the most flagrant example of the inequality between the various social classes of the Turkish population. But it is known that 50% of these women with higher qualifications are the daughters of managers or men who themselves are university educated.

Table 2 *Educational achievement of middle-class women in Turkey*

Year	Primary	C.E.S.	Lycée	L.E.T./ L.E.P.	University
	%	%	%	%	%
1930	28.3	26.1	22.4	30.8	6.0
1950	30.1	26.1	21.5	20.9	20.7
1960	33.2	27.6	27.8	23.5	19.3
1970	38.6	28.5	30.3	35.0	19.3[10]

These figures are the most tangible evidence of the social and cultural gaps in Turkish society. In 1975 48% of women were illiterate. But it is also instructive to observe with Mrs Dino that in literature 'the two most striking and novel trends of the last twenty years have originated with two social groups whose voice has been longest stifled:[11] that is novelists of peasant origin and women. The author goes on to list the most famous names in Turkish women's literature which has grown considerably in recent years.

Women are at last speaking out. These talented women are writing about everything that affects Turkish women, their feelings, their daily lives including their political struggle and their place in the 'journey' of migrant Turks. The majority of these women are from well-off backgrounds, they have been educated, they have completed secondary school and mix with university people. They have therefore a mainly intellectual and sociological knowledge of the problems of Anatolian women. Until the time when peasant women from Anatolia can speak for themselves it cannot but be a step forward to have these writers speak for them.

Certain of the response we were going to get, we asked the immigrant women if they knew some women writers. Only one of them could give us a name but it was that of a theatre actress. Yet they were quite certain that Turkish women fiction writers did exist and we were struck by the modernity of spirit with which they took our questions about what they thought of the Turkish women city-dwellers and European women.

'The women in the big cities are right, women should be independent. Look, even in the village, things are changing a little; instead of the *chalvar* [baggy trousers] women are now wearing long skirts at home. European women are like the ones in Istanbul — as they should be!'

'They are more educated and thus more advanced. It's logical, they can't be like us in the villages. It would be stupid. European women live according to how educated they are.'

'It's not right that, in the towns, Turkish women should behave like European women.'

'What would they gain from being secluded like us? If I had a social life I'd be better able to respond to your questions. They're quite right to be like that, all of them.'

'Those who can, they should advance and unveil themselves, it's quite right.

European women? they're not as dissolute as we've been told; they are as women should be.'

'They are rich, so it's normal. I approve of them. Frenchwomen are like Turkish women in towns. All women who are working are the same.'

'It's normal that they should be different but they are a minority. I also think that many of us are working so as not to get bored. Frenchwomen are relaxed, they work, they have social security, they have holidays. France tries to make them happy; but in Turkey things are different ...'

'So long as they are honest, they're right to do what they are doing. European women work hard and are very devoted to their family. I won't throw stones at them.'

This passion to take up the cudgels to defend the liberation of women was again confirmed in the responses on the role of education. We asked them if they would like their daughters to study and work:

'If I had to do it over again, I'd do everything I could to study. I wasn't able to finish primary school. You see, my mother is illiterate but she went running to the classes that were organized recently and she was very happy to be able to sign her name for the first time on the day of the census.'

'I would so much have liked to stay on beyond Form 3. My daughters will study for as long as they want and I hope that they will work.'

'I'm so ashamed of being illiterate, it's terrible! Certainly my daughters will study.'

'Look, if I could have studied I could have told you what Ataturk did. My daughter? She'll study as much as possible. So that she's a real human being instead of being ashamed. She'll work. She'll do as she pleases.'

'My family wanted me to study. But I didn't want to because I was lazy. If it were today ... I so much regret it.'

'Education is essential. The more you've read the more your eyes are opened. I only know what I've seen. You, you know loads of things because you've read. I'm illiterate because there was no school in the village. It's the government's fault. I like progress in everything.'

As for the woman who was always more conservative in her responses, she said

'It's good to be educated but primary school is enough for women. You just need to be able to read and write. I would prefer my daughters to do their primary school and learn to be good housewives. Look, my eldest daughter is in Form 2 here (I didn't want her to go on) and, well, she does nothing in the house, she doesn't obey or help me at all.'

Women and emigration

There is no doubt that emigration has changed women from the countryside in many ways. Already, staying alone, after their husbands have emigrated to Europe, they gain respect. Their work in the fields and their role are recognized because they have greater responsibilities. Their rights within the family increase. Emigration also influences the choice of how to invest the money remitted by their husbands, in which the whole family has a say. When the husband goes off to work in Europe, the wife lives with her husband's family. She must obey her mother-in-law. When she herself emigrates, or 'is called for by her husband', she finally accedes to the position of the chief woman in the family, fully wife and mother. In Turkey, it is often the case that from the time of her marriage and until the birth of several children or the death of her parents-in-law, a woman lives in the house of her in-laws and in the eyes of her husband occupies a distinctly secondary position.

When she arrives in Europe she is involved more actively in decisions about the education of the children and has rather more say in planning the size of the family. Nor should we overlook changes in female morphology, in clothing, behaviour, habits and life-style. But at the same time, emigration makes some women more introverted and conservative. They hold to traditional values as if this were a sacred duty. They want to fully live up to these traditions since their guardianship is a special responsibility whch enables a woman to make a niche for herself within the family. We ourselves are convinced that this determination to retain traditional values will not always help their status as they imagine. This voluntary withdrawal cannot contribute to their emancipation.

We asked our interviewees whether emigration had changed anything in their life and whether they would one day return to Turkey. They replied,

'I've only changed in terms of clothing. I don't wear the *chalvar* any more. I was already going out with my husband. Except for that, life is the same, the concrete houses are the same. I'm just better set up here. The chores to be done are the same. Only one thing will change when we go back. I don't want to live with his family. We are having a house built, we'll be on our own.'

'I've changed a lot in the clothes I wear. I would have preferred not to come because here I keep committing sins. Back home, I didn't go out or shake hands. France has done nothing good for me. I've changed, but against my will. I'll go back to the life I had before back home. But my husband wants to live in town. But he agrees with me, I'll start wearing the *çarsaf* (*chador*) again.'

'Of course you change. When you are moving about, you see different things. Back home I didn't even wear short sleeves. But my life indoors is the same. Back home it was even better because I had a garden. I don't think I'll be too changed. You have to respect traditions.'

'I've become a little more open. But I wear the same clothes. As a newly-wed I used to wear the *chador* but it's my husband who made me take it off. If he hadn't wanted it I wouldn't have done it. Yet it's so stupid! In this heat why on earth cover yourself like a ghost? I shall go back changed. It's better that others see me and follow my example. You see one day a girl arrived in the village wearing trousers. Three months later no one was shocked any more and everyone had changed their *chalvar* for trousers.[12] Here when I go out I put on a headscarf because of the gossip of the others. Yet I'm ashamed. Look, I've noticed that people confuse us with gypsies. My daughter doesn't cover herself and I don't want her to cover herself back home either.'

'I've not changed much. I've just replaced the trousers under the skirt with stockings. I don't think that I'll go back very different. Perhaps with a few more advanced ideas.'

Some of the others said to us that the only big change would be their living in a town or small town. The change was thus autonomy vis-à-vis the family. The two women who were working in France had interesting replies;

'I've changed a lot. I'm more responsible. Responsible for myself. As far as clothes are concerned, I dress more fashionably but that's all. And in any case we are the people who make these clothes in the workshop. But here I've lost the possibility of being an activist.[13] I think that when I go back I'll retain the consciousness and the responsibility. I shall work back home too. On reflection, I will certainly go back altered.'

'Back home I just wore a scarf, but I've stopped wearing that here. But I forced myself to wear it again when we were back there on holiday. In fact I wear it for the others. You know I think that I'm only half Muslim. When I go back I think I shall live more in the Western way. And I'll smoke in front of others. If you have respect, cigarettes won't change you. I think too that I won't accept certain things. This summer in Ersurum, in a bus, two women, completely covered, you know, showing off, told me that I should be ashamed to be in short sleeves, that I would not go to paradise. I told them paradise must be very crowded and perhaps I'd try to start filling the other place. I would never have replied like that before.'

Listening to these women, we realize once again the enormous contradictions that come from the differences between regions and ethnic groups. Religious beliefs and how strongly they are held vary according to where the women come from.

All these women are living evidence of the anachronisms of Turkey. It would be most interesting, for example, to carry out a more in-depth survey among immigrant women on their views of motherhood and to try and find out whether emigration has changed anything in plans for the family. For in Turkey itself, it is astonishing to see that while the desired norm in terms of children is 2.6 or 3 children, the national average is 5.2 while in the countryside the figure rises to 7 and in Istanbul falls to 2.65. Our earlier contacts with the wives of immigrants showed us that there had been real changes in this area. And if most also say that on their return they will have to 'fall in line with' customs, we must wonder whether, despite everything, their presence won't have a profound influence in the long term on other women in the village. Finally, it is remarkable, among other things, to see the desire for change that they all have for their daughters . . . All without exception want their daughters to have a higher education than theirs and incarnate the woman 'with the uncovered face' that Ataturk wanted.

What can we conclude about women in Turkey today? Sixty years later, what remains of Kemalism in the area of women's rights? How do these emigrant women see their mothers and daughters and how do they see their own marriage as compared to the Western marriage presented in the media?

'I don't know if women are as Ataturk wanted. Surely not really. But I'm not like my grandmother. My mother, yes, I take after her except that she still does not dare uncover her arms. With my husband I cannot, of course, act like a Frenchwoman. At home, we're not so independent.'

'I don't know whether Turkish women have really changed. Looking at it like that, yes they have, but it's not good in a Muslim country. By changing, they "tempt" others. Look' France has influenced my daughters; they won't listen to me any more. A true believer should be modest, for her husband's sake — it's he who will have to account for her sins. If my husband wanted me to change, I'd change. If women are no longer as they ought to be, it's because of work. That's why European couples are like two strangers. My mother was right to be covered, secluded. I think like her.'

'I think things were rather the same in Ataturk's time. It's normal for the young to be a little more "open". You have to move forward with the world. A Turkish couple is very different from a European couple. With us, there's a host of "taboos" between the two partners, less freedom. As for Frenchwomen, their husband helps in the house and they help their husbands. That's how it should be.'

'Women have regressed since Ataturk. They are more restricted. Ataturk didn't do enough. And now everybody is going to be forced to wear the same clothes. It'll be like in Khomeyni's country. A woman and a soldier, obviously they're not the same. A woman should be free. Look, this summer I saw women covered right outside the Palais de Justice in town.[14] My mother doesn't even go out, she and I are as far apart as France and Turkey are. So things have changed a little. I'm happy my daughters are more advanced than me. When I think about it, what has Islam really done for us? My husband and I have changed a little in our habits here. He agrees more easily when I ask him for something. Back home, he has other models, he becomes less easy going. But in Turkey, when he wanted us to walk arm in arm, I laughed to see how the neighbours reacted! I think European women are happier.'

'I think that women are more open. But it all depends on the men. In Turkey you still have villages where one man alone lays down the law. I've seen more than my mother so I'm more open and my daughter will be more open than me. It's good. And then I don't ask her what my mother used to ask me. You have to progress. In Europe women are freed by household gadgets. So there are fewer problems between couples. We are dependent on what our husband wants, they aren't.

'It's as Ataturk wanted, I think. Women haven't stayed behind. My mother couldn't tell left from right. My daughter has overtaken me. In Europe men help women; women give men orders, it's the opposite of what happens with us. I think that if women want to free themselves, they must be able to give men orders. I always say so.' This woman's husband intervened at this point to say, 'Soon, you'll all become Frenchwomen.'

'I think that women are more advanced. But in the villages, they are marking time. I think that it's because of religion. My mother and my grandmother were even more backward in their life, their language and their clothes. But they were slaves of their upbringing. Young people have to be more advanced. In Turkey the married couple are more reactionary. Perhaps things are better among the rich. But you see, with me, if I didn't work, I wouldn't like my husband to look after the house instead of me. If I work, we share. The man must help in the house. I would have liked things in our country to be as they are in France between husband and wife.'

'It's only the women in the towns, the bourgeoisie, who are more advanced than in Ataturk's time. But in the villages, things are far from what Ataturk wanted, I think. It's only the right to vote which actually works. My mother is educated, she is a teacher but I still think she mixes less than I do. I've got men friends but she hasn't got her own circle, she only has her husband's. The two couples (Turkish and French) are very different. Here husband and wife share much more. Women are more respected. But I think too that the couple here is more fragile; the wife is less attached to family values, she sometimes puts herself before her children.'

The Kemalist reforms seem not to have changed the situation of women very much. As this last young woman put it, some Turkish women may have moved a long way, but they are a minority. The inequalities in the liberation of women remain flagrant. While, legally, Turkish women have nothing to envy European women for, socially, and in customary rights, equality disappears.

The liberation of women varies with the level of their education and the greater or lesser impact of religion and traditions. The seclusion of Turkish women goes hand in hand with the social, economic and political seclusion of Turkey from Kemal's death to the present day. There is a great contradiction between the values of Islam and the secular precepts of a society and a state which officially recognizes women. The family finds it hard to choose a path between these contradictory entities; but it is quite certain, too, that so long as the powers necessary for the implementation of a truly secular policy are not provided and so long as Turkey does not emerge from political obscurantism and become a true democracy, it will be superfluous to be actively concerned with emancipation of women. We do not believe that the status of women will improve separately from the development of the whole people. Before concluding, we must note that few Turkish women have actually carried on a struggle for their emancipation. Rights have been granted, even imposed on, women rather then demanded by them. This partly explains their failure to participate in social, economic and even political life despite having had the right to vote for so long. But listening to these few immigrant women we realize that their consciousness of what they have been deprived of, and their frustrations, are growing. But what do the women who spoke to us so frankly want? (We asked them what was the most important thing for women's liberation and what they wanted for Turkish women and themselves.) We leave them the last word.

'The most important thing is education. Everything depends on knowledge.'
'Freedom. We must be free to work, to earn our living, to have a place in society. If our governments had solved that problem, we wouldn't be like this.'
'Equality. Minds have to be enlightened too. But I must reflect more on this question, you see, I've never even thought about it. Perhaps because no one's ever asked me what I wanted.'
'A real equality. But not only in words. Equality for women to be able to work in equal conditions with facilities. The most important thing is equality in work.

And that women no longer be considered second class.'

'I would like complete equality with men. Education is vital. An individual who has not been educated is only a half a person; I think that's why we are not counted as full human beings.'

Some didn't know how to reply to this last question. They are so unused to being invited to speak ...

Paris, January 1983

Notes

1. F. Grenard, 'Mission Scientifique en Haute-Asie' (Paris, 1898), in S. Dirks, *Islam et Jeunesse en Turquie Aujourd'hui* (H. Champion, Paris, 1977), p. 93.

2. A. Ubicini, 'Journal Universel', in *L'Illustration*, 10 June 1854.

3. Gokalp Ziya (1876–1924), writer and politician; he taught sociology at the university, and was a member of the Young Turk government, then deputy for Diyarbakir in 1920 under Kemal Ataturk. He taught himself French. While admiring French culture he developed nationalist and pan-Turk ideas of a Turkish 'homeland' larger than Turkey itself and which would embrace all the Turkish-speaking civilizations and regions. He was the theoretician of Pan-Turkism and of national union around a 'great' Turkish culture and civilization.

He was an advocate of the 'Turkification' of the language and was also a fervent admirer of Western scientific progress. He proposed to take 'the best' from the West and keep the moral values of Islam without mixing them up with the legislature and the executive. Politically somewhat fluctuating and portraying himself as apolitical, he defended Kemalist policy wholeheartedly.

4. Poems written between 1941 and 1945 in Nazim Hikmet, *Paysages Humains* (F. Maspero, Voiz series, 1973) and in Nazim Hikmet, *Un étrange voyage* (F. Maspero, collection Voix, Paris 1980).

5. Cited in a series of articles by O. Erten in *Cumhuriyet* (a Turkish daily), August–September 1976.

6. According to article 12 of the 1961 Constitution 'all citizens without distinction of language, race, sex, political and philosophical opinions and religious beliefs are equal before the laws', and according to article 42 'work is the right and duty of every citizen'. But article 156 of the Civil Code states that 'the wife may, with the express or tacit consent of the husband, carry on a profession or trade'.

7. Figures published in 1970 by the National Institute of Statistics, Ankara.

8. The 1975 data were obtained from a 1% sample drawn from the 1975 census in *Dunyada ve Turkiye — de Tarih boyunca kadin* (Tan yayinlari, 1981, Ankara).

9. In 1976, 46.3% in the Ministry of Public Education; 16.3% in the Ministry of Health and Social Welfare; 6.5% in post and telecommunications; 3.3% in social security; 3.1% in the State Bank; 1.3% in the Ministry of Forestry; 1.1% in the Ministry of Agriculture. O. Citçi, 'Turk kamu yonetiminde kadin gorevliler', in *Turk Toplumunda Kadin*, published by the Turkish Social Science Association, Ankara, 1979.

10. G. Kazgan, ibid., p. 167.

11. G. Dino, 'Aux avant-postes de la littérature, la femme de la Turquie nouvelle', *Le Courrier de l'Unesco*, November 1981.

12. More and more rural women are replacing the baggy trousers under their skirt or dress with European-style trousers.

13. The most recent women's movement was the Movement of Progressive Women. This movement had pro-communist sympathies and was banned after the September

1980 military coup just as it was beginning to gain a certain audience among women intellectuals, teachers and clerical workers.

14. She is referring to decisions of the state of siege which have recently regulated the clothes of women working in the civil service.

Bibliography

Abadan-Unat, Nermin, *Turk Toplumunda Kadin* (TSBDY yayinlari, Ankara, 1979).

Dino, Guzin, *Le Courrier de l'Unesco*, November 1981.

Dirks, Sabine, *Islam et Jeunesse en Turquie Aujourd'hui*, thesis presented to the University of Paris-V on 21 May 1975 (H. Champion, Paris, 1977).

Dirks, Sabine, *La famille musulmane turque* (Maison des Sciences de l'Homme and Mouton and Co., Paris and The Hague, 1969).

Ataturk ansiklopedisi (Ataturk Encyclopaedia), Istanbul, 1972–5.

Tunisian Women, Their Rights and Their Ideas about These Rights

Malika Zamiti-Horchani

It is generally considered that Tunisian women enjoy the most favourable situation of all Arab women. The Code of Personal Status established in 1956, immediately after independence (and amended several times since), considerably reduced the inequality of women compared to men, an inequality sanctioned by Koranic law (*sharia*) and tradition.

Today, however, we are obliged to say that there is a considerable gap between the rights granted to women and the practice. There are still few women in public life. If the facilities women have for access to education, vocational training and work are compared with the possibilities open to men in these areas, they have remained in a situation of clear inequality. It is this gap between the law and its interpretation that young educated women stress to draw attention to the real situation of women in Tunisian society.[1]

We have tried to look at the ideas of both men and women on the status and role of women, believing that these ideas can be a driving force or a brake on change. Such a study does not tell us about the objective reality of the place of women in society; but it does allow us to grasp the psychological mechanisms that lie behind behaviour and block any improvement in the condition of women.

The sources of information

The survey was carried out nationally and a sample of 400 adult persons of both sexes was chosen.[2] The data from the 1975 census served as a basis for the composition of this sample and all social categories are represented in it. If we group the responses we can see how the ideas of female roles vary according to the sex, age, urban or rural origin and level of education of the respondent. The replies range from very liberal to highly conservative.

The most liberal respondents thought that women should be freed from all control, represented at all levels of responsibility and free to dispose of themselves and their income as they saw fit. This is the model of the 'modern woman'.

These are the attitudes:

- of virtually all the young female subjects aged between twenty and forty, who have completed at least secondary education and who live in towns, even if they are of rural origin;
    - of only a minority of male subjects with the same profile;
    - of some of the older women, aged over forty, illiterate and of both rural and urban origin.

The most conservative responses refer to the traditional model of the woman devoted to home and children, incapable of taking on high level economic and political responsibilities.

These are the attitudes:

- of the majority of male subjects aged over forty who have at least secondary education and live in towns;
- of virtually all men aged over forty, with little or no education, whether living in towns or in the countryside;
- of some of the rural women aged over forty, with little or no education.

The intermediate responses were contradictory and reveal an ambivalent attitude. They refer to a model of women with the same abilities as men but denied an equivalent economic and political status.

These are the attitudes:

- of the majority of young male subjects (between thirty and forty years old), educated and city-dwellers;
- of some of the women aged over forty, educated and city-dwellers;
- of some of the men aged over forty, educated and city-dwellers.

Thus sex, whether male or female, seems to be the most determining factor in the attitude that the subjects surveyed adopt with regard to the emancipation of women. Contrary to the universally held view that attributes to women the role of guardian of tradition, it is, in Tunisia at least, the man who fulfils this role.[3] Are women who suffer dependence every day and are deprived of control over their own existence better placed to question the lot assigned to them than the men who benefit from it? The responses of men and women are consistently disparate on three issues that our survey has chosen to bring out: the position of women in the family, as part of a couple and in social and political life.

Women in the family

It seems that there should be no other place for a woman than in the family. All her upbringing, including the models she sees around her, points to her sole role being that of wife and mother. Her status is constantly being devalued compared with the boy whose prestige is infinitely superior to hers; her chances in life are correspondingly reduced. From their earliest childhood, this difference in social esteem, which is universal in traditional society (and brought out in numerous studies), shows itself in the attention given to girls and boys. Boys are suckled longer, and they are more likely to be taken to the doctor when ill — which explains the higher incidence of infantile mortality among girls.

45% of those surveyed stated that in their family the boys were favoured as compared with the girls. Curiously, men seem more conscious than women of this situation; almost 50% of them, as opposed to 40% of women, recognize it. Have women internalized the cultural models so deeply that they find this discrimination normal, or do they deny it and therefore refuse to admit it? Most parents refuse to admit the difference in treatment accorded to sons and daughters. But discriminatory practices are very common. 84% of women participated in domestic chores from their earliest childhood (against 5% of men) and 52% of women began by the age of six.

Girls are obliged to perform a variety of domestic tasks in addition to the household chores: shopping when they are very young, and, in rural areas, fetching water, collecting wood, looking after animals. Boys are much more rarely called on to do this sort of work and it is accepted that they can play while girls are obliged from a very early age to learn the tiresome and routine work of the adult woman.

Other aspects of behaviour within the family testify to the great differences between the two sexes:

* more than 50% of men questioned said they ate their meals separately from their wives. From puberty, boys eat at the men's table and the women are generally served after them. A quarter of the sample continues to carry on this tradition in the family today;
* virtually all the men state they didn't have to account to anybody when they went out during the day or at night from the time they were adolescents;
* women on the other hand, until they were married, had to seek their parents' permission for even the shortest trip;
* the majority of the men, as soon as they began to work — while they were still living with their parents — had complete control over their incomes whereas 50% of women in the same situation had to hand over 50% of what they earned to their father and 50% could only spend it with his consent.

Opposition comes from men

Despite the high proportion of women who asserted that they had not been the object of discriminatory treatment in the family, 73% of women in the sample say that they met opposition from one or other male member of their family when the question of their going to school was raised, as against 60% of the boys.

It is important to stress that opposition to the schooling of boys is justified generally by cases of *force majeure*, such as the need to take the place of an absent or elderly father, whereas for girls, it is usually a matter of opposition on principle. Opposition to sending the girl to school rarely comes from the mother. It comes essentially from males — fathers, grandfathers and in some cases brothers — who seem more attached than women to the traditions that keep women in the home.

As for the level of education, 81% of men consider that girls should go as far as possible, that is as far as university. This seems to be in contradiction to the attitudes previously mentioned; but in fact, it is usually with a view to better preparing girls for their role as wives and mothers that most men want to see women educated. 'So that she can help the children in their studies ...', 'So that she can help her husband professionally if necessary ...' 'Because an educated woman understands her husband better and brings up her children better than one who knows nothing ...' Such are the most common arguments put forward by men. Women's arguments are more demanding and refer more often to the social role that they intend to play outside the family. 'So as not to be out of tune with the times.' 'So that she will be a rounded person ...', 'To understand what is happening around her.'

While they accept that girls should be educated, men are less willing to accept the idea of vocational training. If the educated woman is an ornament for her husband, one who has a skill appears as a competitor of men both economically and in social standing.

Thus 8% of women are in favour of vocational training of daughters whereas 60% of men (evenly distributed over all the categories of age, education, and geographical origin) are against it. The justifications given by men and women are different. For men who are in favour of the training of women in a skill, this is still envisaged in relation to their future role as wife and mother, the skill being seen not as a necessity but as a guarantee for the future or something to fall back on in the event of bad luck, 'in case she doesn't get married'; 'in case her husband doesn't earn enough'; 'so as to be able to feed her children if she becomes widowed'. Women, on the other hand, seem to adhere more to the image of the 'modern woman' who is economically emancipated. They see acquiring a skill as a means to economic liberation and self-affirmation, 'So as not to be at the mercy of father or husband for the least little thing', says one of them. 'When she contributes to the household expenses, she has a say in how the money is spent', adds another. Some women see in work a means of escape from the role of minor that is usually assigned to them, 'To be socially respected' is an argument that recurs often.

Finally, some women mention the need to keep up with the times and respond to the needs of the age, 'So that she should be up to date ...'; 'These days it takes two to provide for a family ...'; 'It's not done any more to stay in the house.'

In the way in which they conceive of the education and vocational training of girls, the men surveyed express themselves more in terms of traditional models while Tunisian women tend to be looking for progress.

The women's responses are more coherent. In fact, while overwhelmingly recognizing the need to push girls' education to the highest possible level, men assert equally overwhelmingly that vocational training is scarcely desirable, if not downright useless.

Conversely, only 8% of them want their own daughters to be housewives and only 5% would like to see them do handicrafts which is a job that can fit in with home life. Men dream of the best qualified and most attractive professions for their daughters: higher management, liberal professions, directorships in trade, industry and agriculture. No man in the survey mentioned the occupations of teacher, secretary, typist or nurse — jobs that many women in fact do.

Women give equal support to the vocational training of girls in general and of their own daughters. They wanted the same occupations for them as they wanted for their sons and these were always the most prestigious occupations of doctor, lawyer or managing director. In theory at least, the traditional image of women would seem to be seriously undermined.

Women in the couple

How do Tunisians adjust to the traditional and modern models? How do they conceive of relations between husband and wife? Is participation of the wife in the family budget and its management, in decisions about family planning, in the future of the children or the purchase of possessions conceivable or acceptable? And how far?

Contrary to all expectations — given the fact that we are dealing here with a patriarchal Muslim society — 58% of Tunisians (men and women) do not accept the idea that the main responsibility for supporting the family should fall on the man. Only 32% of women still support it. 45% of them believe that it doesn't matter whether it's the man or the woman who works (as against 13% of the men). Is this a reflection of economic conditions? A number of the women are the wives of part-time workers or unemployed men and have the experience of the responsibility of supporting a family.

On the other hand, the men showed a very strong attachment to their traditional privileges as far as decision-making was concerned: 55% of men as against 25% of women give priority to the husband. However, 59% of men and women overall consider that the decisions must be taken jointly, thus demonstrating a trend towards a closer collaboration between husband and wife.

The man is always free from household chores

While agreeing to consult their wives, husbands do not go so far as to agree to sharing in household chores, seen as 'unmanly' activities. The majority of women, moreover, don't want them to. Only 19% of men and 33% of women believe that the men should participate in housework. The overwhelming majority of both sexes feel that houswork is an optional or exceptional activity for a man.

The stereotype of 'female tasks' is so strong that even among the women who felt that the man should help, most accepted that he should not do the washing or clean the floor and gave him only minor tasks. 'He could lay the table or clear it while I do the washing up', said one of them. 'A man bent over a mop, no, it's not nice, but he could make the bed or look after the children', added another. It is important to stress that all these women are from a young and educated milieu. Even here, where we find the most advanced ideas of equality between the sexes, the traditional model persists and gives a privileged place to the man and assigns to women routine domestic chores.

The majority of those surveyed implicitly accept the principle that women should combine domestic and professional tasks, since they want to see women occupying positions of responsibility in social, political and economic life. They do not agree that the husband should fill in for his wife if her work should temporarily prevent her fulfilling her domestic responsibilities.

58% of those surveyed believe that the woman should manage alone. But a majority of men feel that a woman's domestic and maternal role should come before her professional duty. 'Her home and her children come first . . . she just has to manage!'; 'If she's organized she won't need her husband's help'; 'She can ask her mother or sister to help her'; 'If she earns enough, the problem won't arise, she can pay someone, if not she'll just have to stay in the house'. These were the most frequent responses.

Even greater priority is given to the maternal role when it is a question of deciding between career and motherhood. 58% of Tunisians questioned don't accept that the wife has a right to refuse to bear children unless she has already had at least three.

Conflict between male and female models

Since the aspiration for equal education of boys and girls is equally shared by men and women, it was interesting to see how this principle fitted in in terms of relations between the couple. Overall, 58% of Tunisians surveyed believe that the guarantee of agreement within the couple was for husband and wife to have the same level of education.

But here again, the sex variable shows up a distinction between the responses. Only 15% of women still adhere to the model of the man enjoying a higher educational level than that of the wife. Conversely, the majority of men (58%) remain faithful to the image of the husband dominating his wife, even intellectually. These men are from almost all backgrounds. There again, the attachment of men to the traditional model which gives them privileges goes against the egalitarian aspirations of women.

It is important to stress that the ambivalent attitude of keeping the woman in her traditional role — while at the same time affirming the principle of equality between the sexes — is a dominant attitude explicitly confirmed by every official speech. The President of the Republic himself, who has done much for women's liberation, doesn't hesitate to assert that the woman's primary role is in the home and as mother. 'Society must help women harmonize their various social roles as wife, mother and full citizen ... Society's first obligation consists in making women aware of their family responsibilities as wife, mother and mistress of the house. This will reduce the causes of disagreement that lead to the break-up of the family. It is equally the case that women should be made aware that their role in public life may sometimes have to take on a secondary character for them.'[4]

It would seem that, ultimately, the reference models for very many Tunisians are ambivalent and oscillate between tradition and modernity. The extent to which these models are systematic and coherent varies generally according to sex, age and level of education, sex being the most determining variable. It is generally among women, and more particularly among young women with a relatively high level of education, that the images are structured into systematic, progressive and coherent models.

Among men, the images are more contradictory, more stereotyped and more ambivalent. The most ambivalent images exist essentially among men who are relatively young and educated. They seem to indicate the malaise among men faced with having to question their age-old privileges. They also testify to the transitional character of the period in which they live.

Women in social and political life

After trying to understand the images of women in the family and in marriage, the survey attempted to discover — still at the level of ideas — the role theoretically assigned to women in social and political activities. It used as indicators the assessment of women's capacity for professional success, attitudes towards a hierarchical female superior, towards the highest level of responsibility that a woman can exercise or the attitude towards measures seen as particularly liberating such as access to contraceptive devices or the promulgation of the Code of Personal Status and the amendments to it. Such attitudes are even more ambivalent than those towards the roles of women in family life.

Capacity for professional success

The majority of Tunisians questioned (58%) believes that, given an equal level of education, women are as capable of succeeding professionally as men. The proportion of women who take this point of view is higher than that of men (62% of women and 53% of men). Moreover, the 31% of interviewees who deny that women have an equal chance of success compared to men give different reasons depending on which sex they are. Whereas women generally mention objective obstacles (maternity, domestic responsibilities, opposition from the family), men tend rather to attribute women's lower success to their nature: 'Whatever she does, woman is always inferior to man'; 'God created woman inferior to man, she can never equal him' are typical of the justifications frequently used.

While a significant proportion of Tunisians recognize that women have the ability to succeed professionally and run a business or a service as well as men, many men still prefer not to work under the orders of a woman (45%). Those belonging to the 'young and educated' category had most reservations.

Women unsuited to political responsibilities

While many Tunisians may agree that women can succeed as well as men in the economic sphere, fewer of them see her as having the same abilities in the political sphere. A large majority (68%) believe that in the leadership of state affairs (in the post of prime minister for example) a woman would do less well than a man. In this sphere more men than women dispute her political competence (76% as against 63%). The reasons adduced to explain women's political incapacity relate in a number of cases to her nature. 'Women are easily influenced, they can't be objective'; 'God made women more sensitive than men, they couldn't be harsh when it's necessary'; 'In the early months of pregnancy, a woman becomes irritable and moody, she couldn't govern properly'.

In the reasons adduced by women, we find more references to social than to biological obstacles. The problem of the affront to male authority is often mentioned. '(If she were Prime Minister) her husband would have to be President of the Republic otherwise she would be unhappy at home'; 'Men don't like women doing better than them, so they put obstacles in their way'.

This attitude of reserving politics for men is an accurate reflection of the dominant ideology in the country where, despite the affirmations of principle and some striking exceptions, women are kept out of political responsibilities and are virtually absent from all decision-making bodies both in the ruling party and in the opposition parties and movements.

The ambiguity towards the capacity of women to succeed is emphasized further when we compare the aspirations for sons and daughters on the one hand, and the assessment of how competent women are for positions with a high level of political responsibility on the other. Although they consider women to be unfitted for positions of political responsibility, the majority of Tunisians want their daughters to be able to accede to these positions. It is still the case that more of them want it for sons (83% as against 72%) but the

117

percentage wanting it for daughters is still considerable and gives a glimpse of major changes in models of male and female roles and of the participation of Tunisian women in political life.

Since motherhood is often adduced as a justification for saying that women are less suited to political, economic and social responsibilities, it seemed interesting to look at the attitude of Tunisians to modern contraceptive methods and abortion. Only one-third of men, as against three-quarters of women, believed that modern contraceptive methods were necessary for the improvement of the status of women in society. The reservations expressed by men related in the main to the fear of losing their ascendancy over women if these methods were to be used without their knowledge, to religious prohibitions and to the decline of morals. (It should be stressed that religion was only mentioned by a small percentage of women, mostly old ones, with a low level of education, and only in the case of abortion.)

Contraceptive methods are better accepted by men when they are presented as contributing to the happiness of the married couple 'on condition that they are only used with the prior consent of the husband', several of them specify. In this case, 60% of men think that they are useful.

Men's fear of losing ascendancy over women also shows itself in their attitude towards the Code of Personal Status promulgated in 1956 in a modernizing attempt to reform mentalities and morals. The attitude towards the Code of Personal Status raised the problem of the fact that women are less well informed in legal matters even about problems that affect them directly. (51% of women in the sample were not even aware of the existence of the Code of Personal Status.) Women's lower level of information may be attributed to their lower level of literacy. As for women who did know, three-quarters of them thought that it was very good because it protected them against the abuses of power that men often subjected them to. Its most positive contribution, according to these women, was the suppression of repudiation which gave an excessive and arbitrary power to men.

Most men hostile to the Code adduced either religious factors or the fear of losing their acquired privileges. The most often mentioned reasons are of the type, 'It's against the spirit of the Koran' or 'Family life isn't possible if the man has no authority over the woman', 'Women only do what they feel like, you can't control them any more'.

The differential analysis of male and female images and representations concerning the status and role of women in society reveals a certain lack of congruence. The gap between men and women persists in the deeper motivations and determinations which govern the views of each.

To recapitulate, while the mother conceives, for example, of a high level of education for her daughter guaranteeing self-fulfilment and integration into the modern world, the father rather sees in this training an opportunity to learn better how to adapt to the traditional role; he opposes any change.

Tunisian women can be seen as being more innovative than men, whereas the men endeavour, through a strategy of retrieval, to hi-jack the new by integrating it into the old. This thus contradicts (as we have already observed) the widely held view that women are (or should be?) the guardians of traditions.

In the context of 'underdevelopment' it might be wondered why women internalize the dominant ideology of male superiority to a lesser extent than in the customary modes of existence. Is this because of the influence of Western models or because of material constraints? Whatever the case we must say that Tunisian women are beginning to fight together both against the oppression that is customary in the old structures of social life and against economic exploitation linked to present-day forms of wage-labour.

In doing so, in the throes of an uneasy, even traumatic, situation, they are attempting to grasp a future that is more open than the limited horizon to which men would like to restrict them.

University of Tunis, February 1983

Notes

1. See Samya el Mechat, 'Femmes et Pouvoirs en Tunisie', *Les Temps modernes*, no. 436, November 1982.

2. The data analysed in this study are drawn from a survey carried out on behalf of the Union Nationale des Femmes de Tunisie (National Union of Tunisian Women) (the only officially recognized women's organization), *L'Image de la femme dans la société tunisienne*, by Ali Belkadi, Annie El Amouri, Tahar El Amouri, Abdallah Maaouia, Abdelaziz Mejeri and Malika Zamiti (National Union of Tunisian Women and the El Amouri Institute of Applied Psychology, Tunis, 1981).

3. Similar conclusions are drawn for Algeria in Hélène Vandevelde-Daillère's *Femmes algériennes*, a study of the condition of women in the area of Constantine since independence (Algiers, OPUA, 1980).

4. Speech by the President of the Republic, Habib Bourguiba, 'Harmoniser les rôles sociaux de la femme', 13 August 1976, quoted by Samya Mechat, see note 1.

Being a Woman in Yugoslavia: Past, Present and Institutional Equality

Mirjana Morokvasic

On contradictions

Women in the socialist countries are getting themselves noticed: several works have appeared in the last few years, especially in German and English, but also recently in French: Scott, H., 1976; Holt, A., 1978; Kirsch, 1978; Rind, A., 1980; Volgyes, 1977; Wander, M., 1967. The picture that emerges from these books reflects the contradictions experienced by women in the socialist countries. Socialism manifests itself to them on the one hand as an extraordinary conquest of rights, a victory, a breakthrough in society and, on the other hand, as the betrayal of a promise of emancipation and liberation that has been only partially kept. Most authors are careful to avoid speaking of one aspect without mentioning the other.

There are very few people, even in the socialist countries, who think that everything has been resolved. But it remains a great temptation, especially for those who take the West as their reference point, to say that, when all is said and done, nothing has been achieved and to lambast socialism as if, after a revolution, the position of women would, by some miracle, be entirely transformed. And yet Clara Zetkin and other socialist women had no hesitation in saying at the beginning of the century, well before they were in a position to confront their ideas with a socialist reality, that even in a socialist society there would have to be a long fight by women to achieve their equality. Economic transformations — which were certainly the essential prerequisite — would not imply *ipso facto* immediate changes in the relations between men and women nor in the attitude of men to women and vice versa.

In Yugoslavia, almost twenty years after the war and the socialist revolution, Z. Pesic reiterated Clara Zetkin's message:

But these new relations (between men and women) don't develop spontaneously with the change of economic structure. They are achieved by a long and difficult process that depends above all on the will and conscious effort of the people concerned, once the material conditions have been attained. The time when a socialist society will be realized depends on the way in which people conceive the construction of human relationships suitable for

120

the new society and their interest in struggling against the legacy of the past. (Pesic, 1962, p. 4)

So people didn't expect a wave of a magic wand. What has not, however, been clearly defined is the type of struggle to be waged and the type of human relations and socialist family towards which we should aim.

Authors who have recently looked at the question of women in socialist states have all overlooked Yugoslavia. Yet Yugoslavia has features in common with other socialist countries in Europe. Yugoslav women share with other socialist women the weight of contradictions; they have won rights, and access to education and a career and cultural life. At the same time, the old inequalities and values in the relations between men and women have persisted. It is as if, institutionally and legally, everything had been done and settled and yet all the most important issues remained untouched.

In Yugoslavia, as in other socialist countries, there exists a great gap between the ideals proclaimed and the actual condition of women. The reasons for this vary from country to country. Yugoslavia stands out because of the great socio-economic variety of its regions and peoples, its market economy and the stress laid on consumption and the mosaic of historical and cultural influences. In Yugoslavia women took an active part in the revolution. Ethnically, historically and culturally, Yugoslavia is the most complex country in Europe. Differences between regions, within regions, between the country and the city are the source of the main contradictions of Yugoslav society and of the position of women within it. In 1971, Yugoslavia had one of the highest rates in the world of university-educated women; yet at the same time, a quarter of the female poulation was illiterate.

In such a context, any attempt at generalization may appear misplaced and useless. In most of the country, the old and the new coexist. Traditional values, those of the consumer society and those of socialism are all jumbled together; this inevitably creates contradictions, conflicts and ambivalent situations for women and men. The time needed to bring about change varies considerably between region and region, between village and town, between one social group and another.

The socialist revolution brought industrialization and change in the socio-economic structure of the country. It also laid the foundations for changes in social relations, notably in relations between men and women. However, it is precisely in these latter relations, the domain usually called 'private', that the grip of patriarchal values is most tenacious. The gap between the achievement and recognition of women in public life and the position of women in the private domain remains very large. A double sexual morality is dominant and often hinders the implementation of egalitarian legislation. Public opinion still judges men and women's conduct differently, while women are considered to be inferior to men and of lesser value. The worst insult for a man is to call him a woman. Women,

121

in Yugoslavia can be economically independent, socially active, recognized and respected at work and yet remain mere servants at home, where the man retains authority.'As a consequence of the artificial distinction between the private domain and the public domain the position of women in public life has evolved differently from women's position in the family. Legislation has set out the position of women at work, in education and so on, and much has been done to prevent discrimination. But in the private sphere, legislation was unable to resist the old values and replace them with something new. They have survived. They have even often been supported and have in turn affected the position of women in public life. 'Politics and private life have remained two distinct and separate spheres, the former reasserting itself as essentially for men, and the latter for women' (Denic, B., 1976).

We will first outline the disparities within the country which affect the condition of women. The next section will analyse the reality for Yugoslav women behind the framework of institutional equality. The past and the values of the consumer society are often seen as obstacles to the implementation of socialist ideals: these two parallel influences are considered later. Finally, we shall attempt to outline the continuing debates on the emancipation of women and their place in society.

Regional differences: the country and its people

The diversity of Yugoslavia is reflected in the numerous groups that make up its population — Croats, Serbs, Montenegrins, Macedonians and Slovenes, then Albanians, Hungarians, Italians, Turks, Germans, Slovaks and Gypsies. Several languages are spoken in Yugoslavia, two alphabets are used, Cyrillic and Latin, and three main religions are practised: the north, east and south are Orthodox, the centre and south are Muslim, while Catholicism dominates the north, centre and west.

This diversity arises from a separate historical evolution. For centuries, since their invasion of the Balkans, various groups of southern Slavs (Yugoslavs) have come under various influences. Some parts retained their independence for a very long time: Dubrovnik, for example, was a prosperous and independent republic until the 19th Century whereas the rest of the country (below the Sava-Danube watershed) was occupied by the Turks for almost five centuries from the late 14th Century onwards. Serbia was the first to free itself from the Turks in the 19th Century. The northern and western parts of the country belonged to the Austro-Hungarian empire and Italy. The Yugoslav state is a recent creation: the first unified state to appear was the kingdom of the Serbs, Croats and Slovenes after the First World War and later the kingdom of Yugoslavia. With some exceptions, the country covered the present territory inhabited for centuries by Yugoslav peoples.

These different historical origins are today partly responsible for the persistence of cultural and economic contrasts. Whereas some parts of the country have a GNP per head equal to that of a developed European country, others have many features typical of a Third World country. The disparities in the condition of women throughout Yugoslavia are only the reflection of these differences that have grown up over the centuries.

In 1976, the total population of Yugoslavia was 21,560,000, covering a territory 255,000 km^2 (according to the 1981 census, the population has risen to 22,354,219). Half the population is rural while one-third lives in what in Yugoslavia are called 'mixed households',[1] that is households in which at least one member works in industry while at the same time the household also derives part of its income from agriculture.

In the demographic structure of the country as a whole, women are a majority. However, in the least developed regions such as Kosovo and Macedonia, men were in a majority until very recently and women's life expectancy was lower. Conversely, the birth rates there were very high: according to the 1971 census, there were 36.5 live births per 1000 inhabitants in Kosovo and 23.2 in Macedonia. The average for Yugoslavia at that time was 17.8; in the developed republics it was 13.9 for Croatia, 14.8 for Serbia strictly so called (less the autonomous regions) and finally 13.00 in the Vojvodina. In these same regions the natural growth rate of the population is very low.

Infant mortality in Yugoslavia is among the highest in Europe. The average of 55 mortalities per 1000 births (31 per 1000 in 1981) hides regional variations. In Kosovo, 96 children per 1000 (66 in 1981) die less than a year after birth, in Macedonia 88, in Slovenia 28 (1971). Only half these children would have received medical attention, in Kosovo no more than a third (*Zena u Drustva privredi Jugoslavije*, 1973, p. 19).

Women in education

Despite the considerable improvements in the level of education of the population as a whole, women still lag behind men. Once again, there are considerable regional disparities, although fewer than there were in the past. Whereas four years of compulsory schooling was introduced for children in Slovenia, Croatia and the Vojvodina in the second half of the 18th Century, in some parts of the country this was not implemented before the end of the Second World War (Tomsic, 1980).

In 1933 more than 80% of the women in Serbia, Bosnia and Macedonia were illiterate, while the rate in Croatia was 35%. After the war, in 1948, the rate of illiteracy among women in Yugoslavia as a whole was still 57% (for comparison, in the same year it was 5% in France and the USA). In 1953, more than half the female population aged over 35 was still illiterate, in Kosovo 91%. The legacy of the past was not eradicated two decades later: the illiteracy rate in the population aged over 35 was still 40% for women and 20% for men. Illiteracy persisted even among the young (Yugoslav census of 1971).

The improvement is due to the introduction in 1952–3 of eight years of compulsory schooling. Despite this requirement, which is enforced for girls as well as boys in the developed republics, 30–40% of girls do not go beyond four years or do not go to school at all in the less developed parts of the country.

However, at the level of secondary schooling, there is practically no disparity in school attendance between girls and boys. In higher education women were 40.4% of the total of 271,032 students in 1976–7.

Women in economic life

The proportion of the working population engaged in agriculture has been constantly declining in recent years for both men and women. In ten years, from 1961 to 1971, the proportion of working women in agriculture fell from 68% to 59%. But there were still more women than men. At the same time, the proportion of women in the working population as a whole rose from 24.8% in 1954 to 34.5% in 1976.

According to the 1971 census the proportion of women working was 30.7% (in 1981, 36%), a much lower figure than that in other socialist countries, and here too there are very pronounced regional disparities, ranging from 40.8% for Slovenia to 8.4% for Kosovo.

Women represented more than half the unemployed (people looking for work, the translation of the term used in Yugoslavia in 1976 *Women and Development*, 1977). Right from the time of the economic reforms of the 1960s, which affected women more than men, they formed the majority of 'persons looking for work'. In the period between 1964 and 1976 the number of unemployed tripled, rising from 222,800 to 665,000, of whom over 300,000 were women. According to some observers, this figure seriously under-estimates the size of the potential female labour force (Wertheimer-Baletic, 1972). It must be stressed that women who are highly skilled have more difficulty than men in finding a job. This is not the case for very highly skilled or skilled women who are only one-third of persons seeking work in this category. But it is not at all certain that the jobs they find are really appropriate to their level of skill.

The institutionalization of equality and women's reality

In pre-war Yugoslavia women were subjected to specific political and economic discrimination. They had no rights, and received lower wages for the same work. Religious norms and the law varied considerably from one to another but, everywhere women were treated as minors, dependent on husbands, brothers, or even sons (Tomsic, 1980, p. 17).

With the socialist revolution women entered into public life, equality was institutionalized and a socialist ideal for the position of women in society was established. It is a view that is often officially upheld that as 'soldiers of the revolution' (Pocek-Matic, M., 1976, p. 96) women have secured their new roles and place in society.

By linking their destiny to that of all the oppressed, women become an inseparable part of the revolutionary potential, and of the consciousness of revolutionary strength ... No revolution could be won without the massive participation of women, without their contribution to the strength, goals and results of the revolution.

Yugoslavia has some of the most progressive legislation in the world on women. The new socialist constitution laid the foundations for equality between the sexes. Not only did women secure political and legal rights that they had never had before, but they won access to most spheres of public life. The industrialization and reconstruction of the country theoretically opened up to women new possibilities outside the family, in production, education and political and cultural life. The entry of women into the ranks of wage-earners was officially seen as an essential condition of their economic independence and emancipation. Yugoslav legislation protects women as workers, as mothers and as wives. It is impossible to give here a complete list of all the legal measures that have been introduced (see Tomsic, 1980, pp. 157–90). We shall only mention some of them, those which best illustrate the *legal* position of Yugoslav women.

The sex of an applicant cannot be a condition for his/her access to the job. Women have the right to a year's maternity leave on full pay. Within marriage, the woman and the man are treated as equals. Divorce by mutual consent is possible everywhere but, in some republics, conditions have been introduced to protect women. In some republics, there is no legal distinction between marriage and a free union. The right to decide freely whether they (women) want to have children or not is a basic right specified in the 1974 constitution. Abortion has been legal since 1952.

In spite of these measures, the old values and the image of women as inferior have not disappeared. Effectively, as Tomsic stresses,

> Constitutional and legal norms have had a limited impact on the *de facto* equality of women. They are an important instrument in the process of change underway in human relations, but only as part of sustained social action (1980, p. 85).

Socialism has not succeeded in removing the enormous national disparities. The real position of women and how they live effectively shows that reality still lags far behind the ideals of the law. Women are conspicuous by their absence from many decision-making positions and representative bodies. Consequently, although the participation of women in the work force has been constantly increasing, they are under-represented in work force representative bodies and almost completely absent from key positions in these bodies: in 1972, only 5.5% of workers' councils had a woman presiding officer and only 0.9% of all the managers of enterprises in Yugoslavia were women. In workers' councils their representation is 16.8% and in the councils of agricultural cooperatives it is only 5.5%.

Their position is no better in socio-political life: 'Given the situation of delegates in the assemblies, the declared equality between men and women has not yet been achieved, particularly in recent years' (*Materijalni i drustveni razvoj jugoslavije*, Federal Office of Statistics, 1973, p. 36).

Women's participation varies according to their level of education and qualification. At a low level of education and qualification, the participation of women may even be higher than that of men whereas at the highest levels there are few women (4% among highly skilled workers for example). They are concentrated in the highly labour-intensive manufacturing industries and in the typically female sectors: textiles, clothing industry, services and administration. However, although they are over-represented in these sectors there are only 8.8% of women in management positions. Among teachers, more than half are women. Two-thirds of medical personnel are women. Their wages are on average 18% lower than men's (Suvar, 1980).

A study of the position of women in the social system in Yugoslavia shows that despite the constant increase in the participation of women in economic activity, the vertical mobility of women is less than that of men; women are concentrated in the sectors listed above and in occupations where low wages have always been the rule (Buric, 1972, pp. 61–76). In all the key positions of responsibility, women are very poorly represented, despite the constant improvements in their level of education and skill. It seems that, as in other socialist countries, revolutionary change has lost its steam and in the areas of senior positions, decision-making and participation in political life, women are not only regressing but are withdrawing into passivity and silence.

This stagnation and even regression of women's participation in public life has been openly debated. Tito himself said,

> As for the general principles, there can be no misunderstanding, yet the ever-increasing participation of women in industry, agriculture, health and education and their declining participation in self-management and representative organs is in the process of becoming the most tyical characteristic of current social practice (*Zena*, 1971, p. 29).

Studies illustrate this trend: Erbeznik Fulks (1972) interviewed over 2,000 women in Zagreb, all former fighters in the revolution, in their fifties, and thus still some way from the normal retiring age. Over half of them were members of the League of Communists. Where were they now? Their representation in political bodies was only symbolic (0.2% of them); 73% were not working. Among those who were working, the majority earned salaries lower than average for salaries in Zagreb. Those in retirement (often taken early) received lower pensions than their male comrades. Simisevic's study (*Zena izmedju rada i porodice*, 1975) of a representative sample of 1,479 working women showed that fewer than 1% of women were in management positions or in self-management bodies. Over 90% played no active part in these bodies while only 5% of those interviewed were active or belonged to professional, cultural or sporting organizations. The author drew the odd conclusion that women were not interested, whereas 85% of them gave as their reason too much work in the house and with their children.

This trend,towards political passivity found its symbolic expression in a letter written by 84 housewives in Pancevo (a town near Belgrade) (*Slobodna Dalmacija*, 23 August 1973). This letter, addressed to the Constituent Assembly before the public discussion of the new constitution, was widely reported and discussed throughout Yugoslavia. These women's request[2] that housework be recognized as productive work with similar benefits pinpointed a subject that is currently under wide discussion in feminist literature on the value of housework. But the arguments these women used to support their request mostly reflected an acceptance of their inferior and less important position in society. Their request was rejected as conservative.

For women it seems that the whole post-war experience has been artificially divided between the private and the public spheres. The most far-reaching and fundamental changes have taken place in the public sphere whereas the private sphere has been abandoned to chancy influences of all sorts, those from the past being the most tenacious. However, there is also a regression of women in the public sphere, mainly due to the persistence of old customs, attitudes and values. This, in turn, has influenced the position of women in the public sphere where patriarchal men–women relations have been preserved despite progressive marriage and family legislation. This mutual influence shows up the artifice of separating the two spheres.

The socialist revolution has not always been able to cross the threshold of the family. Open forms of discrimination are repressed (although they are not uncommon). But women suffer more from hidden oppression. The role of women as domestic servants is never questioned, nor is the lack of responsibility on the part of men for domestic chores and looking after the children. As in other socialist countries, women's emancipation (notably their enhanced participation in production which should *ipso facto* bring them economic independence and liberation) consists in reality in working a 'double day': alongside a full-time job in the factory, the school or the office, women had to manage the home, look after the children and remain socially and politically active.

The difficulty women have in continuing to be active in all domains is well reflected in the responses of the women interviewed in the survey of 1,479 working women, mentioned above (Simisevic, *Zena izmedju rada i porodice*, 1975). To the question, which in itself says a great deal about the alternatives open to women, 'should women work or be simply mother and housewife and why?', almost half the women declared themselves in favour of the mother-housewife alternative only. However, 51.3% still chose the mother-housewife-worker alternative, despite the difficulties that every woman listed. These latter thought that part-time work would be a solution for them (since it would enable them to devote more of their time to domestic chores).

The existence of the 'double day' is openly recognized and condemned: 'If women work and at the same time have the burden of domestic and family chores, this cannot be the basis of their emancipation but the doubling of their slavery' (Suvar, 1980, p. 19). After the revolution, services (i.e. other women) and domestic appliances were expected to perform the domestic duties of the working mother. This solution turned out to be altogether impracticable; there were not enough or appropriate institutions or services while domestic appliances, which were to revolutionize a 'technologically primitive' family, have not reduced the amount of time women spend washing and cleaning but only their efforts and their suffering. But it remains the case that the socialization of family functions (meaning implicitly the functions of women) continues to be the officially declared goal. How near is it?

The access of children to pre-school institutions is a valid indicator of the possibility women have of being able to work outside the home and be involved in other public activities. Given that, in Yugoslavia, since the revolution the accent has been on enabling women to work, it might have been expected that the problem of child care would have been solved. Not at all — a Yugoslav child less than three years old has only a 2.4% chance of getting into a creche, and if he is between three and seven (schooling in Yugoslavia begins at seven) this probability rises to a mere 11.6% (*Women and Development*, Principal Statistical Information, 1977). It is true that women have between six months and a year of unpaid maternity leave (and even between one and two years) while their jobs remain open. But it still remains the case that the number of nurseries and creches is absolutely inadequate to meet the need. Most such institutions are in the developed regions and in the urban centres. In the villages and small towns, it is the traditional family structure that still continues to be the main framework in which children are looked after and educated.

Whether the child is among the few who go to an institution, such as a creche or a nursery, or is looked after at home, the model of socialization is not radically different: the working mother almost always has a female substitute to perform part of her role: grandmothers, aunts, cousins, older girls or sometimes, in well-off families, house-girls. In pre-school institutions it is again women who are responsible for bringing up the children. Fathers and men, until they become grandparents and retire, have little to do with the bringing-up of children and their responsibility for socialization is less.

The availability of female substitutes, within or outside the family, might be partly responsible for the persistence of the age-old division of sexual roles and the infrequency of disputes between men and women on this issue. Women themselves do not think of their male partners as potential helpers or participants in housework. In the representative survey cited above, only 7.6% of the women mention the possibility that their husband might help them in the house, in their response to the question, 'How could the burden of housework be lightened?' Twice as many mention a house-girl or a paid help. But the majority thinks of the organized services or the help of their own children along with labour-saving devices (Simisevic, *Zena izmedju rada i porodice*, 1975).

The socialist idea of women's emancipation is often limited to the public domain. The little that is said about what happens in the family rarely questions the sexual division of labour. On the contrary, hypothetical solutions are advanced to alleviate women's work in the house — as if it was naturally the role of women to carry the burden of both the house and looking after the children.[3]

Men are spared household chores and they continue to consider them demeaning. This domain of private life remains open not only to influences of all sorts from the mass media but also to discrimination even in the framework of institutional equality. It is most apparent in matters directly linked to sexual relations. Women are still beaten and molested, rape being the most extreme but still common example. In his study of cases before the Zagreb tribunals, Sklevicky (1979) shows that public opinion still generally believes that rape is provoked by the woman. Before the tribunals women are treated more as the guilty parties than as victims, whereas rapists can often count on extenuating circumstances. Consequently, rape is not always reported.

Abortion is another example. Legally abortion is available up to the tenth week of pregnancy. For later terminations of pregnancy beyond this limit, the woman must be examined by a doctor and obtain the approval of a commission of several doctors. According to the survey that I carried out among emigrant Yugoslav women (Morokvasic, 1980, 1981) this whole procedure, including the abortion, can be extremely humiliating and distressing.

Parallel influences

The open recognition that the position of women in Yugoslavia does not correspond with the proclaimed ideal is often associated with the view that in this area socialism runs up against two sorts of obstacles: the legacy of the past and foreign influences, notably the values of the Western middle classes and the consumer society. We shall now consider these obstacles.

The past: historical and cultural roots

The socialist revolution in Yugoslavia took place in a backward country where capitalism was only in its infancy. Erlich's study (1971, 1976) covering 300 Yugoslav villages in 1939 is a valuable document on the period preceding the post-war changes. The work covered seven 'historic' regions of Yugoslavia (excluding Slovenia). These regions, according to the author, embraced all the area of modern patriarchalism.

The basis of the patriarchal system is the *zadruga* (Byrnes, 1967; Karadzic, Djuritc, 1967), a type of extended family that used to be found in all parts of the country except in Slovenia. Within the *zadrugas* a subsistence economy developed and the nuclear family had a specific place in it. Because it represented an age-old way of life, the individual as such did not really count; he or she belonged to the family group. The sexual relationship between men and women was only one possible relationship in the *zadruga* and not the most important one.

At the time of Erlich's survey, the *zadrugas* were intact in some regions, whereas in others they were disintegrating under the influence of the money economy. Today only a few *zadrugas* survive, although the values on which they were based are preserved in the modern nuclear family (Buric, 1973; Vujacic, 1973). The position of women must be analysed in the context of their relations with other members of the family. The basic principle of most *zadrugas* was that the male members did not leave the house, the family nucleus; it was women who were exchanged. This is reminiscent of other similar formations in the Mediterranean (Tillion, 1974). When a girl married, she acceded not only to the status of spouse but, more importantly, to the status of daughter-in-law. She entered the house of her parents-in-law's family; by marriage she acquired the lowest rank in her new house and 'many years, even decades passed before she reacquired any position of respect' (Erlich, 1976, p. 228).

The men's authority was almost never questioned. Erlich noted however that it was gradually being undermined particularly in the regions that had never known Turkish rule (Slovenia and northern Croatia). Everywhere the subordinate position of women was enshrined in rituals: a woman kissed the hand of old men, she had to take her husband's and her father-in-law's shoes off and wash their feet, she stood while they were eating, she served at table and never ate with them herself.

The husband's authority was declining, particularly in regions where emigration was widespread (the coast and the islands). Apparently, migrants returning from Australia or America treated their wives with respect. Added to this was another source of respect for women which still remains valid today: in the absence of the men, women undertook farming work normally done by men and thus acquired equal rights and won their respect (Erlich, 1972, p. 292). Women generally accepted their lot with resignation. The only protests were individual ones without consciousness of the fact that other women shared the same lot. Women usually explained this individual resistance in terms of how hard their work was or by their contribution to the household through their dowry. Women's resistance was particularly strong in Serbia where their subjection was most marked and where they were harshly treated by their husbands. The author maintained that, in many regions, wife-beating was part of the prevailing ethos to such an extent that a woman who was never beaten might consult the doctor, thinking that there must be something wrong between her and her husband (p. 260). Sayings cited by Erlich illustrate the position of women in some parts of the country:

'Woman is the most backward of creatures.'
'Boast about the quality of your wheat when it's in your barn and your wife when she's in her grave.'

'Trust neither dog nor woman.'
(Bosnia)

'The husband has the right to beat his wife.'
'Beat a woman and a horse every three days.'
'If you don't beat a woman she'll go mad in forty days.'
'Every woman has an extra rib.'
(Serbia)

Dr Vera Smiljnanic, a Belgrade psychologist, is currently analysing Yugoslav sayings and proverbs in order better to understand the condition of women in the recent past (*Svijet*, 7 August 1981).

According to Erlich, the position of women was bad everywhere in 1939. Women had to be submissive and remain as invisible as possible. But the author concluded that profound changes were underway, notably in places where women were putting up resistance and where structural changes were being made. Where the patriarchal system was being shaken, as in Serbia, violence towards women had increased but so too had women's reponses. In the regions where the patriarchal system has disintegrated violence was rare and women showed a degree of consciousness and self-confidence (Slavonia, the Vojvodina and the islands notably). Where the patriarchal system had remained almost intact relations between men and women were without cruelty and violence, provided women observed the rules — which they did resignedly and almost fatalistically.

In more recent Yugoslav works the woman question is treated in the framework of the sociology of the family. Buric (1973–7) endeavours to show the continuities between the *zadruga* and the modern family. While the structure of the *zadrugas* is disappearing, some aspects of it are perpetuated today in behaviour, values and even in institutional forms. While the practice of more than one family living together has virtually disappeared from Yugoslav society (1973, p. 97), very strong family ties still exist between the core family and members of the family. Modernization and urbanization have not been able to weaken these. One of the important features of the *zadruga*, collectivism, is reflected today in feelings of solidarity extending beyond the confines of the family.

Principles of egalitarianism and democratic decision-making were applied in the *zadruga* as an economic unit. But they did not apply either to women or to the private relations between men and women in the framework of the nuclear (conjugal) families constituting the *zadruga*, in which the master was always the man.

> Given this, the present-day nuclear family could not inherit the egalitarianism and democatic decision-making of the nuclear family within the *zadruga*. The oppression and subordination of women in the nuclear family in the *zadruga* were later only strengthened by the legislation on marriage. Women had to fight for egalitarian relations within the family . . . This struggle is not yet over (Buric, 1973, p. 97).

The Halperns, American anthropologists, have carried out several studies in Yugoslavia (Halpern and Halpern, 1967, 1972, 1975). They stress the changes that have taken place in the roles of men and women and in the perception of these roles. Like Erlich and other authors, they assert that conjugal relations cannot be understood outside other kinship relations. Their most interesting papers are their monographs on the Serbian village of Orasac (1967 and 1972). The first gives a picture of village life in the 1950s against a historical background. The second one deals mainly with changes that took place in the following decade. It brings out the continual clashes between the old values and the new socialist values, the market economy and industrialization, and examines the consequences of these clashes.

> In Yugoslavia, social evolution in a technological context is occurring in terms of vigorous interaction with the still existing although greatly modified traditional rural subculture. It is out of this dynamic, and reciprocal interaction, where urban-derived ideologies and technologies affect rural life, and where village values temper the ways in which towns grow, that the future is being shaped.

Contradicting Erlich, who speaks of the disintegration of the extended family, the Halperns observe that the *zadrugas* have only undergone a 'reformulation' by moving from a rather lateral organization to a linear extension over several generations, implying the progressive disappearance of fraternal kinship links and the strengthening of the husband–wife relationship. At the same time, the modernization of the countryside has brought more agricultural work for women (p. 81), and more respect. As before, the position of the newly married bride (*snaha*) is far from enviable but she apparently acquires a higher status as soon as she bears a child (p. 103–4).

The consumer society

Despite the stress officially laid on the role of women as workers and producers and on their increased participation in public life, in everyday life and in the mass media, women are housewives, mothers and above all consumers.

International Women's Day, 8 March, is one of the numerous contradictions confronting Yugoslav women. They are given flowers and a little more attention than during the other 364 days of the year. But the buffet food in the enterprise is prepared and served by women. The choice of texts about the revolution used in schools is sometimes such that you might wonder whether Yugoslav women took part in the socialist revolution and the war at all, other than as mothers and sisters of male heroes who died for the country. Yet it is known that 20% of the female population took an active part in the revolution and that one-third of the two million dead were women. The day marked by festivities and banners proclaiming 'Long live 8 March' is becoming more and more, in a consumer society, like Mother's Day in the West.

The mass media are full of advice about 'the most suitable gift for your mother or wife'. The gifts suggested are ones considered useful in the home: pressing irons, cookers or other household gadgets, home management books or beauty guides. These things are generally very expensive and represent a real sacrifice for the family budget. Many cannot afford them, they become a sort of ideal, a model to aspire to.

Not only are women pushed into buying consumer goods, but their names and bodies are used to sell products. Advertising is often degrading and humiliating to women. Their bodies are portrayed vulgarly in numerous women's and other magazines. This portrayal of women in the media has already been strongly criticized in Yugoslavia (Pavlic, 1980).

Discrimination may begin from birth: the birth of a daughter can still be considered as a family tragedy by the father (but the times when women could be beaten for having given birth to a daughter are dead and gone). It is still believed that the woman is 'responsible' for the birth of a daughter whereas a man will be boasting of the son he has just 'made' — if the newborn is a boy.

The differential socialization that girls and boys undergo prepares them from their earliest years for their roles in society. The toy-seller will ask, just as in a shop in a Western country, whether the toy is for a girl or a boy. Books for children and picture-books (often quite simply translated from Italian or French with no concern at all for the values being peddled) portray girls as weaker, not always intelligent, in women's occupations, surrounded by pretty pink things and flowers. Rajka and Milan Polic's study (1979) reaches conclusions similar to those of studies made in France or Great Britain. There are fewer female characters in the books, women have the stereotyped roles of mother, housewife, nurse or teacher, and they are given more negative traits than boys.

By the time they reach adulthood women are very well prepared. But their training continues; many handbooks, guides and encyclopaedias for women aim at helping them to become perfect hostesses and mistresses of the house, and good cooks, while at the same time keeping their beauty; the professional side is only touched on in passing; girls are advised to become air hostesses or secretaries. All this has nothing to do with the socialist idea of the place of women in society. Yet it is the image peddled in the media, books and pamphlets that are on sale in the shops and which, with skilful advertising, affect consumers sensitive to any innovation that does not simply make a *tabula rasa* of the past but gives it a modern dress. It is perhaps useful to stress that the media are made by and for urbanized populations and that the image of the urbanized woman remains for the rest of the population a desirable model; but it is one that is difficult to attain unless they migrate to towns in Yugoslavia or abroad.

Of socialist ideals: old struggles and present debates

We have already stressed the gap between the ideals, law and reality. The women's question is not completely settled. At the present time in Yugoslav society there is a debate on the direction emancipation should take.

This debate has a basis in tradition. Between 1870 and 1880 a Serbian socialist, Svetozar Markovic, had resolutely come out in favour of rights for women. He had defended their right to education and work in an essay, 'Are women capable of being equal to men?' His successor, one of the leaders of the Serbian Social-Democratic Party, Dimitrije Tucovic, promoted the setting-up of the secretariat for social-democratic women in 1910. In their newspaper *Jednakost* (Equality) they distinguished themselves from bourgeois feminism and linked the women's struggle and the class struggle.

With industrialization, which accelerated after 1945, women moved into production in large numbers. But the fear of seeing an independent women's organization develop still prevails today and there is a tendency to cling to the view that the struggle for women's emancipation will progress through their participation in all sorts of social activities. But people continue to discuss and this discussion itself is provoked by the reaction of women to the situation assigned to them: the fact — as we have already stated — that they take refuge in passivity and, crushed by the multiplicity of tasks to be done, give up participating in political life.

This is because economic independence and active participation in political and social life are seen as the key to their equality with men (*Nin*, 19 March 1976) with the responsibility resting on society to 'take their place in the functions that they presently have in the family'.

Djorjevic (1975), however, in the introduction to his anthology of Marxist texts on the women's question, defends another position; he stresses that working women in Yugoslavia, as in other socialist countries, are all victims of a specific exploitation because of their 'double day'.

> There exists a conservative position, defended not only by men, according to which housework is naturally women's work and this work is not socially significant ... Whence the guilt feeling among housewives who do not perform socially useful work ... It does not accord with a Marxist approach to eliminate domestic work from the concept of the social division of labour ... only an extremely formalist and economistic approach does not recognize housework as labour ... Progressive circles suggest that housewives should receive wages, including retirement pensions ... and one can find no justification for the exclusion of housewives as productive workers from the group of producers and workers (Djorjevic, 1975, p. 110–11).

Since women, precisely because of their double day and their unrecognized domestic burden, cannot become more active in political life where decisions are taken, the chairmanship of the Central Committee of the League of Yugoslav Communists can conclude that what is needed is to struggle 'against all deviations and types of resistance ... to overcome various conservative and backward conceptions such as the patriarchal, feminist or economistic approach' (25 June 1981).

Among sociologists, those who condemn feminism have a tendency to see it as a homogeneous movement of women against men (Suvar, 1980; Letica, 1980). Suvar attributes to feminism conceptions that few feminists today would consider as theirs, for example that women are slaves in the family because production takes place outside the family. Letica (1980), in his manifesto against feminism, asserts that the women's question has been solved in Yugoslavia, and that in comparison to other more important questions (such as housing, or the peasant question) it has received too much attention. The majority, however, are against these extreme positions and reject unilateral conceptions of feminism as a 'sex war'; seeking rather to see in it a theoretical and practical attempt to change the position of women in society (Papic, 1980; Cacinovic-Puhovski 1980; Pesic, 1980).

One thing is certain: for the time being, there is no independent school of thought in Yugoslavia, whether described as feminism or otherwise, reflecting the needs and problems of *all women*. What could be called a feminist school, if it is seen only as the expression of a small stratum among urbanized intellectual women, will probably find it difficult to have any impact in a country where over half the female population lives in the countryside. But all beginnings are difficult and that should not be a reason for giving up.

Conclusion

Socialism has institutionalized equality. It guarantees women legal protection against abuses and discrimination. With the structural changes that it has brought about in society, it has opened the doors of public life to women, whereas in many more developed countries women are still more or less excluded.

However, in the area of relations between men and women, at the level of attitudes and behaviour, we can see few changes.

Deeply rooted customs and values are difficult to uproot if men and women together, consciously, in their struggle for socialism, do not also struggle to change their relations.

It would seem that apparently contradictory value systems operate in Yugoslavia: socialism, the consumer society and the old patriarchal values. The first two affect mainly the urban and developed parts of the country, while the third is found almost everywhere but takes the most oppressive form in the rural and least developed parts of the country.

The villages have, to a degree, retained a pure, even puritanical, image of women, as opposed to the rather vulgar sexual object that can be found in the mass media. For this reason, in the eyes of the village people, the emancipation or liberation of women often means becoming 'easy women', who adopt the loose morals of the towns — virginity is still highly prized. It is feared that once young women go to town or abroad they will not even think of returning to the village to get married.

The case of Yugoslavia, like that of other socialist countries (Scott, 1976), shows that change in the relations of production is not automatically followed by a radical change in the position of women in all areas of social life. Social cultural and economic forces make it difficult to put socialist ideals into practice.

As for Yugoslavia in particular, it can be said that the achievement of the socialist ideal of the equality and emancipation of women through their active participation in production and public life, and the appearance of a new identity for women and new relations with men, are constantly being hindered by the values transmitted by the mass media and upheld by the old patriarchal system.

The country's transition to socialism, although necessary for the emancipation of women, is not sufficient. 'Women's' questions direct thinking to more universal goals. It is thus that change in the position of women in society must go in tandem with change in the position of men themselves and their relations with one another. So long as that is not achieved, women cannot be satisfied with mere formal equality with men.

Clara Zetkin before the October Revolution and Alexandra Kollontai after it, like many other socialist women of their time, drew attention to the need to continue the fight. But what fight, for what type of relations between men and women, for what type of family? Socialist theory, like socialist practice, has remained silent about the 'private' domain and has paid attention only to defining the position of women in the public domain. Faced with this silence, the door has been open to influences of all sorts which have variously affected women: to feminism, which has affected a small stratum of women intellectuals and which still seems foreign to the vast majority, to the influences of the past and to an image of women peddled by the mass media which has an enormous impact and affects the vast majority of the population.

Deeply-rooted views on the natural character of sexual roles and the sexual division of labour have not been counteracted. The result of this is that most women in Yugoslavia, rather than getting involved in the fight to change their condition, simply opt out.

But Yugoslav women are more and more conscious of the rights that socialism gives them. They have all adopted the idea that the strength of women lies in their economic independence vis-a-vis men and more and more of them are seeking paid employment. Those of them who have not found any in Yugoslavia have sought it abroad (about 10% of the non-agricultural working female population).

Paris, June 1982

Notes

1. In Serbo-Croatian: *mecovita domacinstva*.

2. The letter from the 24 housewives is too long to be translated in full. Two main points in the letter should be stressed: the first concerns the housewives' request to be officially recognized as workers with social security (sickness insurance, old age pensions, etc.) and other rights that workers have legally. The difference between a housewife and a house-girl, says the letter, 'lies in the fact that the house-girl works in other people's homes, eight hours a day, with paid holidays, sickness insurance and the right to a pension'. The second point concerns the argument in the request in which it is agreed that it is appropriate for women to work at home. It is even postulated in the letter that if a solution could be found, many working women would leave their jobs so that 'young people could more easily have access to jobs and not have to go abroad'.

3. Some writers see obstacles in the population and think that the progressive ideology about the family cannot be welcomed favourably in some strata of Yugoslav society: Buric (1971), for example, says that the material, cultural and other resources of the *lower strata* (my italics, M.M.) did not correspond to the progressive ideology proclaimed by Yugoslav society.

Bibliography

Buric, O. (1971), 'Modernization of the Family and Inconsistency of its Structure: A Model for Family Transformation Research', *International Journal of Sociology of the Family*, Vol. 1, No. 2, pp. 1–16.

——— (1972), 'Polozaj Zene u Sistemu Drustvene moci u Jugoslaviji' (The position of women in the system of social power in Yugoslavia), *Sociologija*.

——— (1973), 'Novi tip nepotpune porodice' (A new type of incomplete family), *Sociologija*, No. 2, pp. 245–75.

Byrnes, R.F. (ed.) (1967), *Communal Families in the Balkans: The Zadruga*, University of Notre Dame Press, Notre Dame, London.

Cacinovic Puhovski, N. (1980), 'Pokusaj teoretskog odredjenja feministicke poszicije' (Essay to situate the feminist position theoretically), *Zena* (Zagreb), vol. 38, No. 4–5, pp. 56–8.

Denic, B. (1976), 'Urbanisation and women's roles in Yugoslavia', *Anthropological Quarterly*, vol. 49, No. 1, pp. 11–19.

Djordjevic, J. (1975), *Zensko pitanje* (the women question), Belgrade, Radnicka stampa.

Djuric, V. (ed.) (1967), *Vukovi Zapisi*, Srpska Knjizevna Zadruga, pp. 63–4.

Erbeznik-Fuks, M. (1972), 'Drustveno ekonomiski polozaj, zdravstveno l socijaino stanje zema boraca koje zive na porrucju Zagreba' (The socio-economic position, living conditions and health of former women combatants presently living on the territory of Zagreb), *Zena*, No. 3–4.

Erlich, V. (1971), *Jugoslavenska porodica u transformaciji* (the Yugoslav family in transition), Zagreb.

——— (1976), *Family in Transition*, Princeton University Press.

First, R. (1969), 'Struktura autoriteta u seoskim domacinstvima' (The structure of authority in rural households), *Sociologija*, No. 23–4, pp. 53–60.

——— (1973), 'Struktura moci u porodici zaposiene zene' (The structure of power in the family of women who work outside the home), *Sociologija*.

Halpern, J. (1967), *A Serbian Village*, New York, Harper and Row.

Halpern, J. and Halpern B. (1972), *A Serbian Village in Historical Perspective*, Holt, Rinehart and Winston.

——— (1975), 'Promene u shvatanjima o ulogama muza i zene u pet jugoslovenskih sela', (Changes in the conceptions of women's and men's roles in five Yugoslav villages), Belgrade, Museum of Ethnology, January, pp. 161–73.

Kirsch, S. (1978), *Die Pantherfrau, Fünf Frauen in der DDR*, Rororo, Rowohlt Taschenbuch Verlag, Reinbeck bei Hamburg.

Letica, S. (1980), 'O Vaginocentricnom konceptu zdravlja zene i patologiji emancipacije',

Zena, No. 4-5, pp. 62-5.

Markovic, S. (1960), *Sabrani Spisi* (Complete works), vol. 1: Je li zena sposobna da bude ravnopravna sa muskarcem? (Can woman be the equal of man?), pp. 212-24.

Morokvasic, M. (1981), 'Prendre les risques: femmes immigrées entre la contraception et l'avortement', *Temps modernes*, May, pp. 1933-52.

––––– (1980), *Yugoslav Migrant Women in France, Germany and Sweden*, Paris, CNRS and FNSP, p. 642, mimeo.

Mosely, P. (1976), 'The Peasant Family: The Zadruga, or Communal Joint Family in the Balkans and its Recent Evolution' in: Byrnes, R.F. (ed.): *Communal Families in the Balkans: the Zadruga*, University of Notre Dame Press.

Papic, Z. (1980), 'Emancipacija u granicama tradicionalne svesti', (Emancipation in the limits of traditional consciousness), *Zena*, vol. 38, No. 4-5, pp. 94-7, Zagreb.

Pavlic, B. (1980), 'Sredstva masovnih komunikacija, element odrzanja postojeceg' (The mass media, a factor for maintaining the status quo), *Zena*, vol. 38, No. 4-5, pp. 94-7, Zagreb.

Pesic, V. (1980), 'Skica za kritiku ideologije o zenskom pitanju' (Outline for a critique of the ideology of the women's question), *Zena*, vol. 38, No. 4-5 , pp. 59-61.

Pesic, Z. (1962), 'Moraini problemi u odnosima izmedju muskarca i zene' (Ethical problems in the relations between men and women), Belgrade, Rad.

Pocek-Matic, M. (1975), 'Svoju novu ulogu i svoje mjesto u drustvu zena je stekla kao vojnik Revolucije' (Women have acquired their position in society as soldiers of the Revolution), *Zena*, No. 2.

Polic, R. and Polic, M. (1979), 'Djecji udzvenici o (ne) ravnopravnosti medju polovima', *Zena*, No. 1, pp. 12-28.

Rind, A. (1980), *Etre femme à l'Est*, Paris, Stock.

Scott, H. (1976), *Women and Socialism*, London, Allison and Busby.

Seferagic, D. (1973), 'Pokreti za oslovodjenje zena — zapostavnjeni problem radnickog pokreta' (Women's liberation movements, neglected problems of the workers' movement), *Pregled*, No. 2-3, pp. 241-52, Sarajevo.

Simisevic, I. (1975), 'Funkcija Zaposlene zene u drustvu' (The function of the economically active women in society), *Zena izmedju rada i porodice*, (Woman between work and family), Zagreb, Institute of Social Research.

Sklevicky, L. (1978), 'When a woman says no it means no', in: *Drug-ca zena* (Women's question: a new approach), Belgrade, Student Cultural Centre, pp. 62-72, mimeo.

Stora-Szandor, J. (1971), *Alexandra Kollontai: Marxisme et Révolution Sexuelle*, Paris, Maspero.

Suvar, S. (1980), 'Drustveni polozaj i uloga zene u razvoju socijalistickog samoupravijanja' (The social status and role of women in the development of self-managing socialism), *Zena*, vol. 38, No. 4-5, pp. 13-23, Zagreb.

Tillion, G. (1974), *Le Harem et les Cousins*, Paris, Seuil.

Tomsic, V. (1973), 'The Status of Women and Family Planning in Yugoslavia', *Faits et Tendances*, No. 10, pp. 57-80, Belgrade.

––––– (1980), *Women in the Development of Socialist Self-Managing Yugoslavia*, Belgrade, Jugoslovenski Pregled.

Vujacic, M. (1977), *Transformacija patrijarhalne porodice u Crnoj Gori* (The transformation of the patriarchal family in Montenegro), Belgrade, Slovo Ljubve.

Volgyes, I. & N. (1977), *The Liberated Female, Life, Work and Sex in Socialist Hungary*, Boulder, Colorado, Westview Press.

Wander, M. (1978), *Guten Morgen du Schöne, Die Frauen in der DDR*, Luchterland Verlag, Darmstadt.

Wertheimer-Baletic, A. (1970), 'Demografske rezerve zenske radne snage u Jugoslaviji', *Ekonomski Pregled*, No. 2, pp. 3-21.

Zena u Drustvu i privredi Jugoslavije (Women and society in the Yugoslav economy) (1973), Belgrade, Federal Bureau of Statistics.

Zena izmedju rada i porodice (Women between work and family) (1975), Zagreb, Institute of Social Sciences.

Zetkin, C. (1980), *Batailles pour les femmes*, Paris, Editions sociales.

Fatna and Her Village in Fayoum (Egypt)

Evelyne Porret

At the end of Lake Karoun, in the Fayoum oasis, there is a small hamlet called Ezba Tounes. The road there goes across cultivated fields, there is no road all the way round the edge of the lake. It is a very bad road, it doesn't go into the *ezba*, a path runs down to the houses behind the village across desert-like terrain. In front, crops are growing: fields of onions, tomatoes, corn and sesame are interspersed with palm trees that go down to the lake — a very blue lake, with sand hills in the distance; no modern buildings spoil the beauty of the place. The village is built of yellow ochre, corn and sand, with a few houses of stone. All the people are peasants (*fellahin*). They have animals, sheep, goats, cows and cow-buffaloes (*gamoussas*). Some fish. One single *fellah* owns a boat. Some families sell tea, sugar, rice and cigarettes.

It is said that the largest house in the village was built by a stranger (*khawaga*) called Karam. This man was a Copt. The grandfather of the people living there now, who own most of the land, is said to have bought it from this *khawaga*. That was in the time when 'the English with their big red faces came to sell them cigarettes' — it is even said that they used to take women and children to make them work. People were afraid of them. So it was Hag Ibrahim who, having bought the *ezba*, brought in most of the people, the parents and grandparents of those there now. Almost all the *fellahin* work for the family of the rich men, they till the land and share the harvests — half goes to the owner, half to the tiller. Some of them have their own pieces of land, but most are poverty-stricken. So, for several years now, the men have been going to work in Libya, Saudi Arabia and Kuwait to earn more; they come back, buy land and build a better house. Their children look after the crops. They have the *sherka* system for animals too, and they buy a cow between them, put it with a *fellah* who has some *bersim* (Egyptian alfalfa) and each gets half the profit when the calf is sold. In the village, some are poor and some are richer, but all live very simply with few possessions. There is still no electricity, they say it's coming, you can see iron poles along the path, but nothing seems to be happening. There is one tap for drinking water for the whole village. But it is dry almost every summer and sometimes even during the winter. So all the women fill their jugs at the stream, and let it stand in the *zir* (a big pot) to allow the impurities to settle before drinking it. Each family makes its own bread. You cannot find bread to buy. Fatna or her daughter fetch water every day on their heads. Another woman comes to sell butter, and eggs, a third makes us a bread oven or large mud and sun-dried straw pots to store the grain, or other things we need for our work. While they work, drinking tea, they talk. Our watchman, Abdel Bassir, also passes by, sits down on the mat in the workshop and tells us about the village and everything. He's a great story-teller. People in general enjoy laughing and talking and telling stories. Few can read.

Fatna, 1978

'Tell me how you were circumcised.'
'I was afraid when the midwife came. She comes to the village for two days, she takes a pound from each mother with a daughter of ten, twelve, thirteen. My mother said to me, "It's nothing, don't worry, it doesn't hurt!" She took me on her knees, and, quickly, she cut. I screamed, it hurt. I couldn't walk. The pain lasted for a month or two, and then they took this powder . . . You know, the termites eat the dry fronds of the palm tree, that are on the roof and it leaves a powder . . . It's the only thing that cured me.'
'And will you have it done to your daughter?'
She turned towards Amel, her daughter, 'Do you think you couldn't have it done to you?' Amel laughs.
'Do you know that where we come from no one does it?'
She looks at me, amazed. 'Listen: here the only woman in the village who still has a little bit of clitoris left, she's sick about it, she doesn't dare go out, she's afraid of getting married. All the women who still have a little bit of clitoris left want to go back to the midwife.'
'And what would happen if you didn't have it done to your daughter?'
Silence.
'But listen, that's impossible, no one's ever tried. It's not possible. Yes, I know, in Cairo they say it's not done any more. The doctors told two of the Hag's daughters, the rich man in the village, that they shouldn't do it. But can you see them staying with this great big thing?' And she shows me a whole finger.
'Don't you think that men work rather less than women?'
'Oh yes, we can all do what they do: go to the fields, pick the weeds, take the spade, the hoe, build cupboards of mud and straw, make bread ovens. But what about them, can they cook? Can they look after babies? Can they make bread? And when they come home who makes them their tea? And if they are a little off colour, they complain a lot, so you say to them, my brother, what's the matter? You tap him on the back, you take his hands, you feel his neck.' She mimes it all. She speaks more softly.
'You say to him: here, take the blanket, be careful not to catch cold. Then he takes all the blankets you give him and goes to lie down waiting for someone to look after him. And when we are sick, can they do anything except go and buy pills? And when my husband was in Libya, I was the one who did everything. I looked after the cow that I had hired, I went to the fields, and I had the children. When he came back from Libya, he had presents but all his money had been stolen. So we had a big row. When I don't agree, I say so.'

*'Do you know that where we come from, women are fed up with all that and they
march in the streets saying that they want no more of men like that?'*
'Yes, we, too, we get angry, we go back to our fathers — and then a week later, the
husband sends someone to look for us and we go back. Can you live without
men? I was about sixteen when one day my friends said to me one morning as we
were fetching water, "Mabrouk!" (congratulations). I didn't know why. I went
and saw my mother. "What's happening?" "Last night Mahmoud came, he read
the *Fatha* (the marriage *sura* in the Koran) with your father. He's for you."'
'Were you happy?'
'Happy, unhappy, what do I know? I was young, I didn't understand
anything.'
'Did you know him?'
'Yes, I used to see him when I went to fetch water. Sometimes he used to joke
with me. Yes, I quite liked him. He was better than the others. But from the day
when I learned that he wanted to marry me, I ran away when I saw him. When he
used to come to the house, it wasn't me who took him tea — I used to hide. It's not
like the girls now who take tea to their fiancé, who go into the room if he's there!
Six months later he married me.'

As I wanted to know whether circumcision prevented her from reaching a
climax, I asked her details about the beginnings of her marriage.

'The first week, it was rather hard. It hurt. You want to go back to your mother,
then you get used to it.'
'And what is it like? Do you enjoy it?'
She sat down and looked round to make sure we were alone. She took on a
special look, her eyes were shining. She said, 'Look, he comes to you, this man —
he takes you — he puts his penis between your legs — he moves around a little
and then he enters. After a short time he begins to move about a lot, he starts
breathing heavily — his whole body is thrusting and then, he comes — then you
too, you begin to thrust, you feel something coming and then you come too. And
you stay close to him, and then you get up. You bring him water to wash with.
You're happy, and that's life.'
'But do you always come?'
'No, sometimes you go for a month or even two without coming. But he comes
every time.'
*'Where I come from there are women who never come, have you ever heard of that here,
are there any women like that?'*
'Never, never, no I've never heard of a woman who never comes. I don't know.'

'My first child died. He lived for 55 days. It was a Friday. He was twisting and
turning. He had stomach ache. It was a boy, he was called Mohammed. The
others, the people in the *ezba* said to me, "He'll get over it!" But I was afraid. And
on Saturday morning, when I wanted to go to the dispensary, he was dead.
Mahmoud said, "It's what the Lord sends us, can you be angry with God?" And
can you guess what he did? He switched on the radio and sat down on the *hassira*
(mat). I thought that I ought not to be sad, but each time I saw his little clothes, I
cried. One night I dreamed that a woman and a young man came to my house,
they were carrying some sugar-cane and brought me a white cotton dress, like
you find in the *souk*, for my baby. I said, "But he's dead!" They said, "No, take it",
and I saw my baby. I said, "But I've got no more milk, how am I going to feed

141

him?" They held out the sugar-cane and I sucked it — the milk came back, I took my baby and he drank. I was so happy that I woke up. I looked for my little Mohammed everywhere. He wasn't there, of course. Then I told my mother-in-law about my dream. She said to me, "Luck is with you, you'll soon have another son, don't worry." From that day my bleeding didn't happen again and I had a second boy.'

(Fatna is pregnant again, for the seventh time.)
'I've got a pain in the belly, I've a headache, I don't understand what's happening, yet I'm used to it.' She is twenty-seven.

'I wonder why I feel ill. Do you know that yesterday I walked past a man who said, "Hallo, Fatna! You're looking very good, what's happened to you? Are you eating for two?" I didn't pay any attention to him, I thought he'd said it as a joke. And then, in the evening, when I really had a bad headache, I suddenly thought about him again and thought he'd given me bad luck. The evil eye. When I was small, my father always used to say, "When you feel that someone is saying something nice to you, paying you a compliment that seems to be hiding something, say to yourself secretly, God is great, between Him and me there is nothing. In this way, you don't annoy the person who's giving you the evil eye and if he wants to hurt you, our Lord will take away from you the evil he's done you." But I didn't think about that then, I didn't reply to him and I said nothing to myself. I think it's because of that everything is hurting me.

I got angry with my sister-in-law and her husband. I haven't been on speaking terms with them for a long time. When Mahmoud went to Libya, he asked his brother to look after us. Isn't he the eldest brother? In the beginning, they didn't ask how I was and I didn't have the time to go and see them. I was looking after everything on my own: the fields, the bread, the shopping, the children. One holiday when everybody here ate meat, I didn't have any money. I was out the whole day in the fields and in the evening I met servants of the Hag's family (the land-owners) threshing corn. I helped them until sunset. They gave me fifteen piastres. I bought five piastres' worth of rice, ten of butter. I already had onions and tomatoes, I did some cooking so that at least the children should have something cooked to eat. When I was out at the front of the house I heard my sister-in-law's daughter call my friend Kherna, who lives next door. Her husband was in Libya too. They were bringing her a plate of corn with some meat on top. When you have something to eat on festival days, you ought to send something to those in need. When Kherna saw that no one had given me anything, she was surprised. "What, not your family?" and she wanted to give me what she had left. But I said to her, "I would never touch anything that comes from them!" And yet when Mahmoud sent a parcel from Libya, there were some *galabeyas* for them and for us. In the fields sometimes I couldn't do everything on my own. I needed one or two men to help me. In the evening, when they came home, of course I made them a glass of tea — after all they'd helped me. Then, do you know what they started saying? That men were coming and going all day long in my house. I even saw Ahmed, Mahmoud's brother, on top of the wall opposite our house. And with all they were saying about me, do you know what happened to them? They had a daughter who was getting quite big. One day she was alone in the house — you know Deif — he managed to get into her house and take her and stroke her breasts. Men are like dogs, as soon as they see something they fancy, they can't control themselves. And they said that men did the same things to me.

When Mahmoud came back he didn't believe it, he wanted me to be reconciled with them. But my sister-in-law didn't want to be. I think they are jealous of me because I can do everything, and need nobody. Mahmoud believes and agrees with me now.

Mahmoud went to Libya a second time. He left his money with a Syrian who was to give it back to him in Cairo. When I heard about that I shouted, I cried and wanted to go back to my mother's. And then I calmed down. He went back a third time to Libya. He found the Syrian and got his money back. He sent us *galabeyas* made of shiny cloth and then when he came back he again left his money with the Syrian. This time he never found him. He looked all over Cairo but the Syrian was not to be found. He went away three times and we're no better off than before.'

'No, I don't plant vegetables, why plant vegetables in fields that are not ours? So that the rich family can take half and the children trample all over the rest? The fields are not near our house and you can't watch them. Children have no respect for other people's plants. We have no fields of our own. All the ones we cultivate belong to the Hag's family. There was even a fine eucalyptus tree, a tall one, that no one had planted. One day they came and cut it down and didn't give us anything, not even a scrap of wood. And also a palm tree, one given us by the Lord, well they cut it down without saying a word to us.

Madiha, my daughter, worked in their apartment in Fayoum. She left home with three *galabeyas*. When she came back on holiday with them, I could see that her clothes were all torn, you could see her legs through the tears. The Hag, who was smoking outside his house, said to her, "Couldn't you put on a newer *galabeya*?" The Hag's daughters had left the other ones in Fayoum. I told him. They told him the opposite. We decided that Madiha would not go back to them. Then, one day, one Friday, he came and took away our door. When Mahmoud arrived, he said, "They took the door away?" "Yes they took the door away." "Then let them keep it. It'll let us get some air! You sleep inside with the children and I'll sleep in the doorway." And we didn't let Madiha go again. The sheikh, who comes on Fridays, wanted us to make it up, but I didn't want to. I didn't want my daughter to go away again. After three months, the sheikh spoke to the Hag and they brought us the door back! All that would never have happened in the time of the *Sett Donia*, the mother, may God rest her soul. She was a good woman and knew how to manage her affairs. Now, look at those who are left. Can they do anything but smoke hashish?'

Abd el Bassir

'Fatna asked me for something to eat again today.'
'Who else can I ask, tell me?'
'Yesterday, it was rice and some pomade, the day before yesterday it was money and there's no end of it. Should I say yes, or should I say no? What should I do? It's the never-ending problem. Sometimes yes, sometimes no. But Fatna knows what to do to make me feel guilty. She's very good at that. That's how she manages to keep her house going.'

Mahmoud gets tired very easily, so she has to be able to look after things. Abd el Bassir says that Mahmoud is lazy.

Today, it is hot, the lake is two different blues. Noise is dulled by the heat. The children have taken the sheep near the stream, so that they can soak themselves. The sheep sometimes get sunstroke. The pigeon-house is ochre and the houses in the village a rather brighter ochre. Some grey-greens and blue-greens, the onion fields, the cornfields, strings of onion bulbs wait swaying gently for someone to pick them and sell them at 25 pounds a kilo. It's also the day for flour. One after another, the women pass with their thirteen kilo sack on their head, the flour for a fortnight. In the distance I saw Abd el Bassir in a big *galabeya* and scarf, despite the heat; he's the one I ask about anything that I find surprising. He's the one who talks the best, he inspires confidence, his eyes are bright and he has speaking hands.

'Why are there those palm trees over there, in places that aren't much farmed, that look as if they're drying up?'
'There', says Abd el Bassir, 'pray the prophet: one day a big red ball came down from the sky, a piece of a star. It passed over the trees and they got a bit dry afterwards. But they are not dead.'

I made him repeat it three times — was it lightning?

'But come and see the other strange palm tree, with its little ones, which have started growing up there where the fronds begin.'

And it's true, small palm trees are growing a metre and a half above the ground. One day, even down there in the fields, there used to be one like that, and the mother brought forth dates at the same time as her daughter, another little palm tree stuck on to where the fronds begin.

'Ah yes, you went to Nemous. The people there are very nice, they've got good land. The water has been coming over their fields a long time and everyone over there has a field of their own, no one works for anybody else. They are happier and richer than the people in our *ezba*. In our *ezba*, they are all sons of dogs! I know them!'

The noise of a motor can be heard far away, you can see a cloud of dust moving forward along the road, it's the second *sherka* (company) going past. A bus is called a 'company' because one day some company or other had brought a bus to these parts. People say, 'Are you waiting for the company? It's in the west, it's coming. It goes to the end of the lake and then comes back. If it hasn't broken down . . .'

From up on our terrace you can see everything that's going on, Abd el Bassir's flock is moving in front of the four palm trees at the end of the village, on the sandy bit. The sheep are moving fast, all their legs criss-crossing one another very fast, a music of dull sounds.

'I know all my sheep; in the evening, I bring them in and I put all the little ones with their mothers. I think that even the others know which are their little ones less than I do.'

The little dumb girl is behind the flock. She's the second dumb girl among Abd el Bassir's eight daughters.

'How am I going to marry them, they work hard, they know how to milk cows and look after sheep, but who will take them?'

No one. He has only one son.

'How old is your son?'
'Oh, my wife doesn't hang about, they're coming one after the other, there are already two after him, count for yourself.'

He's proud of his son, he's going to have him circumcised soon. He was keeping two rams for that, but now he's sold them. The calf will have to grow, he'll kill it and invite the whole family and the whole village to a feast. There'll be a loud-speaker and a man who chants the Koran. It'll be a big party and Mohammed will be very proud. There'll be a *zikr*, a religious dance for men, that lasts almost all night. That's what Abd el Bassir promised the sheikh if he had a boy. Now he has to honour it. But Mouftah and Azouz are in prison in Alexandria. Can the festival be held without them? They'd wanted to go to Libya. They took a car, all six of them, as far as the frontier, and then they walked with a guide to get across clandestinely. They were caught, all their money was taken. They'll be six months in prison. One of them had hurt his leg and he said that he was going to see someone at Matrouh. They took twenty pounds from him and let him go. He's the one who came back to tell the news. Mouftah had already been to Libya before. He brought back money, and married another wife, he'd got no money left, he borrowed, he went back to Libya. He's already had four wives, two are with him. Each of them has children, each has a room in the house. There's a black one and a light-coloured one.

'Each as stupid as the other', said Abd el Bassir. 'He can't choose, he likes women and that's all.'

Yet he's an artist, he has a flute that he paid 25 piastres for in the market fifteen years ago. He always carries it with him. He plays without drawing breath — he manages to take it in through his nose. He's very funny. He wants to marry all our friends. He comes to borrow a pound. He pays it back and then borrows two, because he has guests, one of his mothers-in-law.
    And there, now he's in prison. His brothers all have to get together to pay the hundred pounds. And the two wives and the children have to manage as best they can with a little butter, some eggs, a few rabbits, but it's not easy! 'It seems that they're right at the top of the prison and you can't even see them.' Yet the brothers have travelled to Alexandria. They don't let one of their people down, even if he's in the wrong.

Abd el Bassir says, 'Pray to the prophet' and he stops a moment as he does every time he's going to say something important.

'This girl got married a few days before you came. So her husband went into the bedroom with the midwife. She showed him how to put his fingers, his two fingers into his wife's vagina. He was in a hurry, all the men were already

145

knocking on the shutter and shouting behind the door. If he was not to be beaten by them, the midwife would have to show them the blood-stained handkerchief fast. How he did it, nobody knows. But certainly too quickly, like an animal, the blood came and didn't stop . . . she lost one litre, two litres. The doctor had to be called and he told them that such things weren't done any more. But he knew perfectly well that the same thing would happen at the next marriage.

'At my wedding,' said Bassir, 'I didn't want to rush things and they beat me. But it's a sin to hurt a woman so much, to rush her like that. How can you make them understand? I was afraid for my daughter, I sent her mother to tell them off and make them patient. Then, when this girl's blood began to flow without stopping, she began to cry out, "I want to go back to my father's, I don't want to stay here", and she threw herself about like a mad woman. She carried on for several days. So they thought the evil eye had been put on her. They went to the man who undoes the evil eye. It's quite a distance away. He wrote a paper for her, a big paper, from the elbow to the finger tips. He wrapped it up in some tin, he said some special words and they went away. Since that day she's been all right.'

'A dark girl? A dark skin, my God, no, why would anyone marry her, here they like light skins. Look at Mona, Ali's daughter: she's nice, she works hard, she's reliable, she doesn't steal. Well, she's the right age, someone should have asked for her already. But, no, no one wants her. I try, I'm looking for someone for her, I tell them she's a good girl. They laugh in my face. I even said to someone, "Listen, I'll lend you some money, such and such will give you three pounds, that one two and soon you'll have 25 pounds and you'll be able to marry her, it won't be dear for her." But even he doesn't want to. And yet he himself isn't worth a piastre. I ask myself what he's hoping for, we'd found him two rooms he could have lived in. He doesn't want it. And they don't like the father and there's nowhere to sit in their home. so what would the fiance do?'

'The young man goes to the girl's father's house to drink tea: he looks everywhere to try and see her. He goes back a second time, he sees whether he's given decent food to eat, whether the father is rich enough for him; and perhaps he even goes back a third time: but this time he must read or say the *sura* in the Koran for marriage. He gives a sum of money to the father who puts in more or less the same amount and goes and buys the furniture.'

'My daughters, are they beautiful? No, not at all, it's for their father that the men come', says Abd el Bassir.

'But it's sad for Leila, Ali's daughter, I'm sad for her, I really like her. No, no don't get angry. It's her luck, it's her fate. Can you be angry with fate? And my daughter Zeinab, she is promised to her cousin Deif. Others have come for her but if she doesn't marry her cousin all my brothers will be against me. The other day, he wanted to come to the house when Zeinab was alone, she slammed the door on him. When her mother found out she wanted to go and blast them. I said to her: "No, wait." This boy is not good, he thinks he's a cut above the others. Zeinab doesn't like him but she doesn't say anything. She only weeps now and again. We've forbidden him to come back to the house before he brings the money for the marriage. We don't like him much either.'

Then don't let the marriage go ahead.'

'It's impossible', says Abd el Bassir, 'He's her cousin, we can't have the whole family against us. In the end we'll ask for a lot of money and as he won't be able to find it, we can hope that he will decide to find someone else or that she will be married to him for six months and then they'll have a row (because he'll beat her) and we'll take our daughter back and give her to someone else.'

Another day, Deif says to me, 'People don't marry dark girls in the village. Zeinab, you know, she's my cousin, but if she wasn't I wouldn't take her.' *But then, if you don't like her, don't marry her.'*

'How?' he says, annoyed. 'She's my cousin, you can't leave your cousin. This summer, God willing, when we've sold our tomatoes, I'm going to marry her before I go and do my military service. God willing, when you come back, you'll find Zeinab in my house.'

That's how things stand. No one is happy, but it's got to be done. It's duty. We didn't know that that was only words.

And then Deif didn't go into the army. One day when he had a little money because they had sold their tomato fields, he went to Abd el Bassir to ask him for Zeinab and read the *fatha*. Abd el Bassir said, 'No, I won't give you my daughter for 250 pounds.' Zeinab was crying in her corner, in a room. Garia, Abd el Bassir's wife, pinched him slyly to remind him that he shouldn't give her. 'And then I still need my daughter. Who will go and fetch the water, who'll do the housework?' Then Deif got angry. The next day, Abd el Bassir was almost on the point of agreeing to give her. For the whole week they talked about it and then suddenly one day they all got angry. Deif battered on Abd el Bassir's door, but he wouldn't open it. They were both furious. And then Deif went away with his brothers. They went all round the village and went to ask another cousin in marriage. Her family agreed and the wedding took place very quickly.

'She's ugly', said Abd el Bassir, 'she's got spots on her legs, and he'll beat her, but anyway, so much the better, we're rid of him. And I know another man. I've already promised him Zeinab, but not now. She is young and works hard and helps her mother. Her sisters must grow up. In our house, everybody has to do something, the little ones look after the sheep, Samra milks the *gamoussa* (cow buffalo) and their mother goes to the fields.'

One morning, Abd el Bassir and Garia found their camel dead in the stable. A camel costs at least 300 pounds. They said nothing to anybody. In the *ezba*, they would have been saying, 'Oh, he's lost a lot of money', and there would have been a lot of discussion about it. They waited for the evening, they brought a cart to take it and bury it away from the village. Abd el Bassir thought the camel had died because he had annoyed Deif. The others would have said so too. You mustn't make people talk. Now Deif is ill, his illness rises from his stomach to his liver and goes back down to his thighs. He screams a lot. The doctor has said that it's a kidney stone. He gave him an injection and some pills, he gets a little better and then it starts all over again. They brought in the sheikh who reads in the Book. He is thin and very small. He opened the Book, looked at Deif and said to him,

'You've walked on a corpse, on dead meat, on a man. Since then you've felt ill.' Deif said, 'It's true, one evening we went with Abd Allah, we wanted to fish down there, in the big canal. When I sat down on the edge of the river to fish, my foot struck something and I saw an officer, with his uniform, dead, under my *galabeya*. I was very afraid. We fled: government people were already looking for him. We mustn't be seen, they might have thought we'd killed him. We ran and we reached the *ezba* all trembling.'

The sheikh said, 'You should have come straightaway to me to make a talisman, a good luck charm. Now what can be done? I'm going to put some incense on you, some incense in your house and pass my hands over your body. It's no good you going to hospital, the doctors can't do anything for you. It's not a stone.' The next day they went to find a cart to take him to the hospital in Fayoum all the same. They said it was his liver. Now he seems better. His wife is nice, but he beats her.

'Abd el Bassir, what do you think about honour?'
'Pray the prophet. As I watch my sheep, so I watch my daughters. Yes, I've got eight daughters. Shouldn't I look after them? I look at them when they are in the fields, I see whether they are looking all round. And if I see something wrong, I say to my daughter, "What's the matter with you, what's going on?" I make her come home, I try to find out if there really is something wrong. But if it's her mother who sees it, and I don't know about it, then she looks after it. She fetches a woman. She gives her something and makes what is in her belly come out without me knowing.'
'She can do that without you knowing?'
'Yes, she can. If she can do that without God wanting me to know and she's succeeded, then it's fine, I've got nothing to say about it. Let's see what happens when a man wants to take her and marry her. Among our people, you have to show the handkerchief. You go into the room and the man has to put two fingers in to see if she is a virgin. So you know who she is and you know who he is. Her mother is with her. If her mother is clever and she's done what she ought to have done with the man who is going to take her daughter and she's said the thing to him, the operation is what it is, but you and I are before God. We are there, you and me alone before our Lord, so please, no scandal! Then they take a little chrome mercury or pigeon's blood and just before putting his fingers in, he rubs them against the pigeon; when he put them on the handkerchief, the handkerchief is red and it can be shown. They do that in place of honour . . .' (He laughs broadly, he imitates the cries of the marriage bed, he taps his hands.)

'And so everything is arranged. If the man has taken her, if he has put his fingers in and the handkerchief has come out, people can say what they like, it no longer matters. But if the man gets angry suddenly and after a few months he no longer wants her, and says to her, "Get out, daughter of your mother's religion, I no longer want to see you — I want to divorce and I'm going to remarry", and he wants to take another wife, "Have I seen anything of the world? I took one who was not a real one."'
(Abd el Bassir plays all the roles, as if the man was speaking to him and he was replying.)
' "As if when you take one like that you don't see the world, this son of a dog but you've got one wife, is it your fingers that are going to give you the world? You can't hide their mistake, you can't bear it?" — "No, the one I took wasn't a girl, she was a woman".

'Then he sends her back to her parents and marries another one. The woman's parents are very sad; they can neither marry her because the scandal has become known, nor kill her, they don't know what to do. They can't kill her because people know about what happened. In the end, if the husband keeps her, there are no more problems.

'Something happened nearly five years ago in Abadeia, the next village. There was a girl who was always going everywhere. One day her mother found out she was pregnant. "Where did you get that, daughter of a dog, may your house collapse!" The daughter replied, "I've got it and that's it." The mother said, "Well, then, come. Daughter of a dog, I'm going to go mad, I'm going to kill you." And then she managed to get the baby out. It was already rather big, she wrapped it up and threw it away. She kept her daughter in the house for a week saying that she was ill. No one saw her. When she was better, she found her a fiance and married her. That's intelligent women for you. And she got a good husband. He is still with her, now.'

'When I married my cousin, who is more careful with money than I am, she said to me, "Don't stay out in the evening, don't spend money for nothing. You're always spending, you don't think that we've got daughters and we have to marry them." "But no", I say, "what do I spend more than for my cigarettes?" "You spend a lot." "But I don't go anywhere, where do I spend?" She said to me, "Look, we have ten daughters, each will cost 500 or 600 pounds. I give a little, but you've got to give some too." '

'She has her possessions, her rabbits and chickens, eggs, butter that she sells, geese, ducks, she fills the house with things. And I have nothing to do with that money. She buys scarves for her daughters, necklaces, bracelets, and she says to me, "Have you got any money for *galabeyas* today?" I reply, "No, and you, you get some with your eggs and your butter." "No, it's up to you to pay, you have some money, the cloth-seller is here, outside the house, be quick, are you going to leave your daughters naked?" '

'So, what can I do? I have to go and borrow if I don't have any. I have to pay for the *galabeyas* even if she has money of her own.'

'Let's come to my daughter who is getting married — (he swears) — after the divorce, I'm not giving her plates. With us, when a girl gets married, she must have a set of plates and glasses, and it's her mother who provides her with these things. No, I'm giving none of that. Why should I give glasses and plates for her to go and eat away from me with others? So her mother goes out and brings back the plates, the glasses, the *babour* (oil stove), the lamps and all the small things and yet I know it's my money. And when it's done and everything has been brought, I say to the husband, "come, boy, come". A paper is prepared and someone writes down all the things that are there — counts the plates, counts the cushions, the pillows, the bed, the lamps, the copper items, counts everything. And then, "Come and sign" and he signs. And then one day, if he's a bit short of money, he takes a dish and goes and sells it in the souk; perhaps even she too agrees. If she says no, he cannot go and sell them, but she is happy, because he's going to bring back something to eat with these things. At the next souk he sells her ankle bracelets, he ends up emptying the house. And then, if he wants to send her away, he says to her, "Did your father give you anything, daughter of a dog?" Then when this happens, we go to the government, I take this paper and I go to the police post. The officer makes him give up everything that's written on the paper, despite her mother's eyes looking on. They make us both go into a room. He judges and decides the sum of money that I should take home with me.

But if the woman leaves because she is angry with her husband, I can't take anything back'.

'And then, there are men, sons of the Crescent, who are good and honest and never sell their wives' belongings. And if I see that my son-in-law is intelligent and doesn't sell any of the things they have, I say to my wife, when my daughter is going to deliver, run fast, my dear, take Quimeya with you, take these things, take some sugar, some tea, kill a goose — am I not her father? And each time that she has a child, if her husband is honest, we send the same things.'

Abd el Bassir tells the story of Chagara, a strong woman in the *ezba*.

'Abd el Sattar, he's my eldest brother. We were still living all together at that time, with my other brothers and my mother, one *tableia*. We all ate on the same little table. He was married, indeed he got married long before the rest of us. He is older. Because my father had married a woman who had gone away and left him two children, and then he had married my mother, she had two children, Abd el Sattar and another one; my father wanted another wife and my mother went back to her family. He had two daughters by the other one and he said, "Oh, who is this woman who gives me nothing but girls." He went to find my mother and had five children by her and eleven by his other wife. One day then, we prepared for Abd el Sattar's marriage. He married Chagara — that woman who speaks loudly and dances so well at weddings. She's got character. Abd el Sattar got married "under the ground".'
What? What does "under the ground" mean?'
A smile, a slight hesitation and then:

'He'd been married, a calf had been slaughtered. He went into the room, the handkerchief had been brought out and then they had stayed, the two of them, in their room, in our house. In the morning, Chagara came out crying, "I want to go home, I don't want to stay here." "Why?" "Abd el Sattar is sick, I don't know what's the matter with him, I want to go home."

'She screamed and cried. We said to her, "Listen, stay another night, don't make us look ridiculous throughout the village." So she stayed. The next morning, she was still crying. "I don't want to stay, your brother is a woman, he does nothing to me, I want to go." People were beginning to hear. On the third day, she could bear it no longer. So my mother took Abd el Sattar and went to see her family. She was crying too, her honour was wounded, and he was her favourite son. In her village she went to see "the man of the Book" and he opened the Book and said, "Your son has got something, or someone, who is frightening him. Or perhaps he has the evil eye on him. Give me fifty pounds and we'll try and do something. I'll come with you; make him go back into his room, prepare perfumes for him, lay him down on a cushion, with his legs raised against the wall. He'll be alone and he will wait. A woman will come out of the ground. If this woman frightens him and he doesn't dare look at her, he will not get better. If, on the other hand, he sees her and wants to make love to her, he will have children and be happy with Chagara. But from that day, he will have to be alone on Monday and Friday nights, in his room. These will be the nights for the woman from under the ground." '

'They went home and everything was done as he has said. The next day, Chagara, who had returned to her father's, was summoned and she spent the night with him. In the morning, she came out of the room looking happy. She said to the "man of the Book", "Everything's going fine, you can go home. I'm staying with Abd el Sattar."'

'Since that day, they have been happy, they now have children and the children have children too: but right up to this time, on Monday nights and Friday nights she never goes to his room, he stays there alone. She is not annoyed about it, she knows that this other woman is only a dream, and she loves her husband.'

'This sort of thing still happens, only the girls now are often young when they get married and they are shyer than Chagara. So they wait without saying anything, and then it works! In Abadeia, the next village, there is also a man who arranges these things, the little "hitches". It happened to me too (says Abd el Bassir). With Gazia, my dear wife, we waited eleven days. But it was just a little hitch and that was soon cured. It happens like this. You go to the man, he takes an iron bar, he waves it to the right then to the left. He says things like, "Who did this to you? What are you afraid of?" And with the iron bar, he creates a climate of fear. Then, the sick person sometimes says something he has never told anyone before. If he says the name of somebody, the man repeats it seven times with the iron touching him, and he says to him, "Come out from there. Why delay, come out!" and he shouts and gesticulates and then it's all over. He gives you a paper to put under your *taeia* (a small cap worn by men) or under the pillow, and you go home. If women don't have problems, it's because they know more about it. Mothers and aunts discuss the facts of life among themselves, the intimate side of marriage, the girls hear and they understand. But men don't talk about those things, it's a sin. Yet there are women who go mad when they get married. They come out of their house screaming, you can't restrain them. Then they go with a member of the family to a man's house — a sort of doctor, really — sometimes it's the sheikh (religious title) and they do as they like, they shout, they jump about, they dance, they gesticulate, they lament — anything goes. He puts a stone near the woman's head to see whether it's a lie or not. If the woman is not lying, and she really is ill, she cries out and says, "No, I don't want to stay with that husband of mine." He replies, "But of course you must go back to him", and he really tears her off a strip. "Well, I'm not going to keep you here, I don't want you." "Yes, keep me here." It's as if she's in a trance and she begins to say what is going wrong. "He wouldn't give me a green *galabeya* when I wanted one, I need this, I need that," and the sheikh tells her whether it's all made up or not. And they go back to the house, sometimes with some writing on a paper and the husband is told what he has to do to make her calm down. She still doesn't know what she's said.'

'And the *gamoussas*? It's the same thing. Three days ago our *gamoussa* had dropped a calf. She was coming back from the fields, she was kicking out at everybody. She was butting into doors. You couldn't get near her. I said to my daughter, "Whom did you meet?" "I met uncle Holum and Sabri" (for example). So I go to the "man of the Book". He opens his book and says to me, "Who put the evil eye on her?" and gives me some writing on a paper. In the house I burn this paper with phisians, a sort of incense. You burn it all together, she inhales it and then it's all over. Since then she's been giving a kilo of butter a day.'

Guimeya

'I've had fourteen pregnancies. I've still got four daughters in the house: they are too small to help me. The older girls are married. Three of my boys are dead, they were already grown up when they died; I had twins, they were big, stocky boys. One day, they drank some tea in Holum's shop (Abd el Bassir's brother who has a little maize and corn lying around at the back of a room, that's his shop). They never got over it. He offered them some tea and then said to me, "Let them drink some tea, they're your sons, they're big and handsome." They came back home later, and went to bed. They never got up again. Holum had put a spell on them, but why? He told me they were handsome, he wanted sons like that. Did he intend to put the evil eye on them? Since that day I don't speak to him. In the same year, one day I was drying my other son who was younger than them, he too was strong and stocky. Abd el Bassir's other brother passed by. He said to me, "That one's yours?", to show that he found him healthy and that I was lucky to have him. At the end of the day, I saw his neck go stiff. He couldn't bend his head. I realized that he too was ill. In the morning he had said to me, "So, this fine boy is yours?" He had put a spell on him.'

'But didn't you go and see the doctor?'

'The next day he was dead. Can the doctor do anything for sicknesses like that? He can give pills for diarrhoea, he can mend a broken arm, but will he know anything about things like that?'

'And did you talk to Holum?'

'Yes, I said, "Holum, you're the last one who saw him, who said anything to him, you put a spell on him." He laughed and went on his way.'

'Do you think he really wished him harm, that he intended to put this spell on him?'

'No, he didn't intend to. I was the one who thought about it. But you mustn't let yourself have such thoughts. They came, but what can you do? As far as the twins were concerned, the women all said to me, "But you buried them alive, it's not possible, they were so well yesterday." Then I went mad and ran to their graves. My husband said to me, "What's the matter with you? I'm the one who closed their eyes. There was no life left in them. I know."'

Hussain

Hussain is nice and handsome. But he can't get married yet because of his elder brother. This brother got married — one day, his cousin came from some distance to see him. Then he said to his wife, 'Kill this chicken quickly to give my cousin something to eat.' His wife replied, 'What, the chicken my father gave me that is soon going to be producing chicks for me? No, never.' And she went back to her father's. He had to borrow to buy eggs and butter. The next day, his wife's father wouldn't let her go home. Shortly afterwards, the children in the *ezba* had a fight. Because one of the children of Hussain's brother's family was slightly hurt by someone from his wife's family, the story took a peculiar turn. The whole village became involved. Sayed ended up having a stone hit his head and had to go to hospital. All the other people went to the police. Abd el Bassir went with them to calm things down. They talked about it all day. It was agreed that Hussain's brother would return the furniture to his wife's family and divorce her.

Fayoum, 1978–81

Women and Corsican Identity

Anne-Marie Quastana and Sylvia Casanova

Is it wise to claim a 'Corsican identity' today if you are a woman? The question is an uncompromising one and may even appear scandalous at a time when this claim to identity is mobilizing the whole of the Corsican people. Yet many women have answered this question in the negative, rejecting 'Corsicanness' as you would break a chain, leaving their country as though it were a prison, despite all that this separation involves in the way of heartbreak and suffering.

Without passing judgement on their choice, we must ask ourselves why they have fled and what the position of women in Corsican society is. It is only if we start from here that we can at least understand why this question arises.

Women in traditional Corsican society

Many apparently contradictory clichés are current about the position of women in traditional Corsican society. For some people, Corsica is the country where machismo rules, where women are closely subject to the authority and control of the men of their family: father, brother, husband. You only have to read *Astérix en Corse* to see that this cliché is very much alive, even though it's not new; in the 18th Century French travellers were already spreading the image of Corsican women as the 'real slaves' of scornful tyrants. For others, on the other hand, women in Corsica 'have always been in command'. They even go so far as to claim that Corsican society is a matriarchal society where the men couldn't take the least decision without the women's agreement, and where the mother is the real authority within the family group. The role played by women in vendettas is brought up, as is the cult of the *Madonna*. Is not the Corsican national anthem *Dio Vi Salve Regina*?

But the contradiction between one image and the other is only apparent. One thing should be made clear before we go on. When people talk today about women in traditional Corsican society, it is almost always women in the inland village communities that they are talking about. It is not that the towns along the coast have played no role in the economic and social life of the country; but they were populated on the one hand by outsiders —

154

Italians, Frenchmen — and on the other hand by Corsicans more or less recently come from the villages whose culture had been forged there. That is why the collective memory of the Corsican people today relates essentially to the agro-pastoral way of life in the mountain villages.

We shall not go over the historical and economic causes of the structure of these communities. We will simply recall that traditional Corsican society was structured around the family group and a village community made up of the web of alliances and kinship groups. What makes a community strong in the face of enemies is the solidarity between each group; if one tie weakens, the network of alliances is overturned and the whole community may be in danger. This is no doubt why the strength of the family group and the authority of the head of the family has such importance in Corsican society. In this system the single individual has no weight, does not exist. There is a proverb which says: *Un tizzonu solu face pocu focu* (a single poker doesn't make much fire). Each person has his role to play within this group, and only has value to the degree that he plays it appropriately. Institutions all work together to keep each one in his place, under the authority of the head of the family.

The head of the family is the man. All the sayings say it ad nauseam, all mothers remind their daughters of it. And laws are there to punish those who forget it. In her work, *L'honneur des femmes en Corse du XVIIIe siècle à nos jours*,[1] Madeleine Rose Marin-Muracciole shows how customary law, often strengthened by government legislation — Genoese, French or Paoline — institutionalizes this total submission, in particular by women, to the authority of the head of the family, the father or husband.

To get married both boy and girl, whatever their age, need their father's consent; for a long time there was no question of children reaching an age of 'majority'. And the father could marry them without them even being present at the signing of the contract. If the father died, the eldest brother or the paternal uncles took his place. A woman who became a widow came under the authority of her paternal family and could not remarry without its authorization. It could happen that the suitor, in order to force the father to consent, 'kidnapped' the girl. In this case the father scarcely had a choice: he either consented to the marriage proposed as reparation or he killed the dishonoured girl and her ravisher — and set off a vendetta with the young man's family. In order to prevent the father's authority being flouted in this way, Pascal Paoli condemned the ravisher to death with no question of reparation; there was no mention of the fate of the girl who had been 'dishonoured'. What was important was that the authority and power of the father had to be defended.

Equally significant were the laws condemning adultery. Not only could the husband exact justice himself — without any need for intervention by the courts — but the man who had committed adultery with a married woman was also condemned to death. He could only escape this sentence if he could show that the married woman in question was not of irreproachable morals. As Madeleine Rose Marin-Muriacciole stresses, what was condemned was the injury done to the husband, an injury so serious that it demanded the blood price — the same as for the seduction of an unmarried girl.

Of course, these laws are no longer in force and they are only partial evidence of what the reality was for women in traditional society; they say nothing about everyday life or individual relationships. But what they do say is that in the eyes of the community, women had only one role, the role of obedience to their father, their brother, their uncles, their husband — men; they also say that the liberation of women was a serious threat to the honour of the group and the balance of power within it. That is evidenced too by the fact that when a girl was seduced, or when a woman deceived her husband, the label *curnudu* (cuckold) was attributed not only to the cuckolded husband but to all men in his family as well as to the father and brothers of the girl.

That partly explains why even today the 'protection' of women's virtue is a family matter mobilizing not only the father and the mother but also the brothers, uncles and cousins. As Ravis Giordani stresses,[2] the purity of women and the virility of men are the cardinal virtues that govern relations between the sexes in a traditional society. But when you say virility you are saying power, that is the capacity to protect the women of one's group from other men. It is not for nothing that *curnudu* implies a certain sexual inadequacy in the man to whom it is applied.

That does not mean, however, that women were locked up in order to protect them. They worked in the garden, helped in harvesting and fruit-gathering, went to the fountain and the washing-place, went out to sell fish, cheeses or harvest produce in neighbouring villages. But all these outings were linked to a specific task. Corsican society was based on a strict separation of the sexes, both in the division of labour and in the very organization of the village space. Women occupied the fountain, the *piazzette* in front of the houses, the gardens, while the men met in the central square, and generally in all the places involved in public life — fairgrounds and cafes. Even in the church each sex had its separate place on either side of the central aisle; this is a custom that is still very much alive today.

In the home, it was women who bore all the responsibility for running the family. While misogynous proverbs are legion, there are also many that stress the essential role of women in the prosperity of the family. But we need to look more closely at the role of women in the family.

Corsican society places the highest premium on blood ties; the individual does not exist outside his family. In Corsica, people don't ask, 'Who are you?' but 'From whom are you?' — that is 'From what family do you come?'. And the effective ties binding the members of the family are thus all the stronger. A proverb says, *Gira monti, gira castelle, maritu trovi, micca frateddi* (roam mountains and castles, you will find a husband, but not brothers). That is no doubt why in Corsica marriage between cousins is preferred. The Church has been unable to eradicate this tendency towards endogamy. It is true that, for a woman, it was better to be married to a more or less close cousin, since custom dictated that she live in her husband's family house. If she married a stranger she came into a family united by powerful affective bonds. In Corsica nothing has any value outside blood ties; the 'stranger' is nothing and many women remember that in their in-laws' family, they were often made to feel it. It is significant that in customary law, the widow comes under the authority of her parents after her husband's death: there is no 'adoption' by the husband's family. It is as if the conjugal bond had no reality. And until recently it was rare to see a husband and wife together outside their house. The husband/wife relationship was impeded by a double separation: separation of the sexes and separation by blood. Marriage is an association with a single purpose — the begetting of children. The woman is nothing so long as she has no children. Many Corsican women report that their situation vis-à-vis their in-laws changed the day they had a child, particularly if it was a son. For even if there is a proverb that says that a 'fine family begins with a daughter', it is still the case that newly-weds are wished 'seven sons and one daughter'. The *sterpa*, the family line, is continued by men.

As the mother of a son — and with luck of several, for the larger her family, the more powerful she is — the Corsican woman finds in this role what some have called her 'revenge'. For it is on her that the duty of raising and educating the children falls; in the sexual division of labour, she rules inside the house, whereas the main part of the man's activity takes place outside the house. In the childhood of Corsican men, it is the maternal image that dominates, and the relation between mother and son becomes special. (Relations between brother and sister are also special; it is said of a poor little boy that he is 'orphan of his father, his mother and his elder sister'.) The father, physically absent, is also symbolically absent, and Ravis Giordani stresses that in the Corsican family we can see the emergence of 'a peculiar oedipal triangle: that of a family in which the son wins out over the mother's husband, and with her complicity'.

This cult of the mother which is to be found in all Mediterranean societies is particularly strong in Corsica. When they declared their independence, the Corsicans did not set up a republic — which would have accorded with their constitution — but a kingdom whose queen was the Virgin Mary: Pascal Paoli, the head of state, was only the 'general of the fatherland'. This testifies less to the religiosity of Corsicans than to the place held in their symbolic universe by the 'universal mother'.

In his essay, *Les Corses entre l'insularité et l'exil*,[3] Professor Giudicelli stresses the fact that the Corsican man, like most men in the Mediterranean area, remains throughout his life a 'big child', a son whose wife or sister will play the role of mother. Corsican women know all too well what that implies in terms of men's dependence on them, many still seeing in it the proof of their 'power'. But is it really power?

So long as they remain under the paternal roof, Corsican women receive a strict upbringing that aims to make them internalize male values: the preeminence of men in everything is inculcated in them, they are taught that they owe submission and obedience to their father, their brothers and their future husband, they are reminded that the shame or the honour of the family depends on how they behave. They do not get much from the relationship between mother and son. While their affective relations with their brothers and their father are very strong, they know that sooner or later they will leave their family to go and live with strangers. We have seen what it was like for the newly-wed wife in her husband's house. It is thus absurd to say the 'women have always been in command' in Corsica. This is a man's view, a son's view; the women who hold it are only conforming to male expectations. If the mother dominates within the house, it is in the role that has been assigned to her by patriarchal society, and she only retains her power by never moving outside this role. It is in this way that she, 'the outsider', will transmit to her children the values of her husband's family, the traditions of the *sterpa*. She counts for so little, as a person, that the husband can oblige her to bring up with her children the children he has had by another woman, even after the marriage. This happened several times in the villages, and if the women refused, everybody would blame her; the man's children belong to the *sterpa*, they therefore have their place in their father's house, and the wife has a duty to accept them.

To say that the mother 'is in command' in the home is indeed a son's view, for it completely ignores the presence of the father in the house. Certainly, most male work is done outside the house, but at meal-times and in the evening, the father is there. Corsican women have no place of their own where they can be themselves: they are constantly under men's eyes, and they cannot escape.

Even if the power of mothers — and thus to some extent of women — is considerable in Corsica, it is only exercised through a husband or a son. It is an indirect power which has no public reality, which is based on the psychological dependency of men and not social recognition. To obtain it women have to deny themselves, and agree to make themselves the vehicles of male values. It is Corsican mothers who teach their daughters submission to men, it is Corsican mothers who make their daughters-in-law feel that being 'outsiders' they are nothing and that they must obey their husband. It is a very strange power that leads to wanting to destroy others like you — it is destroying yourself!

There is thus no more a 'matriarchate' in Corsica than there is in the other Mediterranean societies and there is no contradiction between the obedient wife and the all-powerful mother; these are but two sides of the same coin. It was only after the Second World War that things began to change; though it remains to be seen how far and in what direction.

Corsican women today

In appearance, at least, there have been major upheavals between yesterday and today: there seems no longer to be anything in common between the life of the young girl who rides a motorized bike where she likes, goes to the lycée, the university or her work, goes out in the evening with friends, collects amorous conquests, and the restraint her mother or grandmother experienced at the same age. But we must look beyond appearances.

The traditional society rested on an agro-pastoral economy. The integration of Corsica into the French economic system ended in the destruction of this Corsican economy and society. Exile, rural exodus and the penetration of French culture, have continued the trend. The rural communities no longer have an economic base, and if some few vestiges of it do remain, it is more in the subconscious of the inhabitants, in the feeling of belonging to one particular place, than in concrete reality. Similarly, the maintenance of a powerful family group, with its network of alliances and kinship, is no longer an economic and political imperative and tends no longer to have any reality except in the collective unconscious.

The Corsican people, living for the most part in the towns along the coast or outside Corsica, are today divided between a way of life which no longer has anything to do with that of their ancestors and a collective memory which still keeps alive the culture and value of these same ancestors.

Yet there is one section of the Corsican people that never expresses any regret for what is called 'the times before' — that is for the time when the villages still had an active economic and social life. In the villages today, if you listen to the men talking, the conversation turns around two subjects: politics and the 'times before'. The old men express nostalgia for what is no more, and the young listen with regret for not having known those times when Corsicans 'lived like Corsicans'. But if you listen to women talking, you hear something very different. The old women make no bones about how lucky the young ones are not to have known those times when they 'slaved like beasts'. And if a young woman expresses a hope of seeing this traditional life revived, the response is a sharp, 'you are mad!' It should also be noted that the women who express this wish are always young women brought up outside Corsica, who have no memory of having seen their mother patiently wear herself out working and who were never told by their grandmother, 'You are a girl, you are nothing, you have no right to anything. Everything is for your brother. He is the King and you must serve him.' For the truth is that exile, rural exodus and the penetration of French culture have been perceived by women as responsible for their 'liberation'. This cannot be disputed even if we question this so-called liberation.

For young women especially, exile often appeared as the sole means of acquiring a degree of independence; they would escape the control of the family and family duties and above all they would be able to try and live as they wanted, responsible for themselves and for themselves alone. For what was most oppressive in Corsican society was not so much not being able to do what you wanted — for no one anywhere can do that — but knowing that everything you did engaged the collective responsibility of the whole group; the whole group bore the burden of the mistakes of one individual and paid the price for them in the community. This notion of 'collective responsibility' is still alive today and no individual, however detached he believes himself to be from family ties, escapes from it.

We are not claiming that Corsican women massively chose exile; it was forced on them by economic and political conditions. But some did choose it, and many have 'profited' from it and admit that they cannot now contemplate returning to live in Corsica, for fear of getting caught again in the 'family strait-jacket'.

For those who did not leave 'for the other side of the sea' rural exodus was — and still is — a means of escaping from many constraints. Living in a flat, however tiny it may be, in the suburbs of Ajaccio or Bastia, means no longer being forced to live with in-laws. It is easy to imagine how attractive such a prospect might be. Girls brought up in the village have mostly only one idea in mind; to find a job in town, marry there and live there. The village is fine . . . for the weekend. The attraction of town life may have something to do with it, it is true. But added to that is the desire for a relative autonomy vis-à-vis the family, and for life as a 'couple'. Today, Corsican women want to 'be part of a couple', create their own family. That is in flat contradiction with the traditional values of Corsican society, in particular with the notion of being part of a pre-existing family group.

For Corsican women, France, and integration into it have been synonymous with freedom. That is why they have sought, more than men, to conform to French cultural values. Frantz Fanon marvellously portrayed this 'complex of the colonized', and there was certainly something of that in Corsican women. Doubly oppressed, by the patriarchal system and by colonialism, they believed that by conforming to the dominant cultural model they could escape this double oppression.

One significant feature is the way in which women have abandoned the Corsican language. In traditional Corsican society the French language was used by the upper class, and until the Second World War, it was only the men who mastered it; a few years of primary education were not enough to inculcate it in everyone; outside school, it was soon forgotten. But men had other occasions on which to use it, if only during their military service.

But today the situation is reversed. As Fernand Ettori notes,[4]

> Corsican tends today to be the privileged idiom of the male community, while women and children 'understand but do not speak' it. Boys join men at adolescence, developing a use of Corsican which is seen as a symbol of a belonging.

This is confirmed by a survey carried out by the INSEE in the third quarter of 1977 and published in 1980.[5] To the question, 'Do you speak Corsican?' the gap between men and women responding 'yes' was between 10–12%, in every age and social category. Women usually speak Corsican in the family, or in the village. Whereas men speak Corsican both in the family and in the cafe or at the workplace, it is rare to hear women speaking Corsican in a public place, or in an office. And it is common to see, in a group, the men speaking Corsican among themselves and speaking quite naturally in French to the women in the group, even during the same conversation.

This rejection of the Corsican language was partly deliberate on the part of Corsican women. The young woman of the 1960s found it 'chic' to declare proudly, 'I don't even understand Corsican!' although she had never left Corsica and was living with her grandmother who only spoke this language. Does this mean that Corsican women today have lost their identity and that no trace remains of the values of the traditional society?

But the essential values are in fact far from having been abandoned. While the extended family group no longer has an economic or social basis, it is still very much alive in the collective unconscious. It is still family that gives each individual an identity, and all 'closeness' between individuals is based on it. And women are still expected to see that the family is kept up and ensure its survival — as in the traditional society. It is on women that the main work of this network of family solidarity falls in everything to do with life and death. Women who work leave their children with their mother, their mother-in-law or their sister; sick people and the elderly are still largely looked after by the women in the family. Of course, over the generations, the network of solidarity has narrowed, but everything still functions in the same way as before. Even for the young, the family remains an essential value.

Another particularly significant fact testifies to this strength of traditional values: the respect — for so it is called — that Corsican men have for women in their community. You often hear the same story, told with varying details: a young woman hitch-hiking or leaving a dance-hall in the summer feels that the men around her are becoming more pressing, almost aggressive; she tells them she is Corsican, from this or that region . . . and immediately the attitude of her companions changes; the bantering continues, but the tone is no longer the same and she knows that the danger is over. Some of the very young ones who were being the most pressing and the most aggressive will go so far as to criticize her for taking 'risks' and advise her to be more careful . . . as if she were their sister or cousin. Corsican women are always taboo; they belong to the men of their group and it is as if they still cannot be offended without risking the vengeance of the group. It must be added that as the Corsican community has become narrower, Corsicans have developed the feeling that they all belong to the same land, that they all belong to the same community; for a Corsican man each Corsican woman is a sister or a mother. This makes the taboo all the stronger. Quite obviously, it concerns only the women of the community, and only to the extent that they respect the laws; others, or women from outside, are all lumped in the category of 'fair game'.

This attachment to the family, and alleged respect for women, should be seen in relation to the cult of the mother that is still very much alive — as shown in contemporary literature and songs — and to the dependence of men on women that 'modern life' has not eliminated. Outsiders, above all Frenchmen — for men from other parts of the Mediterranean the problem doesn't arise — are amazed to see men over thirty and not yet married still living with their parents. And they only contemplate leaving the maternal home the day they marry, whereas girls often seek their independence much earlier. Even more striking, it is quite usual for a man who has got divorced to return to live with his mother. Everyone finds that perfectly normal, 'He can't live alone, can he?'

All this means that Corsican women today live with total contradiction. In appearance, there is nothing to distinguish them, in terms of life-style and consumption patterns, from women from any region of France. But at the same time, they would not like to be like Frenchwomen. They do not recognize themselves in the dominant cultural model, and they continue to think, react and behave as their mothers and grandmothers did before them. The values to which they remain attached are those of a society that has disappeared and they do not in the least wish to see restored.

This contradiction stands out all the more because women have broadly embraced the 'Corsican national cause' and have participated in very large numbers in recent years in the nationalist movement. Their participation has been in the mostly traditional form and in accordance with the role that has always been theirs; they have supported the action of men in the struggle. When the repression began, they came forward to organize support for their 'husbands, brothers and sons' who were imprisoned and to take the places left empty by those who were in prison, or in the maquis, most women quite naturally went back into the house, where they continue to support 'their' militants.

But some women began asking themselves exactly why they were fighting; for what identity, what future, what society? They asked it all the more forcefully because misogynists of every stripe made no bones about turning Corsican nationalism and the demand for cultural identity against women. When we remember what women were in traditional Corsican society, we can see how easy this was. Any manifestation of emancipation became synonymous with treason. But this is not the most important thing. The Corsican nationalist movement is not aiming to bring back the traditional society from the ashes; even if some might want to, economic conditions would not allow it.

The problem is that the Corsican nationalist movement implies the resurrection of the values on which the traditional society was founded. And all the symbolism of the national movement is a male symbolism. It is in fact a men's movement in which the motherland, fraternity, and arms are exalted. Women are physically present in it as mothers/sisters/wives — in relation to men — or, worse still, as 'equals of men' — doing what men do. In the most popular cultural group, the one that has done most to spread the idea of nationalism inside and outside Corsica — the Canta u Populu Corsu — there are no women. And yet its name means 'The Corsican People sing' . . .

But the absence of women can be seen best in the issue of language. We have said how, and why, Corsican women have, more than men, abandoned their language. Today many, among the young, are returning to the Corsican language, learning it and speaking it again. But Corsican women have much more difficulty than men in resuming their maternal language. Many women recognize this, but none really explains it, as if, subconsciously, they continue to reject this language and all that it implies. For it is not that they don't know it; some can even write it, but cannot speak it. The problem is a mental block, and this block is something men don't have. Even men whose command of it is not perfect have no hesitation about speaking it. So, though it is the language of the people and the language of the national movement, the Corsican language remains, despite the cultural revival, 'the privileged idiom of the male community'.[4] And if it is held out as 'a symbol of a belonging',[5] it is above all of belonging to a male community. We only have to see how the young use the Corsican language to show that they are 'among men' and that girls — even if they are present, even if they understand — are not involved in the discussion. Women who have always spoken Corsican are the very ones who want to be 'the equals of men', similar to them in everything, even in misogyny. The coincidence is too common not to be significant.

Women do not want to take the risk of assuming a 'Corsican identity', for they do not see a role for themselves as Corsicans. But even less do they identify themselves with the dominant cultural model — which can no longer even be called French.

Ajaccio, February 1983

Notes

1. Madeleine Rose Marin-Muracciole, *L'Honneur des femmes en Corse du XVIIIe siecle à nos jours* (ed. Cujas, Paris, 1964).

2. Ravis Giordani, *La Femme corse: images et réalités, Pieve e Paesi* (CNRS, 1978), p. 195.

3. S. Guidicelli, *Les Corses entre l'insularité et l'exil*, Presenza Corsa edition.

4. F. Ettori, *Langue et Littérature — Les Problèmes actuels*, in *Corse, Encyclopédies régionales* (C. Bonneton) p. 182.

5. *Parlate Corsu? Economie Corse*, no. 18, January–April 1980, INSEE.

Neighbourhood Relations and Social Control: The Role of Women in Maghrebian Communities in Southern France

Sossie Andezian and Jocelyne Streiff-Fenart

We propose to show in this chapter how Maghrebian women succeed in maintaining, as immigrants, a system of social relations that has many similarities with the women's society typical of Maghrebian culture, and how through this women's network a collective control of the changes necessarily induced by immigration in the definition of family roles is exercised.

The role of the family and community networks of immigrant workers has often been referred to to explain the processes by which the immigrant labour force is introduced, employed and spatially distributed in the labour-importing countries. Interest in the immigrants' own networks has, however, been limited to observing the links that bind the *worker*, that is the man, to his kin or home village, whereas the relations established and maintained by his wife, who does not usually work, have been regarded as of no importance because they have no apparent effects on the modes by which contact is established between the immigrant communities and French society.

Most studies of Maghrebian women in France make no mention of the bonds that women may form within their community group and resort heavily to the notion of isolation to characterize their mode of relationship with French society. The literature on the non-working immigrant woman lays great emphasis on her isolation and lack of understanding of the world around her. How could it be otherwise, since, says Juliette Minces describing the Maghrebian woman, 'She does not speak the language of the host country; of course, she usually does not know how to read or write and since she does not work has no income of her own, and moves in a "narrow" circle, at most meeting only other women, her neighbours, usually of the same age as her, and of the same socio-cultural level.'[1] In the same vein, Isabel Taboada-Leonetti and Florence Lévy characterize one of the types of immigrant women they are studying by the term 'isolation' and add, 'the circle of relations is *reduced* (our emphasis) to the family and her compatriots'.[2]

Here, we maintain, on the contrary, that the relations formed among immigrant women in their country of residence are not only important for them but also form a network which mediates between the host society and the group to which they belong. Being always at home, and being free from direct institutional pressures (such as those exercised by the factory and the

164

school), women seemed to us to be better able, as immigrants, to provide a focus for a collective reinterpretation of behaviour and social norms.

Immigration and family roles

Immigration brings a new situation which, at the same time as it weakens family bonds, increases the number of alternatives and hence the uncertainty about decisions to be taken in all areas of social activity. This almost inevitably results in a calling into question of the division of roles between members of the nuclear family, which is usually reduced to the parental couple and the children. Because of the absence of the mother-in-law and other female members of the extended family, responsibility for domestic tasks falls totally on the wife whose role within the family thus takes on a new importance.

Most authors interpret the situation of the non-working Maghrebian 'confinement' to the domestic space and isolation from any form of social life. But our observations lead us rather to think that women's management of family life, far from being purely private, almost inevitably brings them into contact with the outside world.

The intervention of the state in most aspects of family life brings the woman into contact with a large number of institutions such as dispensaries, schools and social services. She is the most likely member of the family to go to social services offices during opening hours to seek an explanation or make a request on behalf of the family, whether it be seeking accommodation, collecting benefits or dealing with health problems. She is also the one who receives home visits from social workers such as child specialists, welfare and family advisers and teachers.

When the family home becomes the place where private family matters and contact with the 'host' society come together, the boundaries between the inside world and the outside world, between private space and public space, between domestic activities and extra-domestic activities tend to dissolve.

To deal with the problems posed by everyday life in a society dominated by bureaucratic communication, women soon realize that they cannot rely on their husbands, who are often as illiterate as they are and are tied to working hours that leave them very little free time. It will mostly be another woman, the social worker or a daughter at school who will help deal with the countless problems with papers.

So in France the man loses some of his power in the public domain. All women's conversations about male roles revolve around two topics: the ideal husband (he doesn't drink, lives up to his responsibilities towards the children, looks after the running of the house, respects religious obligations) and the way this model is impaired in the immigration situation ('get it into your head that men in France (Maghrebian men living in France) change completely, they're all the same; as soon as they begin to drink it's finished, they don't want to know about their wife and religion')[3] and the use of physical violence which is all the less tolerable because men are evading their duties as husband and head of the family. The combination of these two topics, which appear as linked and opposed ('she was fed up with *being beaten* by a husband *who didn't look after the house*'),[4] reflects the upsetting of the balance between sexual roles on which, in Maghrebian societies, recognition of the legitimacy of male authority rests. Immigration cannot but lead, therefore, to the calling into question of the principles on which male supremacy is established.

Women's neighbourhood relations

As immigrants, the Maghrebian women are called upon to face new problems for which they are unprepared without having an extended kinship network to turn to. The development of very close neighbourhood relations, which we observed in all the districts in which we conducted investigations, may, in this context, be seen as a product of the problems posed by immigration. These relations, which take different forms depending on the form of dwelling and the make-up of the population, fulfil important functions. Links between neighbours are used as channels to convey information from various sources and of various sorts: news from the home country, information on administrative procedures, policies on immigration. They also provide material and moral assistance at times of personal tragedies (deaths, accidents) and advice in the event of difficulties in relations with French institutions.

At the same time, neighbourhood relations help to maintain collective control over the behaviour of individuals by opening up their private lives. The gossip that forms the core of the flow of communications passing through the women's network seems to us to play a vital role in the exercise of this social control. The works of Bott and Epstein[5] stress the importance of gossip in the consolidation of group relations. Gossip always implies the existence of norms to which behaviour is compared and condemned.

Gossip is both a means of social control and an instrument for reaffirming established norms. As such it takes as its target individuals and topics that have some particular meaning for the immigrant community. By the same token, it serves to mark off those who belong to a group from others, the marginals, those whose behaviour is devoid of meaning or interest. The absence of gossip means the repudiation of the individual who is ignored and so put outside the group. This is the case with women who are totally taken in charge by the social assistance who, since they have abdicated all 'dignity', are more objects of pity than of scandal. On the other hand, girls are a particular target of gossip. Their virginity is essential to preserve the honour and prestige of the family.

In France, young Maghrebian women are even more closely watched than at home because the environment contains many dangers and people know that the least false step will be the subject of comment by the neighbours. If it should happen that someone thinks she recognizes a girl from the district in a bar, or someone meets a girl with a boy or thinks she's wearing too much make-up, that will be enough to earn her an immediate bad reputation. It is the mother who is being watched when the behaviour of girls is being discussed since the bringing up of the girls is wholly her responsibility and the bringing up of boys is largely outside her province. When girls 'misbehave' it's their mother who has to bear the criticism. Girls thus occupy a major place in women's conversations. Along with bringing up children, adultery and the way people keep their homes are favourite topics of gossip. Criticism of the way a woman's conjugal, maternal and domestic roles are performed is an attack on her fundamental existence as a woman in Maghrebian society.

The redistribution of tasks within the family does not seem to be accompanied by radical changes in the representations of traditional sex roles. The increased responsibility that falls on women does not drive them to refuse the duties, which, according to the norms they learned in their home society and that they continue to transmit to their daughters, fall on all wives and mothers. It would thus, in our opinion, be altogether quite wrong to interpret the relative autonomy that women acquire in the running of family affairs as a calling into question by them of the authority of the husband. Performing the functions that the husband is unable to perform is more a matter for them of preserving the order that governs the Maghrebian family than of claiming a liberation in the sense understood by Western feminism.

Gossip about conjugal conflicts is revealing in this respect. If women do sympathize with and comfort women whose husbands behave like 'men in France', it is so as to stress the obligations attaching to the male role. When conflicts arise in a family where the husband has the reputation of being a 'good husband', the wrongs are regularly attributed to the wife; women neighbours will be quick in such cases to criticize her negligence of her domestic tasks, the poor way she is bringing up her children, the fact that she goes out too often, even, in extreme cases, going so far as to hint that she's guilty of adultery.

Women's gossip thus plays a determining role in the establishment of a consensus about the norms that should govern family behaviour. The neighbourhood network of immigrant women is in this similar to Algerian women's society as described by Vasse, 'The judgements made form a more or less tacit consensus that acts as a control that the outside world must ultimately take very carefully into account.'[6]

By setting off conflicts women in fact oblige men, the only ones entitled to defend the honour of the family publicly, to take on their quarrels. If the men's world is shot through with fear of women's conflict, it is because, among other things, men know that sooner or later they will suffer the consequences of 'women's palavers'. In a district of Nice inhabited exclusively by Maghrebians, a Moroccan family, sent to Coventry after a dispute between the mother and other women in the district, was the object of such demonstrations of hostility from the whole neighbourhood that in the end they had to move away. Elsewhere, a dispute between two families ended in recourse to French justice, involving the husbands.

It is scarcely surprising that men look upon women's relations with one another with deep suspicion. Their position vis-à-vis these relations is however very ambiguous: officially, they condemn them and forbid their wives to engage in them. But they are in fact obliged to tolerate this women's solidarity which enables women to take on day-to-day tasks that they themselves can no longer look after. The husband's need to unload most administrative tasks on to his wife obliges him to grant her some freedom of movement. This freedom is only made possible by the existence of this network which, by exercising a constant and niggling watch on each of the women belonging to it, enables the husband to be informed at once of everything his wife does.

While the mutual surveillance made possible by the existence of a very close network undeniably has the effect of exerting a pressure to conform, it does not imply that there is no shift at all in the definition of collective situations. The neighbourhood network widens the women's horizons and makes it possible for them to adapt behaviour. As one of the young women we interviewed explained, people are the more willing to accept changes when they know that other families too have to make them:

Before, young women, I say young women because it's usually always they who are confined, before, they were very afraid of the neighbours. But as in general every family has daughters of an age to go out, and as almost all the girls act as if they had agreed to go out to the same places, the mothers say: after all, the others can't say anything about my daughter because their daughter is doing the same thing.

There thus exists a reverse effect of social control which, by making responsibility for changes a collective one, makes it possible to neutralize the dangers they present.

If, as family immigration becomes stabilized, behaviour becomes less rigid, it is not, as is often said, the effect of adopting the Western model. It is, on the contrary, through a collective manipulation of the crisis situation that immigration really is, that the limits of what is allowed and what is forbidden are constantly being redefined.

Nice, September 1982

Notes

1. Minces, J., *Les travailleurs étrangers en France* (Paris, Seuil, 1973), p. 433.
2. Taboada-Leonetti, I., and Lévy, F.,*Femmes et immigrées. L'insertion des femmes immigrées en France* (Migrations et Sociétés, Paris, La Documentation Française, 1978).

3. Extracts from recordings of group discussions among Maghrebian women.

4. Ibid.

5. Bott, E., *Family and Social Networks* (London, Tavistock Publications, 1957); Epstein, A.L., 'Gossip, norms and social networks', in Mitchell, J.C., *Social Networks in Urban Situations. Analysis of personal relationships in Central African Towns* (Manchester University Press, 1969), pp. 117-27.

6. Vasse, D., 'La femme algérienne', *Travaux et Jours*, April 1964, pp. 85-102.

Notes on the Condition of Women in a Southern Italian Village

Maria Minicuci

'We exist but we don't seem to', an eighty-year-old woman said to us when we had reconstructed her genealogy. The stories that she told about her lineage (*casata*)[1] made me think that women had in reality a much more important role than would appear. In the village studied,[2] women occupy a key position in the reproduction strategies of the society;[3] but ideological writing continually attempts to deny this position, or at least to play it down. The starting point for analysing women's condition is the functioning of kinship structures. For about two centuries (given the available documentation[4] it is not possible to go further back into the past) the community has regulated access to land, property and its use by means of marriage strategies based on village and kinship endogamy and precise modes of transmitting inheritance. These strategies are based on a preference for marriage between cousins.[5] Marriages always take place within the community; the modes of inheritance give the land to women and the house to men. The inheritance must be shared equally among all the children; that is the 'rule', declared to be such, which has to be reconciled with the need (this is really the priority need) to provide all the women in a family with a dowry and to endow them with equal shares. The woman's dowry is made up of land. Only the lack of land justifies payment of a dowry in cash or no dowry at all.[6] But in no case can a woman be deprived of land in favour of the man.[7]

Where land is scarce and/or where there are several women to be provided with a dowry, the men are left with no land; and, vice versa, when there is enough land, the men get some too. It goes without saying that while women have land at the time of marriage, men rarely do. They usually receive it when their parents die or when the parents have grown old and become unable to look after it. For most men access to land is only possible through marriage. And in most cases, the only land a new 'household' possesses is the one it has received as a dowry, brought by the wife as her property. It is obvious that within a 'household' the wife and the wife's lineage must hold a position which is often dominant and always strong. But the fact of entrusting to the woman's lineage the transmission of some of her goods (even if they be the most important ones, as in the case we are discussing here) does not automatically give her power, for matrilineality is of course not the same thing as matriarchy;[8] however, this mode of transmission obviously determines a woman's role to a considerable degree. The mode of transmission of the surname gives us a first indication of this.

In a village where there is a very high degree of homonymy of patronyms and personal names, identification of individuals, as of groups formed on the basis of consanguinity and marriage alliances, rests wholly on surname. This is transmitted mainly by women. The modes of transmission in turn translate the predominance of one lineage over the other and make it possible to reconstitute the history of marriage alliances by reading the relations of force between the two lineages (male and female).[9] Thanks to this key, analysis of genealogies brings out, in most cases, the predominance of the female lineage over the male lineage, the results being confirmed by the history of marriages. It should be added that women do not transmit only the so-called 'family' surname, but also frequently their own surname which may come to prevail over the inherited surname and in turn become a potentially inheritable surname.

The wife is thus the owner of the land that she receives as a dowry at the time of marriage or by inheritance if it should happen, in particular circumstances, that she is unmarried or is still unmarried at the time of her parents' death; she remains the owner throughout her life. When she has received the land as a gift rather than as a dowry, according to the distinction suggested by Davis[10] (as has happened in most cases since about 1930) she retains the right to transfer it or alienate it as she wishes. The community of goods between husband and wife has never been practised. All the legal documents show that husband and wife dispose of their goods separately; they dispose together only of goods acquired after marriage. In all the deeds (of sales, purchases, transactions and gifts) which relate to their own goods, the women appear in the first person; they also often appear as representatives of their husbands and children who have emigrated. It is not only the fact of being the owner of a piece of land that gives the woman responsibility for it, it is also the fact of working this land or looking after it on a footing of equality with the man. Women often work in the fields as much as men; sometimes they carry out different tasks from those of men, sometimes the tasks are interchangeable. When the men are away they sometimes take on responsibility for all the work. When the women are not wholly responsible for them, they participate in all decisions about what to grow and how to grow it and above all in the commercialization of products that they are often the only ones to sell, in the old days in the market of a neighbouring village, today mainly to wholesalers who come and buy on the spot. They look after the animals (donkeys, pigs, goats, chickens, cattle). In addition, women not only work their own land but also their husband's and, where necessary, lands that have been acquired or inherited since marriage. Given the extreme subdivision of property, this implies an obligation to look after pieces of land that may be several kilometres away. In short, the woman is owner, worker and manager and is endowed with a power to decide and to intervene. That is one aspect of reality — the one usually glossed over by women themselves. The other reality, the reality of everyday life, of domestic life, is the one usually mentioned, a reality in which the strength and power of women are diluted and masked and take on metaphorical forms.

The day and the life of a woman are structured around two poles: the land and the house. These are two universes within which the woman moves differently and behaves differently compared with men. From the time she is very small, her life revolves around these two poles. As a child, she enjoys total freedom of movement and freedom in the choice of her friends. Like all children, she enjoys great tolerance from adults. When she is about eight or ten years old, she begins to be given little jobs to do around the house and in the fields. At puberty, she is cut off from the world of men and her world is now wholly female. She continues to have contact with men working in the fields but these contacts are governed by specific norms that mean that she must be reserved and 'serious'. Outside work, the house is now her world and women her only company. This is the time when she learns about her future duties as wife and mother and studies the histories of families, lineages (*casate*), kinship and marriages. She gains knowledge and begins to use a genealogical memory which enables her, even though still very young, to locate individuals within structures of kinship and determine possible husbands. In fact, through the history of lineages, she comes to know the history of lands, dowries, exchanges and all the conditions required to ensure a good marriage. She thus develops her initial criteria of choice which will make it possible for her to choose the right man.

The genealogical exercise makes her even more conscious of what she has known since her childhood: the inevitable necessity of marriage and motherhood so as 'to have someone to leave the land to', so 'that the name will not be lost', so as to continue through her own life the life of the collectivity. During this period she learns too what her duties are as wife and mother: respect and obedience to her husband, and responsibility for her children. During this period when she is kept apart from men, many aspects of her behaviour are repressed. Women know, and old women never tire of repeating it, that they have value, that they have more value than men, to the point of saying to anyone who cares to listen that it is better in a family for a girl to be born than a boy. They will support this statement by saying that a woman is capable of looking after the house and the land, children, the old and the sick, that she is quite capable of taking care of herself and of living alone. A man on the other hand, is incapable of living without a woman, being unable to do without someone to meet his everyday needs for clothes and food. It may be said in passing that food is one of the most important intermediaries between husband and wife and between fiances. In fact, both in public and in the family, the couple behave with a great deal of reserve and never exchange marks of affection or kindness. On the other hand, the taste and smells of food, and the care with which the woman has cooked it are a language of love, an erotic metaphor.

The putting down of men who are, in other respects, looked upon as biologically 'superior', is carried out above all at the level of language, in the conversations women have among themselves about men. The most common weapon is the weapon of irony and contempt. In general, women's language (when women are speaking with other women or about themselves with others) is an allusive, metaphorical and complicated language that — like most spoken language — implies more than it says. But when talking about men, women are explicit, provocative, ironical, mocking, sometimes violent, often without pity for weaknesses and failings. It is above all the old women, the very ones who teach respect and obedience, who use the most violent, indeed often obscene, language. Such language exhausts its destructive charge in verbal violence, and in story-telling from which men are excluded.

The adolescent girl quickly learns that her life will unfold within a complex reality in which her role will be a mixture of importance and suffering. She will have to protect her sexual integrity and her image, unlike men from whom the same behaviour is not demanded. While virginity is demanded of women only, morality is also a male concern although men's morality is of a different kind.[11] Once she is engaged, a woman acquires a relatively greater freedom of movement. She begins to visit her fiance's house (she often helps his mother in domestic and farming chores) and to go out with him in accordance with prescribed forms and at set times — always under the watchful eye of those whose job it is to protect her. Despite this, it is by no means rare for her to be pregnant before marriage; this is not considered particularly bad if the marriage is all arranged. The opposite case (which in reality occurs very rarely) of pregnancy followed by desertion by the man is much more serious and leads to high tensions. 'Dishonour' and shame will strike the woman and her family which will choose to remove the 'guilty' woman to another village where members of her family have already moved. Eventual marriage with a man from outside the area will at least wipe out the shame it caused, if not the memory of what happened, restoring the status quo and making possible an eventual return to the area. The disapproval which arises at the mention of other cases of pre-marital pregnancy shows itself in the form of comments and generalized and malicious chit-chat, a moral sanction which exhausts itself in the very act of asserting and declaring it without being translated into other forms of exclusion, violence or rejection.

It must be stressed in this connection that the concept of honour does not represent a dominant value in the village studied and does not have the same importance there as it does in other villages in Calabria.[12] Honour is rarely mentioned, and when it is it is solely in situations like those just described. Concerning women, it is not a value that has any great compulsive force, or whose transgression will give rise to violent conflicts. Disputes are certainly common, but they are over land demarcation, inheritance, or dowry and not generally over questions of honour. It comes over clearly that because of the real and symbolic[13] capital that is associated with her, woman is a precious object who must be preserved and protected but who cannot be easily lost, despite mistakes and breaches of the dominant rules. When it is a matter of a birth outside wedlock, the situation is rather different. In this case, it is no longer simply the man who is involved but the functioning of society. An illegitimate birth disturbs the order which has to be maintained and reproduced and upsets reproduction strategies.

For the rest of her life, even once she is married, the woman will have to protect her own image and avoid circumstances that could give rise to gossip or suspicions. However, she will, with time, and especially after the menopause, enjoy increasing autonomy, though never to the point where she will have the right to go beyond the limits which have been assigned to her and which she accepts as appropriate.

Outside work in the fields, the woman's world is organized within spaces and areas which are her own, set in opposition to male spaces and areas,[14] just as the roles and competences of the two sexes are different. The motivations that explain and justify the divisions and differences tend to value the male independently of and to the detriment of the female. Women perform roles such as helping other women in childbirth, helping the sick and the dying, organizing marriages and betrothals, taking care of kinship and neighbourhood relations, keeping and transmitting the traditional lore and other roles related to significant moments and situations in the existence of individuals and the functioning of society; but they do not enjoy any particular esteem for doing these things, even from other women themselves, because they are considered 'normal things' which are suited to the 'nature' of women. But being concerned about politics, administrative and major financial problems calls for special qualities that men have and women don't. Male competences of this type are not only varied but also highly valued.

Relations with higher official authorities fall on men where it is necessary to go outside the community. Women, for their part, have direct access only to the imaginary world of the unknown. They are its interpreters and develop techniques of controlling it, acting as intermediaries between the unknown and the known. Faced with the real unknown, it is the man who has to guide them by showing the way. Random observation of male/female roles and the modes of articulation of relations between the sexes shows clearly that women occupy a secondary position in some sectors. The power held by women in the reproduction processes of society is not only not translated into a condition of equality at all levels but is denied by attitudes which affirm, in the last instance, the superiority of the male over the female.

It is at the symbolic level that the subordination of women becomes explicit and obvious and produces an image that is largely at odds with reality. This image is connected with the supposed inferiority of her body and her sexuality. It is drawn from a cosmogony that in this case organizes things, stars, plants, words, according to categories of male and female that are then translated into a dualist system that portrays the male as superior and originator and the female as the opposite. From the time of her conception, a woman's self-image begins to be formed. A whole series of beliefs, spread above all among women, have it that the female has from the beginning characteristics that differentiate her from the male. People believe that the soul is formed after forty days if it is a boy, and later, after between three and six months, if it is a girl. In the event of an abortion, if the foetus is male, it is already fully formed, with all its limbs; if it is female, on the contrary, it is not formed and comes out in pieces. A boy begins to move very early in the mother's womb, a girl later; but the girl moves about a lot and disturbs the mother. The male denotes the fully formed, the essential and the quick, the female the fragmentary, the excessive and the slow. The two sexes are in opposition and the superior sex and the inferior sex, a strong sex and a weak sex are contrasted, according to the system common in all societies.[15] The attribute that, at the symbolic level, best connotes male superiority is blood, associated here, as elsewhere, with sperm.[16] It is believed that blood is transmitted by men only (this motivation justifies the taboo on marriage between parallel paternal cousins) and that sperm is blood. Female blood is milk, which serves not to create but to feed. Male blood is felt to be stronger and purer. The act of bringing children into the world thus becomes less creative than the act of impregnating, a male act (in this connection it might be recalled that women can and do do all the work in the fields except sowing, a task which is reserved to men), because the man alone can transmit the primary and vital element.

Women are thus dispossessed of their power to give life through a series of mental operations that have an effect on both men and women. 'The strength of ideas lies in their being shared, in the belief and confidence in the truth value of the interpretations of the real world that they offer.'[17] The blood of women is not only weak, it is also dangerous — as numerous beliefs about menstrual blood and its evil powers testify. A woman must not cross a field where seeds are beginning to grow from corner to corner with her legs apart on pain of causing their death; similarly, peculiarities of desire and thought are attributed to women. Their physiology is further held to make women weaker, more fragile, less capable than men of taking on tasks that require specialization and skill. In working in the fields, for example, even when the woman does most of or all the work (which is the case with women when the men are temporarily or permanently away), women are supposed to be able to do only the secondary tasks that are complementary to male ones. The dirtiest, lowliest and most repetitive jobs,[18] are her province, while all the domestic work she has to do inside the house is devalued.

It is her sex, her 'woman-ness', that is the 'natural' cause of the inequality of the sexes: 'sexuality, the differences of bodily forms, substances and functions, the anatomical and physiological differences that arise from the different functions of the sexes in the processes of reproducing life, permanently supply the materials with which messages and discourses are stitched together to interpret and justify all the social inequalities existing between men and women'.[19] Men and women both participate in supporting this mythology and thereby combine to maintain a situation in which women can exist without an identity.

Messina, February 1983

Notes

1. The term *casata* in the region studied describes all the descendants of one ancestor in the male line.
2. The research was carried out in 1975–6 over fourteen months, then during brief stays in 1977, 1978 and 1979. The original object of the survey was kinship structures; the topic later became more specific: marriage strategies and the modes of transmitting inheritance. Part of the research, the materials of which have not yet been completely treated, was devoted to the role of women. Here, we are only giving a few outline features of it. Until about 1960, virtually all women were employed in agriculture and only a small minority were engaged in other occupations. Today the number of peasants has decreased and the area of land that is either left fallow or turned into building plots is growing. The research was conducted at Zaccanopoli, a village in Calabria, in the province of Catanzaro. This village is devoted to growing corn, maize and other cereals. It was once a cattle-rearing village where today there are virtually no shepherds. It covers an area of 660 hectares. It has a population of 1,080, almost all peasants or small landed proprietors. There are some small family holdings, but there are no large estates.
3. The expression 'reproduction strategies' is used in the meaning given it by Bourdieu (see P. Bourdieu, 'Les stratégies matrimoniales dans le système de reproduction', *Annales ESC*, No. 4–5, 1972, pp. 1105–25.
4. The sources used are: the *feux* (hearth tax) of 1641, the cadastral survey of 1747, the births, marriages and death registers for 1793 and 1848, the population census of 1851, the births, marriages and death registers for 1959 and the card index of families consulted at the mayor of the commune's office. For the preliminary results of this survey see M. Minicuci, *Le strategie matrimoniali in una communità calabrese. Saggi demo-antropologici* (Soveria Manelli, 1980).
5. Those called and defining themselves as cousins are the children of first cousins and the children of children of first cousins. Beyond this limit, they are kin or distant cousins. In his study of the diocese of Como, R. Merzario uses this definition: *Il paese stretto. Strategie matrimoniali nella diocesi di Como sec. XVI–XVII* (Turin, Einaudi, 1981).
6. Whereas marriage between cross and parallel cousins in the matrilineal line is prescribed, sought after and widely practised, it is forbidden between parallel cousins in the patrilineal line. Kinship terminology distinguishes this latter category of cousins from all others. In the event that there is no land, the dowry is made up in cash which has to be invested in the purchase of a piece of land of which the woman will be the owner.
7. The requirement for the woman always and everywhere to receive a dowry is attested to by a solution that is chosen — even though it is very rare — in the case of double marriage. In this case, if the woman agrees to renounce the land that is hers by right, in favour of her brother this land will be given not to her brother but to his wife while she herself will be provided with a dowry by her husband's father.
8. See on this point F. Héritier, 'Hommes/Femmes', in *Enciclopedia*, VIII (Laborinto-Mamoria, Turin, Einaudi, 1979), pp. 797–812.
9. See M. Minicuci, op. cit., chapter entitled 'Il sopranome', pp. 75–105.
10. See J. Davis, *Antropologia delle società mediterranee. Un'analisi comparata* (Turin, Rosenberg e Sellier, 1980), in the chapter, 'Famiglia e parentela', pp. 175–246.
11. How moral a woman is is measured essentially from her behaviour towards the

opposite sex, whereas how moral a man is is measured from the fact that he is a good worker, and neither a spendthrift nor a drunkard. A man must give the guarantee of being a good father and a good husband. A man who is rejected by a woman because he is considered to be not serious enough or who breaks off an engagement without specific reasons (the only acceptable reason is generally a dispute over the agreed dowry) may well not find a woman to marry him in the area.

12. See on this point Zagnoli's analysis of the province of Reggio Calabria, where he says that 'Calabrese culture is based on the notion of honour. Its corollary, shame, is less important. The first term is the positive aspect . . . whereas the second term is the negative aspect, the one that explains the fact of avoiding certain actions, or certain situations which would be dishonouring'. N. Zagnoli, 'A proposito di Onorata Società', *Quaderni del Mezzogiorno e delle Isole*, nos. 42–43, 1977, pp. 23–40, p. 27. Even if what is asserted by Zagnoli can be verified in the area he studied, it is not proved that it is the same in the rest of the region.

13. For the definition of symbolic capital, see Bourdieu, *Esquisse d'une théorie de la pratique* (Geneva and Paris, Droz, 1972), in the section 'Le capital symbolique', pp. 227–43.

14. On the organization of space in this community, see the article by M. Minicuci, 'Il disordine ordinato. L'organizzazione dello spazio in un villagio rurale calabrese', *Storia della citta*, VIII, no. 24, 1983.

15. F. Héritier, 'Fecondité et sterilité: la traduction de ces notions dans le champ idéologique au stade préscientifique', in E. Sullerot (ed.), *Le fait féminin* (Paris, Fayard, 1978), pp. 387–96.

16. On this topic see especially M. Godelier, *La production des grands hommes* (Paris, Fayard, 1982).

17. Ibid., p. iii.

18. To this it should be added that women generally use implements that are simpler and more archaic than men do. The introduction of agricultural machinery (tractors, cutters, combine harvesters) has led to the exclusion of women from some phases of the productive cycle, for example, for corn, harvesting and threshing, and relegated them to marginal roles. Today, only two women drive a tractor, none a combine harvester.

19. M. Godelier, op. cit., p. 13.

Childbirth, Women's *Jihad*

Yamina Fekkar

Eleven p.m. . . . An imperious alarm bell awakes you abruptly from your first sleep . . . The time for emergencies . . . The tiredness, the anxiety of those on duty . . .

A rush through the night, a maze of roads, dark houses . . . A courtyard to cross and then the entrance to a room darkened with incense smoke where women of various ages, all attention, surround a woman in labour. Summary greetings, examination punctuated by an index finger pointed skywards testifying to the oneness of God . . . and for the uterine contractions. Estimate of how far advanced the labour is and prognosis: still two or three hours to wait . . . Sundry movements, ambiguous silence . . . Everyone is tired, hoping for an early end to this labour which began in the morning. I explain . . . inadequate dilation . . . But no one's interested. They translate it as 'obstacle'.

The traditional midwife whom I replace, visibly annoyed, mutters about being obliged to 'hand over' to a young midwife, who may well have a 'diploma' but lacks *baraka* (good luck) since they still have to wait. The good midwife is one the angels accompany in her travels by lending a helping hand to her intervention.

Long hours of waiting . . . time to be passed with a throng of women torn between the desire to go and rest and the desire to remain to receive the blessings that the angels of childbirth bring with them and distribute at a birth.

For the time being, the young woman in labour rests under the effect of a sedative that I have given her, scarcely raising her *khol*-laden eyelids when her contractions come . . . Attentive silences, talk about nothing and everything . . .

The traditional midwife who has ostentatiously performed her ablutions is praying in a corner and settling her accounts with God. Her busy piety prevents her from scorning all these people who are beginning to doubt tradition by having recourse to modern techniques . . . But Allah is great, He alone has all power over beings both visible and invisible.

The little bag of indigo and salt worn by the young woman on her right ankle effectively reminds us that invisible, powerful beings are abroad in this room and that their neutrality has to be secured. All the women know this but never speak of it because these mysterious beings have great powers.

178

It is said that when a woman gives birth, at the very same moment a *djennia* gives birth too. If this *djennia* should happen by caprice to abandon her child and want that of another woman, anguish invades the atmosphere, the body closes up and fear spreads on the face of the woman huddled over the tears of her belly.

The ingestions of herb tea and cinnamon are followed by drops of water made holy by the diluted ink of a verse from the Koran[1] or by the water used in the washing of the husband's big right toe, making the woman into a receptacle where the vegetable, God and magic are combined in a particular symbolism ... and water. She renews her links with the djinns in space, earth, fire, metal and so with the essence of things, the spirit of matter.[2] Women's Islam is submission to the natural order, the sign of acceptance of her sex, recognition of the Word given to man.[3]

Fumigations, gasping steps punctuated by the profession of faith ... Premature and repeated crouchings over a pushing that leaves the woman panting on the edge of fainting, abandoned on the sympathetic sisterly chests of the other women. Traditional childbirth is a ceremony in which each person present is active and makes herself useful. It is women's *jihad* (holy war). The mention of *jihad* during labour usually stimulates the endurance and courage of the most frightened woman. This offering of oneself in the name of the faith is what (in Islam) gives the human being, even a faint-hearted one, the feeling of surpassing her own limits to attain to the mercy of God. The acceptance of death in one's body to attain the other life, the life of fullness and blessedness, is the ideal of self that every Muslim woman in labour achieves. Already, pregnancy, by suppressing the impure menses, sublimates the creation that is taking place in the woman's body. It is the equivalent of fasting and prayer.[4] In this ultimate offering to God, a woman fully affirms her sex, reminding us that beyond the initial difference (the *infiçal*) she was with man created from a single soul (Koran VII/189).

Going on *jihad* also means leaving without regret and between the uterine spasms the woman begs forgiveness of the throng, getting each one present to confirm that she bears no unforgiven grudges. This forgiveness sought and forgiveness granted is the condition of the agreement of each one with God that binds the community of believers together (the forgiveness that each Muslim, man or woman, seeks before the Departure). At these moments there is total communication and spirituality envelops this night of vigil. In the collected silence, gestures become symbols: one woman gets up and goes to open the doors and the drawers of all the furniture in the room, another prays as she stirs the fire with a pinch of incense, yet another goes out into the courtyard to call upon God in the diffuse pre-dawn light. Dawn is not far off and this is the time the old midwife chooses to go up to the woman in labour. She gently passes her hand over the woman's aching belly and says, 'In the name of God, He who grants mercy, the merciful one, O my child, angel among angels, submit yourself, accept to die so as to live.' A sybilline phrase, that projects the spirit into the world of the metaphysical cycles of the Islamic creation.

Time moves on, the air loses some of its heaviness, the eyelids lift a little, the woman stretched out obeys the advice she has been given. The rhythm of our breathing becomes one with hers. All attention is focused on the appearance of the baby's head as it obstinately endeavours to break through the last resistance of its mother.

The milky light of dawn glows through the window. The voice of the muezzin summons the faithful to prayer and suddenly, the melodic sound of the *Allahu akbar* is mixed with the raging cry of a little creature writhing impatiently. It suffers the aggression of our care which brings it into the world of human beings. Swaddled, warmed, it finds rest in the arms of the elderly midwife, all attention, who murmurs into his ear, '*La ilaha ... Mohammed rassul Allah*'. The task of cutting the umbilical cord has been entrusted to her as a testimony of appreciation for the deep lines of weariness that show her age, and also in recognition of her role as a security-giving mother helping the new-born to cross the line between the closed and the open, the inside and the outside, life and death.

It is with childbirth that a young woman finally dies and becomes a mother at whose feet Muslims speak of paradise ... The old midwife participates in the mystery of this change. For her, each umbilical cord that is cut represents a freed angel who will join the earlier ones to form the joyful cohort opening the road to heaven for her at her last moment. There is another ritual that she performs: burying the placenta in an out-of-the-way corner, this last vestige of the mediation between heaven and earth, mother and child.

With bodies weary, hearts at rest, laughter and joy fuse in the light of morning around the cup of coffee that brings together in a single euphoria the mood of the evening before and of today.

This story was a professional experience that took place between 1950 and 1962 in Oranie (Algeria). At that time, Algerian women trained at the midwifery school in Algiers were few and far between. Since independence in 1962 the Algerian state, demonstrating a desire to modernize, has established many hospitals and dispensaries supplied with sophisticated equipment. Since the number of doctors trained in Western universities was insufficient, as was the number of medical personnel, there was a need to train some quickly: the training of midwives was speeded up (one year instead of two for rural midwives). Today they are among the 'health technicians'.

This project involved accepting a new relationship with the body: the anatomical, mechanistic, Cartesian body replaced the Islamic body — a place where heaven and earth came together. This modernization of medicine at a time of political determination to Arabize and return to Arab cultural sources, had the paradoxical effect of removing a whole Islamic dimension. Free hospital care impelled women — when they could — to give birth in the hospital, and, because of the shortage of beds and personnel, the hospitals cannot cope with the demand.[5] A woman's stay in the maternity ward must be short, and so must her delivery, so she can't occupy a bed for more than twelve hours. There's no longer any question of respecting the labour time of the woman, of taking account of her own physiological rhythms. The sympathetic sisterhood is replaced by the cold authority of 'skill'. The hospitalization of childbirth is equivalent to a deculturation both of the medical personnel and the women in childbirth themselves.

Can we strike a path between an impossible return to the past and the present abuse of power and the relations of force that today characterize the relationship between carer and cared for? Today, the carer incarnating modernity stands armed with a 'knowledge' which incriminates traditional behaviour. Can some aspects of this behaviour be incorporated in a new society?

Gordes, February 1983

Notes

1. One of the recipes for this ink (*smagh*) has been transcribed by Hassan Massoudi in *La Calligraphie arabe vivante* (Flammarion, 1981). It dates from c.300 AH (940 AD): mix the sap of a wild, non-fruiting tree with half a litre of water, 5 grams of salt, 250 grams of gum arabic and 30 grams of grilled nuts. Blend it all and add 40 grams of iron sulphate and 30 grams of honey, boil for two hours and add 20 grams of carbon black, leave for one hour over the fire, strain and put in a bottle.

2. Yamina Fekkar, 'La femme, son corps et l'islam', in *Le Maghreb musulman* (1979 CNRS, 1981).

3. Mohamed Arkoun, in M. Arkoun and L. Gardet, *L'Islam, hier et demain* (Buchet/Chastel, 1978), pp. 228–9.

4. The five basic obligations of Islam are the confession of faith, prayer, fasting, alms-giving (*zakat*), and the pilgrimage to Mecca. On this sublimation of childbirth and maternity see Abdelwahab Bouhdiba, *La sexualité en Islam* (PUF, 1975), new ed. in coll. Quadrige, 1982.

5. Women who receive any medical assistance in childbirth are still very few: 18% in urban areas, 2.3% in rural areas according to the 1976 census. Algeria has a very high birth rate (3.2%) and is unable to keep up with the demand for care that ensues. See Monique Gadant, 'Les femmes, la famille et la nationalité algérienne', *Peuples méditerranéens*, no. 15, April–June 1981.

A Feminine Culture

Rossana Rossanda

> 'The life of women is too limited, or too secret.'
>
> Marguerite Yourcenar, *Memoirs of Hadrian*

It has too often been said that women were excluded from culture until relatively recently (compulsory education for all dates only from the 20th Century), and, more slyly, that they still remain in many respects excluded today or have only partial access to it. But did women during this long period of exclusion, in which they lived alongside or in the service of men, produce a culture of their own, a specific knowledge, repressed or suppressed, which, if it were to emerge, would make a significant difference and not simply be a gloss to existing culture? In other words, have women developed a different way of being?

The new feminism said that culture was male, that it didn't express women, that it denied them. This is certainly true; you cannot express yourself through the opposite sex (and not even through another individual; at most you can be interpreted or translated in this way). This assertion no longer surprises us, since the idea that culture, knowledge, research, even language itself are not neutral has become generally accepted. In the same way that the social order is given or imposed by the strongest classes, who make *their* law as *the* law, the dominant culture and its instruments impose themselves as the sole principle of truth. They are in fact only the projection of the values of that part of society which already *knows* because it *already* dominates. The new feminism went further. As well as seeing so-called 'objective' knowledge as the knowledge of a dominant class, it saw that the sexuality of women and men had been defined by the male — the dominant sex.

The political theories of liberation (particularly those that see in the social relations of production the root of inequality and oppression) define the knowledge of those who hold power as conditioned by a false consciousness and these theories proffer a demystifying reading of them. But how far does this knowledge that is certainly neither neutral nor innocent still reflect a degree of objective reality? And what critique of knowledge defines it as masculine? What alternative demystifying reading does that critique propose? And if culture is not simply a reservoir of notions but a system of relations between past and present, present and present, the world of men and values, in what way does the feminine culture subvert it and what different systems of relations does it propose?

182

The temptation of parallelism

But does feminism set itself this goal? Does the critique of machismo aim, as Marcuse says, at making this monosexual culture 'androgynous' or does it aim at asserting a 'space' where the feminine is autonomous, destined to remain different and not *interested in communication*, accepting itself as *complementary*?

It seems to me that this choice is rarely formulated, even by those who complain very bitterly of the male character of knowledge and language. In practice, already, women are divided into two groups: those whom I would define as radicals who practise separatism. Others, those who practise 'double militancy' for example,[2] accept the two cultures as complementary. And some, among whom we would perhaps wish to be counted, wonder whether it is possible to make of the historical experience of women a principle, not to say a projectile, with which to attack the whole culture of the dominant class and sex, in the same way as the labour movement has attacked the idea of the state and law.

It seems to me to be important to take up a clear position on this point. Politically speaking, women are the most extraordinary of minorities; we say 'politically speaking' because in fact women are not a minority. They make up half the world, they are dominated by the other half and limited in their civil rights. All minorities, once they have realized their subordinate position, have taken to questioning the social and cultural principles and systems that have misrepresented or marginalized them. They have often tried to revolutionize the ruling culture because they have seen in that culture the foundation of the whole edifice of domination.

A minority that is conscious of its own diversity but 'does not rebel' limits itself by contrast to preserving its integrity and its difference; it tends to close in on itself, in a way to stabilize itself in ghettoes that may be smaller or larger, parallel with the dominant culture, hating it without attempting to subvert it. This choice usually leads minorities to a slow extinction or condemns them to remain mere anthropological exhibits, less because of the murderous hand of the powerful than because of the defection of their own offspring who sooner or later prefer to run the risk of losing their culture by drowning it in the dominant one rather than staying in isolation.

To which type of minority do women correspond? In political terms, as we have seen, they may be called a minority; their rights and their powers are subordinate. Feminism does not limit itself to asking for access to increased rights and powers, but fundamentally calls into question their proclaimed universality. What are these rights, what understanding of nature or of human relations support them, when they have been drawn up by a single sex and by a powerful segment of that sex which, historically, has deprived others of a voice? Do women aim at the establishment of a really bisexual total culture (and thus one bearing within it the critique of patriarchal culture) or at the legitimation of their own non-communicant culture?

I tend towards the first hypothesis. I want the 'difference' of the feminine experience to be a scalpel that cuts through the unadmitted bias of the dominant *and* male knowledge (which is not exactly the same thing). I know very well that this choice comes to me as a result of a personal vision of the world as movement, disequilibrium, interaction and struggle. More pertinently, I feel this way because feminism seems to me to have arisen not by chance but because the arrogance of 'culture' is cracking on all sides, subverted by its own internal subjects.

But I know too very well that anyone who aims at preserving the integrity of the difference is less interested in the possibilities of disequilibrium and is sceptical about the possibility of historical change. Can the hypothesis that women have perhaps taken on board as their own a 'non-need' of culture, understood as knowledge, communication and a potentially total system of relations, be disposed of without misgivings? And yet if this option were followed (and I have been asked, 'Why are you so determined to find an interpretation? The feminine is not something that is thought, but something that is experienced'), women would deny themselves not only by acceding to knowledge of themselves, but by being known; in obscurity they would retain the truest part of themselves. The 'experienced' would then be very much like the 'suffered', the 'unspoken' zone that everyone has within them. But silence is a weak identity principle. When women spoke, they would speak of the 'other', male culture; worse still, they are the earliest and most effective transmitters of it (who, if not the mother, teaches the son to command, the daughter to obey, him the need to be recognized and paid, her the need to be loved (and yet . . .) but work invisibly?). Theories on the priority of the incommunicable are elusive; in the way in which this experience does not speak for itself it resembles madness — a secret and inexpressible experience.

But let us agree that by recoiling from the extremity of silence, women tend to legitimize a *separate* culture of their own. This attitude, in changing times, does not shock but, oddly, corresponds to the new 'systems' theories in the social sciences. These pay close attention to the various status groups and corporations, including the cultural ones, which produce a balance of power in a 'political market', in which it would be a matter of circulating 'feminine money' too, if possible with a good price on the Stock Exchange. Moreover, if we are to believe Kate Millett, feminism has tried this path in the United States. But in what mint is feminine money coined?

Obscurum per obscurius or the attraction of anti-reason

There is no codified feminine culture. All cultures are male. But why do women find some more appealing than others?

The first and the most widespread reason is the critique of the 'logos' — the terrible *reason* that has come down to us from the Greeks as ultra-male. Not that this is strange; given that it is certainly on the basis of the 'logos' that law is established, that is the organized political sphere that sanctions the social inferiority of women, the aversion is understandable. However, up until now, it has been more a question of spasms of rebellion than a continuous assault. On the other hand, the critique of reason as *rationalism* and *rationalization* and through that *total regulation* (with a leap from thought to action) is not peculiar to feminism alone. It is a characteristic trend of recent years, and there is no need to go back far to find its roots; they are to be found in the crisis in the dominant political theories of the left — to which, let us not forget, feminism is allied — whether this crisis is apprehended as a crisis of progressivism or as a crisis of the 'rationalizing' policies of programmation, the state and planning.

But the truth is that rationalism had been called into question long before. Hegel already had his Kirkegaard, and before him the critique of historicism was already developing. Irrationalism, in so far as it stresses the irreducibility of the existent and the experienced to a pure logical schema, is concomitant with the history of reason, it is its obsession as well as its complement within the structure of Western thought. But where is its feminine matrix to be found? It cannot be credibly recognized anywhere, not even in mysticism. On the other hand, if what feminism fears in the 'logos' is precisely that it hypostatizes it as rationalization and hence total regulation, it should far rather direct its suspicions towards eastern philosophies to which a certain women's culture is sympathetic. But these philosophies fix as archetypes eternal and equal (but in appearance only) in dignity the principles of domination and dependence which are believed to govern the universe. They explicitly link the male sex with authority, and classify active and passive, heaven and earth, fire and water, dominant and dominated, *yin* and *yang*, as the unalterable cardinal points of the world. With that, in one stroke, the 'logos' is removed, but so too is history as 'change'. Even if we can understand the fascination these theories have for women, who may feel themselves more linked to the phases of the moon and the unchanging elements of the universe than men as immortal 'mothers', it still remains true that in these theories it is the sun that gives life and the moon, sterile, that moves round it. But for the present, I merely want to observe that if a certain feminism chooses mystical thought as more adequate in preference to the fatal 'logos', then that is its business; so long as it does not cheat and pretend these philosophies are something they are not.

The only women (apart from exceptional members of the elite, intellectuals or saints) who have rebelled are witches (unknown women, nameless, except in witchcraft trials). The most savage repression rained down on them, not when they began to exist (for they have existed in all ages and in all civilizations) but when, in the West, between the late 16th and the early 17th Centuries, that is at the time when the state and modern philosophy took shape, there arose a great collective fear, fuelled but not caused by the Counter-Reformation. The faggots then flamed like matches, and if a few males were also those burnt (a hesitant monk, a sympathetic judge, the odd Scottish or Fruilian sorcerer), it was nonetheless a basically feminine society that was consigned to the flames.

What was the culture of this society? We cannot find out from the trials which reflect the culture of the inquisitor, which once again associated the devil with sex (feminine, *vas iniquitatis*), as the repetitive questions asked at the trials make plain. 'Do you go to the sabbath? Do you rub yourself with the fat of children? Do you copulate after initiation?' The sexual imagination is once again male, perhaps sometimes introjected by women because of the need for a semblance of freedom or rebellion. But even when a few fragments permit us to glimpse the experience of the witches, we discover practices associated above all with the fertility of the earth or of animals and a few elements of basic medicine (medicine and esotericism long went hand in hand) which do not reflect specifically feminine knowledge. These fragments reflect at best practices that women transmitted essentially among themselves because they were the ones responsible for providing help; in these practices, they found small elements of authority and perhaps some freedom (we know so little of the unwritten culture of the time).

The interest we now have in feminine witchcraft comes from the hypothesis that pre-existing cultures were repressed by reason (male) and the modern state (male) (there too a certain sort of feminist culture is analogous with the ideas of the extreme left). But if we consider the shift from empirical practice to codified 'science', it is clear that we cannot simply reduce science to the mere authoritarian abuse of trust. 'Modern science' has capacities for knowledge, for development and for intervention which, if they do not prove that it is the 'only' possible 'science', do prove that it is so far the most articulated and vibrant, the only one capable of relations ('scientific' medicine could absorb 'folk' medicine but not the reverse) and self-criticism (the instruments of medical 'knowledge' change, but not those of 'folk' medicine, linked as they are to the eternity of nature from which they claim to derive their inspiration).

While the heat of the faggots in times which are not so far removed from our own, and were relatively short (the massacre lasted about 130 years) leads us to postulate the existence of 'free zones' — dominated by women, who did not (according to the inquisitor) recognize either God or Caesar — which seemed intolerable to states in the process of formation, the most recent research on witches in the villages (which is where many came from) that they dominated but by which they were rejected and then denounced, makes it difficult to pin responsibility for the faggots on the fatal centralizing state. The witch was a marginal among marginals; the countryside was in poverty, weighed down by taxes and wars; the witch's fragility, so far as I know, never at any time allowed her to express the *collective* needs for rebellion and affirmation.

The witch's knowledge is fragile because of the fact that it makes opposition the principle of its counter-culture. This appears nowhere so clearly as in the magical imagination: it is the reverse, pure and simple, of the liturgy (prayers said backwards, a caricature of the mass), of the imposed morality (liberated sexuality, deliberately reversed even in gestures, dancing back to back, the magic circle in which the back is turned inward). This is a subordinate negation; from the viewpoint of culture, it is silence.

In the reassessment of the witch, seen as good because she heals and is freed of the duties imposed by current morality, a certain strand of feminism perhaps recalls a temptation that belonged to the 18th Century and which has reappeared in recent years; the attachment to primitive cultures as a reaction against the unidimensional character of the mass media and of authoritarian, official and elitist knowledge. With the extinction of the hopes that had been put in a 'future of marvellous progress', these other cultures become a refuge. A striking phenomenon deserves mention here: while the culture of the 'noble savage' arose in the 18th Century at the height of the Enlightenment and perhaps as an aspect of the 'logos' reacting against the moral codification of the Church, today this same culture is arising again as a rejection of lay knowledge, as a response to a need for consolation and religious belief.

The place of feelings

But most women lean less on mysticism (although, in recent years, we have been assailed by astrology, horoscopes, the arts of divining and tarot cards) than on a culture of feeling seen as *other* than reason, and supremely feminine.

This choice is more fruitful than the first one, on condition — paradoxically — that its premises are eliminated. These are essentially an unacknowledged conception of feeling as positive (always a 'value') and illicit in its sexualization. The most common equation now is reason = power, feeling = fraternity or oppression. But power does not arise from reason, but rather from passion: of all the 'feelings' it is primary.

There is no logical basis for power; when we look for a justification for it, it is only to be found outside reason (a gift of God, or of the 'natural' order or delegation by one and all, in their inalienable, 'natural' or 'divine' character). This passion exists in all civilizations, ancient and modern; women share it with men and experience it over the young, children, servants, and, in complex and 'seductive' forms, over the male. The male/female relationship can be read largely as a struggle for power, precipitated by man because he is deprived of 'natural' fatherhood, woman being the only true reproducer, the one who holds the power and knowledge of birth. If man does not impose on her a condition of slavery, whether monogamous or some other, he will never have 'his' children of his own, which is a great loss.

It is difficult too to consider other feelings as being feminine in their essence: what about ownership as a substitute for identity? *My* family, *my* husband, *my* son, *my* house; and conversely, *my* dispossession, *my* melancholy, *my* frustration, *my* envy, *my* symbolic attachment. It is a matter in short of a double reduction which turns out to be untenable: the reduction of the feminine to a specific 'affectivity' against a male 'lack of affectivity', the two being understood as natural principles linked to each of the two sexes, but with a relative sublimation of feeling, the human being acting more on the order of the heart than of reason — which leads both to the most splendid altruism and to lynching.

But when we have dismissed this facile approach, the attention given to the specific affectivity of woman turns out to be useful. Women have been placed socially in the realm of feeling where relationships are strictly personal and non-abstract, tinged with emotivity. Such is the case with the domain reserved to woman in modern times; while where relations are impersonal, even the strongest passions — revolutions, powers, wars — can be said to take a 'rational' form of expression. It is the position and the social role that is *imposed* on women that make them seem more attached to feeling.

Is it not the same with reason? In the first issue of *Memoria*,[3] Eva Cantarella says that women have had imputed to them not reason, the fatal logos, but a *hybrid* closer to guile; she calls it, wrongly, I think, 'ineffective' reason. This is the form intelligence takes in situations of inferiority. Dante sees Odysseus as the symbol of human intelligence defying the frontiers of nature and of God, and Penelope as the *hybrid* using guile to foil the suitors and to recognize her husband.[4] If already, in Greek tradition, guile rather than logos is imputed to women, it is because this tradition in a way recognizes that it is the virtue of the oppressed, needed to survive in conditions where freedom is lacking. There too it is the social position that sharpens a faculty. In the same way, we cannot say that if feelings are linked to femininity, it is because the sphere left to women is that in which power, identity and negation (the triad of the logical)[5] are experienced in the direct sphere of the known — family, servants and the site of social reproduction.

It is this latter that explains feminine specificity and not the reverse. Femininity is induced by the division of roles. Does not accepting it as a principle of culture also not imply acceptance of this division of roles? Is not the new feminism tempted to accept it out of despair, faced with rejection by civil and political society? But why does it despair and rebel against this subjection? Is it because of the disproportion of the adversary's strength or because it consents to limit itself to a compensatory identity? Home, children, motherhood are not only symbols — they are powerful principles of identification.

The seductive fantasy

Perhaps we are reaching here the problem of the distinction between what, in sexuality, is historical and what, deriving from a historical determination, has become a value. It is the first time that this has happened to an oppressed group. It is a fact that the very bitter perception that women have of men's attitudes towards them is accompanied by the conviction that they have not only been made 'diverse' but that they 'are diverse' and above all that this diversity is in itself a 'value'.

Here again the study of Simmel in *Memoria*[6] comes to our help. But we cannot read this study without wondering not only whether what we want is simply to get ourselves recognized as *complementary*. One of two half-apples that come together again after such a long separation that the two halves have become two different varieties of apple but above all whether this 'value' of femininity that Simmel postulates is not purely and simply the male fantasy projection of woman accepted today by woman herself as her own and main identity.

That is the ultimate and most disconcerting looking-glass effect. On the one hand, the new feminist, by imputing to the male everything that has been thought, imputes to him wholly the image of woman, who would then only exist as a male fantasy, and so would not exist at all (*Ce Sexe qui n'est pas un*[7]); on the other hand, the feminist who recognizes this fantasy as her truth. As if, although sprung from the brain of Jupiter, she escaped him without his knowledge; and since he wanted her to be seductive, sentimental, emotive, timid, delicate, narcissistic and retrograde, negative and fleeting, attentive above all to her own body, these were really *her*.

Here the ambiguity is enormous. This projection is upheld by a part of the role that has been assigned to women by men over the centuries. Here we are dealing with that part of her subordinate condition that woman accepts, or is tempted to accept, as positive, because she perceives that this fantasy that man has of her is *partly* a terrifying fantasy for him — what makes Don Juan mad, the unattainable 'feminine'. Though we weep because they consider us a 'whore' or as a 'madonna', we are not unaware of the powerful temptation that attracts man towards one or the other. The former, the elusive Ishter,[8] all-powerful and sole mother and reproducer, continuity of life; compared to whom the embrace of man remains ephemeral and leaves him no right unless he imposes it by the violence of his strength or his law; the latter, the inaccessible site of grace and of those virtues that man considers the highest and permanently violates. Woman represents his contradiction. She will be afraid of the strength or brutality of man, but man is afraid of her, and in the first place of her sexuality, obscure, profound, invisible and perhaps devoid of sincerity, the site of the reproduction of life for which she alone holds the capacity and the knowledge.

To what extent is this fantasy experienced by woman as 'her' specific, inalienable power, and thus as an agreeable truth even though it is received from the other? But if she does accept it, at the level of sexuality, the war is fought with less unequal arms than some have claimed. It is at the level of social organization, which refracts bisexuality, that man truly takes his revenge; he assigns woman a limited role and limits her rights because her sexuality escapes him.

And here the problematic nature of man, described wrongly as calm and solid, his fragility and the archaic character of his codification come into play. Even the acts of violence (not more frequent, but more significant than at other times) that women experience today constitute perhaps the extreme manifestation of the crisis of the male/female dyad, a crisis that is due to the fact that each side is now taken over by an unbearable fantasy of the other. Woman sees herself in the mirror that man holds out to her, although she knows that this mirror is not hers; and man loses his reason in this unconvincing fantasy that he has given himself for a companion. If he partly saves his self-respect, it is because society, the site of collective relations, reassures him; it is he alone or almost so who has constructed these relations; this fantasy of woman, in which 'half the universe' recognizes itself and at the same time sees its separation, penetrates right into the heart of this construction. This fantasy woman exists as a real component even in knowledge or knowledges, in society or societies, as the only projection absolutely necessary to the other, the one who creates her (or perhaps only remodels her because she appears to him thus less fearful). If the presence of the rejected Black is a component of the mode of being of the White even in Pretoria, we can imagine what the presence of woman is in the male world. Whether that presence is a void or a fully occupied space, a protrusion or a hollow, it permeates the whole world of culture, even if only as a frontier, a boundary, an absence.

It is all very well for the strictest feminists to affirm 'I don't even want to think of or write about myself because I can't think or write about myself other than in the language of the oppressor'; they cannot not exist as the 'problem' or 'fantasy' of woman in culture and social organization as a whole. This fantasy has a depth, which is not entirely reducible to the product of the male imagination because it does have some relationship to a 'real object', which it is impossible to eliminate; and this fantasy acts in turn on the mode of being of the object and shapes its subjectivity, which in turn is refracted back onto the male fantasy.

Is it possible to construct a history of women's self-awareness without looking for it in the way in which men have thought of women? And, conversely, is it possible for women to codify themselves, by liberating themselves from male thought, asking themselves why such an important and specific 'experience' as the experience of being female has not expressed itself in a language and culture that are themselves specific? This virtual absence perhaps relates to the fact that women receive a compensation from their subordinate position, of which other subjected groups have been deprived. That compensation is no longer sufficient which is why women are becoming conscious that their ways of being are derived from the other. Women are seeking an identity of their own. But where is this identity to be found? In the remains that the experience of women has left historically, or imprinted as a profile, a void, an invisibility — like their work, Illich would say, or their unspoken mediation, Laura Balbo[9] would say, in short in fragments? Again the question arises: what is an experience that has not been thought?

'The life of women is too limited or too secret' responds Marguerite Yourcenar to herself when she asks, commenting on her long study of the Emperor Hadrian,[10] why she did not reconstruct his image through the life of a woman close to him. It is because this woman, although fine and complex, has disappeared without leaving a trace, either of her existence or of her thinking about the world, while the 'memoir' of Hadrian soars to the very frontiers of the empire and from there returns to the most intimate part of his life and his death. What can the woman have known about it? Where were the frontiers of the empire for her? Do we really know anything about something on which we do not act? Even reflection about the private space of old age and death or ultimate destiny appears, oddly, deepened by the size of the stage on which the individual has acted; by the same token *he* — a powerful man, an emperor — seems better placed to express what should belong to the totally interpersonal and affective territory of *this* woman. Conversely (but that is perhaps a male thought), Racine's Berenice, who is not only Titus' lover but the 'queen of a hundred peoples', would not hesitate to leave them to live with him, and it is he who is not able to, as a king, and so does not want to. Thus Berenice is doubly dispossessed, of a public existence and of a private existence; so her destiny is to disappear.

Nature, culture, social position

This perspective, this different way in which man and woman have looked at the same world (and the closer their personal relationship, the more tragic the divergence) becomes even more dramatic in an advanced society than an ancient one, because then it is society that separates them. Power separates men from their companions more than poverty separates the male slave from the female slave; industry separates more than agriculture by dividing the 'field' of presence.

But this division of roles has assigned the woman life and the man knowledge; this is what some of my dearest friends have been saying to me in recent years and they challenge me to choose between the two. Just as the most exquisite essences are pounded and crushed in the mortar, so the essence of woman is at its greatest in 'civil' obliteration, itself become *vertu*, in capacity for attention to herself, to the rhythms of her body and her heart, in not being distracted by the vastness of the horizon. Does not Karen Blixen's[11] essay say more or less the same thing when it asserts that man is doing, woman is being? But does a being exist without doing and vice versa? Are there two modes of constructing identity?

We can of course reply, 'All right, there is no woman's culture. And then? There are *women*.' Their presence and their absence are as old as the world; nature and the seasons do not speak either, they have no culture, yet they are no less real and eternal for that. But if that were true, of what would feminism complain? Even if we admit that women were once satisfied with this condition — which is different from the fact of feeling compensated —

the time for that is now past. This world itself, that man has constructed without giving women the same space and the same rights as himself, makes the fact of being without space and without rights intolerable to women. And it seems to me that there is something poignant in this search for themselves that women pursue, in the attempt they make to save not only their sisters, but their own past; from this perspective, it is a matter of making a *vertu*, a unique wisdom, of the oppression, of turning it from a 'void' into a 'secret fullness'. Not unknown, but only 'unsaid', or said according in ways that could only leave traces in inadequate forms of expression.

And yet I do not think that this is the right path. Not only because it would be highly curious — living in times of extraordinary change when, by questioning ourselves about our identity, we have undermined the universality of knowledge and of male identity — that we should end by recognizing as our only and true nature the 'feminine nature' that the others have assigned to us. As if we were drawn to solidarity with the past by the millions of women bent over a child or a needle or simply in obedience, considered at the best as secondary, venerated mothers, respected wives, whose opinion was sometimes sought, reduced to pleasing in order to be (is seduction anything else?), but usually denied and existing in silence, weariness and resentment. This past weighs on us and scarcely have we turned our eyes away from our personal, privileged conditions than the present weighs on us. But the fact of having escaped from the trap of emancipation as pure imitation of a male model obliges us now to something like the terrible passage, the necessity for and dilemma of which for workers Lukacs expressed in his *History and Class Consciousness* — asking himself how, from pure negation, they could become the positive principle of a new relationship between men.

This is not possible by way of the exaltation of a 'workers' essence'. This temptation was strong and it is not dead; it is resurrected as an alternative solution in all populisms and manifestations of 'proletarian culture'. The sooner we liberate ourselves from the hypothesis according to which the cultures of the oppressed were 'liberated' or 'liberating' cultures, the better it will be. What we will find will serve only — but it is an important 'only' — to restore *the* culture, the great one in its effective historical (and relative) dimensions, and see it in its caste functions.

Certainly the analogy cannot be perfect: the worker was a mere commodity, altogether depersonalized while women have been so only in extreme cases. The functions and symbols with which women are burdened delineate if not a culture, at least a mode of being and are, in addition, the pivot of a system of relations which is missing in all oppression. Research on this specific history of 'femininity' has fascinating aspects that the quest for the essence of labour never has and which — I suspect — resembles what 'negritude' has produced — the Western culture of the noble savage — and the discovery of the delights of anthropology.

In search of the feminine: from alienation to the new subject

There is more. This 'feminine', as we have said, has, not without ambiguity, run through the culture that men have codified, as the 'field' of being, doing and knowing became more a specific field of relationships. If we take four fundamental relationships, the relationship with nature, the relationship with the body, with society and finally with language, the profile of a 'feminine' which is not simply complementary appears obvious if fragmentary.

Take the relationship with nature. What relationship have women had with it? Has it been different or not? This point is very important for understanding whether the feminine experience is or is not a subculture. Dacia Maraini[12] reminds us, in her latest book as in *Sor Juana*, what every woman knows, through cooking, chemistry and botany; an empirical knowledge that non-empirical knowledge is in a position to embrace without waste. The question is to know whether what woman 'knows' about nature is also something that the other science *is not* in a position to know, or whether the feminine mode of knowing might be able to introduce an important variation into the methodology of science. The third point is to ask ourselves whether as 'an object' of science, woman has created an area of unconscious error which, once it has been removed, would modify science itself by its contribution (that seems to me to be undeniable for psychoanalysis, at least in its beginnings). If we find a negative answer to any of the previous questions, it must be concluded that the feminine contribution is only accessory to Western knowledge since it has no trace of any scientific hypothesis — one that Feyerabend[13] would accept anyway as good, in the sense in which they all are — expressed globally, and perhaps 'against method' but in the feminine (it is curious to note how far some utopian women's books of the last century, such as Charlotte Parkins' *Terradilei* are rigidly positivist). If we find no fragment of an 'other' knowledge or method of knowing, there remain only magic, alchemy and esoterism; reading the cards or the stars, whose main importance, as we have seen, lies in the fact of being not an embryonic 'different science', but a contribution to the knowledge of the paths, which are not a little tortuous, of a feminine consciousness in the past, and, suddenly, in our times. The most interesting relationship with nature is vis-à-vis the body. Here the variety not only of morphology but of physiology ought to lead of itself to a different, radically critical, feminine understanding. And yet more than the historical material (the various works of Trotula[14] or again the male difficulties in imagining woman's body) what counts in this case is the extraordinary value that the body has for woman, whether as the locus of the reproduction of life or in so far as it represents the sole card of power (seduction and commodity). The necessity felt by feminism to plunge itself into psychoanalysis, less as an instrument of therapy than of understanding, reveals an acute need to understand the depths of fantasy and of the male and female subconscious.

More generally, women's relationship to the body is interesting because it is so symbolic. Finally, given its specific relationship with sex, and the place it occupies in her life, a woman cannot *not* have a *specific* experience of the body. Perhaps too of suffering, since she knows at least one suffering, that of childbirth, which is a Biblical condemnation, but is the only suffering to be so profoundly linked to life. Yet, what increase, what acquisition or modification of knowledge has resulted from this relationship up to now? The more we advance on to the specific terrain of interrelationships, the more the evidence of women 'being different', or 'having been relegated' develops; but at the same time this tends to encompass wholly their social position. This latter, certainly, throws a new light on all their relationships and the culture that links them or underlies them; but as a consciousness of a limit, not unfathomable or diverse, but unsaid. The shadow work which Illich speaks about, or 'service' works as Laura Balbo says (or its 'mediating' function), beyond the infinite imagination of woman as the locus of values (faithfulness, love unto death, the sense of individual irreducibleness, the oneness of the relationship, piety, the wisdom of suffering, tolerance for what is poor and coercive in the oppressor and the boss, etc.) constitutes a depth, a residue where the specificity and the diversity become also embryos of another possible organization of relationships.

There the feminine experience is a mine. It is an enormous deposit largely hidden by silence. Women are secret because language has been taken from them because language is a form of domination; or better, the language that has been left to them is one that was not designed to pass beyond the territory of their enclosure. What is needed is thus not so much an 'other' language but rather the mixing of language — knowing that the historical experience of femininity will remain irremediably the zone of 'silence' marked by the absence of sources, this fact of passing through life without leaving any trace, without any 'monument' more lasting than bronze.

And yet, if that is true, is not the problem of woman wholly, and in the full sense of the word, 'political'? That is why I think that research on this secret vision or the vision that has come down to us over the centuries through secondary sources (as transmitted by men) or ambiguous when they are primary (when they are transmitted by women, once she has entered the camp and language of men) is necessary.

It is not by chance that the latest issue of *DWF*[15] and the first issue of *Memoria* open a debate on this problem. And I think that we shall also have to pursue tenaciously the redefinition of the feminine. But it seems to me easier to glimpse what, through this confrontation, will be deconstructed in the 'masculine' than what will be introduced as 'feminine'. It seems to me that there will be a lingering look from the 'outside' at the patriarchal world, the permanent denunciation of its limitations, rather than the possibility of bringing to light our hidden pearls. Women still codify themselves as alienated.

Good can only come from the movement of women towards a total identity. It is in this break (without precedents, given the mass dimensions it assumes and the consequences it entails) between what women have been and what they will be, in this questioning of themselves, that is to be found the most important 'feminine', the one that is really and ultimately significant. It is not by chance that, starting from a deeper understanding of their own dispossession and the affirmation of the 'I am I', 'I am me' as a potential identity, demanding and yet still uncertain in its direction, women are nearing a sort of new 'emancipation' without illusions. They are preparing themselves to possess the empire of the other without enclosing it in myth, so as to throw on it the doubt born of their long scepticism, and grasp, as in stories, the tiny grains in the midst of an infinity of wild and infertile seeds. With that, the perspective of women will change forever: but, in the history of humanity, the world too changes depending on the perspective of the onlooker.

This journey will not be a simple one. The suffering and the present conflict-laden relations between the sexes is perhaps the sign of this. But in it the experience of women, by making itself total, will also be made culture in the full sense of the word. And our children and grandchildren will think with a smile of the time when we had to ask ourselves, so as not to make mistakes at every step, 'But who am I?'

Rome, 1981

Notes

1. This text was published in *L'Orsaminore*, (Summer 1981), a cultural and political monthly edited by Maria Luisa Boccia, Giuseppina Ciuffreda, Licia Conte, Franca Chiaramonte, Anna Forcella, Biancamaria Frabotta, Manuela Frarire and Rossana Rossanda. It provoked a wide-ranging debate (Nos. 1, 2, 3, 4 and 5), from which R. Rossanda drew the first conclusions (No. 6, May 1982). *L'Orsaminore*, via Muzio Clemente 68/A, 00193, Rome, Italy.

2. The Italian feminist movement has called 'double militancy' the practice of women who join a political party. As women, they only grant legitimacy to their own movement, for the rest they recognize the authority or the organs of the party.

3. *Memoria* is a feminist historical journal.

4. When Ulysses returns home to Ithaca, after his long absence, he kills all the suitors who were living in the house hoping to marry Penelope. But she hesitates to recognize him and fears a usurper. Night was falling. Penelope, pressed by Ulysses, asked her maidservant to prepare the bridal bed. Ulysses then became angry, deeply hurt . . . This bed that he had made in the hollow of an olive tree, around which their bedroom had been built, no one could unmake it or remake it . . . An old secret of the couple . . . Penelope opens her arms and 'loosens her girdle'. The bed that he describes to her, the secret which only the two of them know, proves that he is indeed Ulysses, her husband (see *The Odyssey*, ch. XXIII).

5. In a famous passage in the *Phenomenology of Mind*, Hegel analyses the relations of Master and Slave, relations of domination in which the Master defines himself in opposition to the Slave whom he subjects and who recognizes his domination. The Slave in turn only overcomes the state of being relative to achieve identity through a struggle in which, risking his life, he accedes to recognition and defeats the Master, thus eliminating his power over him.

6. Gabriella Bonacchi, 'La un e le molti, la differenza "astuta" di G. Simmel',*Memoria*, No. 1, March 1981.

7. Ed. de Minuit, 1977.

8. Ishter or Ishtar (or Astarte, among the western Semites) goddess of the sky, goddess of lust, fertility. Among the Babylonians and the Assyrians who call all their feminine goddesses by the same name, goddess of war.

9. I. Illich, *Shadow Work* (Marion Boyars, 1981); L. Balbo, *Stato di Famiglia* (Etas, Milan, 1976); idem, 'Il lavoro per se', in *Doppia presenza* (F. Angeli, 1982).

10. M. Yourcenar.*Memoires d'Hadrien* (Plon, 1958), new ed (Gallimard, Folio, 1981), p. 329.

11. Karen Blixen (1885–1962), born near Copenhagen, lived in Africa from 1914 to 1934. She published a series of novels and stories in English (notably: *Out of Africa*, *Seven Gothic Tales*, *Last Tales*). This extract is from her essay.

12. Dacia Maraini, writer, film-maker, feminist of Rome. *Sor Juana* (Juana de la Crux, Mexican) is one of her feminist dramatic widows.

13. Feyerabend is an American scholar radically opposed to scientism, whether historical or not, and an adversary of Popper. He has written in particular *Against Method*.

14. Trotula (second half of the year 1000) is the most famous of the women of the 'Salerno school' (medicine). She was the author of a very important written work which has been preserved (exceptionally for a woman's medical work of the time), and she left in particular a treatise on obstetrics and gynaecology. Salerno, as well as a few city-states (in Sicily and Venice) was in the Middle Ages, a 'paradise' for women and for medicine compared to northern Italy and the whole of Europe where people lived in fear of the Inquisition (ban on medicine by the Church) (in *La politica del feminismo*, Savelli, 1978, p. 129).

15. *Nuova DWF* (Donna, Woman, Femme) is a theoretical journal of Italian feminism.